Key Concepts in
Family Studies

Recent volumes include:

Key Concepts in Childhood Studies
Allison James and Adrian James

Key Concepts in Community Studies
Tony Blackshaw

Key Concepts in Social Gerontology
Judith Phillips, Kristine Arjouch and Sarah Hillcoat-Nallétamby

Key Concepts in Early Childhood Education and Care (Second Edition)
Cathy Nutbrown

The SAGE Key Concepts series provides students with accessible and authoritative knowledge of the essential topics in a variety of disciplines. Cross-referenced throughout, the format encourages critical evaluation through understanding. Written by experienced and respected academics, the books are indispensable study aids and guides to comprehension.

JANE RIBBENS McCARTHY and
ROSALIND EDWARDS

Key Concepts in
Family Studies

Los Angeles | London | New Delhi
Singapore | Washington DC

SAGE Publications Ltd
1 Oliver's Yard
55 City Road
London EC1Y 1SP

SAGE Publications Inc.
2455 Teller Road
Thousand Oaks, California 91320

SAGE Publications India Pvt Ltd
B 1/I 1 Mohan Cooperative Industrial Area
Mathura Road, Post Bag 7
New Delhi 110 044

SAGE Publications Asia-Pacific Pte Ltd
33 Pekin Street #02-01
Far East Square
Singapore 048763

Library of Congress Control Number: 2010926864

British Library Cataloguing in Publication data

A catalogue record for this book is available from the
British Library

ISBN 978–1–4129–2005–6
ISBN 978–1–4129–2006–3 (pbk)

Typeset by C&M Digitals (P) Ltd, Chennai, India
Printed by CPI Antony Rowe, Chippenham, Wiltshire
Printed on paper from sustainable resources

contents

Acknowledgements   vii
Introduction   1

Attachment and Loss   9
Biology   12
Care   17
Child Development   21
Childhood/Children   26
Comparative Approaches   30
Conflict Theories   34
Coupledom: Marriage/Partnership/Cohabitation   37
Demography   42
Division of Labour   46
Domestic Violence and Abuse   51
Families of Choice   56
Family as Discourse   58
Family Change and Continuity   62
Family Effects   66
Family Forms   70
Family Law   75
Family Life Cycle and Life Course   79
Family Policies   84
Family Practices   88
Family Systems   91
Fatherhood/Fathers/Fathering   95
Feminisms   99
Functionalism   103
Grandparents   106
Home   111
Household   115
Individualization   118
Intimacy   123
Kinship   126
Motherhood/Mothers/Mothering   131
Negotiation   135

contents

v

New Right   138
Parenthood/Parents/Parenting   141
Personal   146
Phenomenological Approaches   149
Post-Coupledom: Separation/Divorce/Widowhood   153
Power   157
Problem Families   162
Public and Private   166
Rationalities   169
Role Theory   172
Siblings   176
Social Divisions   179
Socialization   184
Transnational Families   187

Index of sub-concepts   191
References   225

key concepts in
family studies

acknowledgements

This collection of key concepts proved a major undertaking and commitment for us, and we had assistance along the way. In particular we would like to thank Fiona Harris, who used her excellent skills as an editor to help us take in hand what was, at the time, an unwieldy mass of notes. In addition to our own appreciation, our readers owe her gratitude as well! Catherine Ribbens also made some of the administrative tasks associated with organizing the manuscript easier for us. Several colleagues were kind enough to respond to our ideas and read some of the concept entries, generously giving us the benefit of their expert knowledge in the field. They include Anne Barlow, Graham Crow, Megan Doolittle, Simon Duncan, Janet Fink, Frank Furstenberg, Harry Goulbourne, Heather Montgomery, David Morgan, John Oates, Georgia Philip, Mabelle Victoria, Jeffrey Weeks and Margie Wetherell. Finally, we would like to thank Chris Rojek and Jai Seaman of Sage for bearing with us.

INTRODUCING FAMILY STUDIES –
WHAT THIS BOOK IS ABOUT

Family studies is a broad and fascinating area. In this book, we set out to offer what we hope is a thoughtful overview of the key concepts through which family lives may be explored, and to provide clear and even-handed signposts to the main debates at stake in many of these concepts, and associated readings. As an area of academic interest, however, family studies is not easy to define, not least because the core term 'family' has become a matter of considerable controversy and dispute.

Although the word itself continues to be widely evident and generally unquestioned in everyday lives as well as in political debates and professional practices, researchers may ponder how to use it, or whether to use it at all. Many academics have grown wary of using the signifier *'the* family' as this draws on stereotypes that fail to take account of, and marginalize, the realities of diverse family lives that do not fit the implicit model in 'the family', of a heterosexual two-parent nuclear family with breadwinning husband and father and home-making wife and mother. There are a variety of responses to these dilemmas within family studies.

- Some researchers continue to use the term 'the family' unproblematically, often in practice referring to interrelated issues of residence, close ties based on blood or marriage, and the care of children. Talk about 'the family', in this way, is most likely to occur in discussions of broad patterns and structures, perhaps looking across different societies or examining how 'the family' as an institution relates to other major social institutions such as economic, employment or educational systems. There are many questions about social life that seem to require the concept of 'the family' as an object that exists and can be studied. Similarly, policy makers may feel the need for a clear model or benchmark of what 'the family' is, in order to develop legislation and general procedures.
- A different solution is to use the term in the plural and refer to 'families'. This acknowledges the diversity of lifestyles and relationships that might be referred to as 'family', offering a way forward which is widely accepted in family studies.

- Other solutions have been to use the word 'family' as an adjective, as in 'family lives', or even as a verb, as in 'doing family' (Morgan, D.H.J., 2003). This takes us away from the idea that 'family' is a noun – an object that can be named as such – suggesting rather that it is a descriptive term which is applied to a wide variety of experiences and interactions and to different aspects of living.
- Yet another approach is to turn the difficulty into a source of new questions, interrogating the word and asking how the term 'family' is used, in what contexts, and with what consequences? Various empirical studies have sought to do this (for an overview, see Ribbens McCarthy, 2008). This way of thinking also opens up the possibility that 'family' may be found in all kinds of social setting, not just domestic sites.
- Some writers find the concept of family so limiting and politically charged that they prefer to use other ideas altogether, such as 'intimacy', or broader terms within which 'family' is seen as one form of living alongside other relationships and experiences, and which may be captured by a notion such as 'personal life' (Smart, 2007).

As an area of scholarship, family studies is more fully recognized and academically organized in the USA than many other countries, and major overview textbooks are often authored from there (such as Boss et al., 2009; Coleman and Ganong, 2004; Collins and Coltrane, 2001; Lloyd et al., 2009). This is not to say that the field of family studies is not recognized as a discipline in its own right in other countries. While this recognition may be more or less explicit, academics in societies around the world produce important work relevant to the field, although there may be some associated differences of emphasis.

Besides theorizing the term 'family' itself, and how it may be used, family studies generally covers an interconnected set of topics, including:

- partnering and childbearing
- household formations and demographic trends
- daily living arrangements and decision making, including resources and provisioning
- parenting and other forms of care
- close relationships and their dynamics, in the context of various dimensions of age, generation, gender and sexuality
- kinship and community relationships
- domestic lives and their interrelationships with other areas of social life, such as education, health and employment

- aspects of social policy, the law and professional practices related to these topics
- diversity, inequality and cross-cultural and global issues.

The last theme raises a further question, about how far any of these topics can be studied by applying the same concepts across all global, social and historical contexts? This points to the need for comparative, anthropological and historical perspectives. Other key disciplines that contribute to family studies are sociology, psychology, demography, social geography, legal studies and economics, while political science and religious studies may also be stakeholders here (Karraker and Grochowski, 2006). But each discipline has its own sets of concepts, and even where they appear to be using the same terms, these may not always carry the same meanings. To engage in true interdisciplinarity is not always straightforward, and, indeed, may not always be desirable. Furthermore, different disciplines may have different approaches to what is meant by 'family' and how it is theorized. In psychology, for example, the focus may commonly be directed towards dyads (such as mother and child, or siblings) rather than more extensive networks of relationships that might be considered to be 'family'.

Indeed, it is important to explain, as authors of this book, that our own primary disciplines are sociology and social policy, and our theoretical and empirical orientation has been to explore how 'family' is understood by people in their everyday lives, such as to consider how parents understand their routine practices of living and relating around the care of children. Our work has also drawn extensively on feminist perspectives over the years. We see the links between feminist approaches on the one hand, and family studies as a field on the other hand, as crucially important in reinvigorating the subject and opening up new questions that had previously been seen as lying outside the scope of social science. Indeed, feminist family scholars have recently hailed progress in 'the ongoing transition from feminism *and* family studies *to* feminist family studies, where we cannot imagine a family studies not shaped by feminist contributions' (Allen, 2009: 3–4, original emphasis). At the same time, each of us have drawn on, and engaged with, most social science disciplines in our work, and we have drawn on these as far as possible in this book, as part of a project of developing broader dialogues and deeper understanding of family lives.

A vital aspect of family studies is to consider the research methods that underpin its knowledge base. We have not provided research methods as a direct entry in the book, but methods are clearly implicated throughout.

Those who want to pursue research methods further may like to refer to *Key Concepts in Social Research* (Payne and Payne, 2004). Texts that specifically consider research methods in family studies include those by Mason (2002), Ribbens and Edwards (1998) and Greenstein (2006), and readers may also like to explore the 'Real Lives' website (http://www.reallifemethods.ac.uk), which is part of the UK Economic and Social Research Council's National Centre for Research Methods, and the online resource for quantitative methods in family research (http://blog.lib.umn.edu/vonko002/research) based at the University of Minnesota in the USA. Again, there may be differences in traditions about the use of various research methods, as well as differences in theories of causality and explanation between disciplines – for example, randomized controlled trials are considered particularly important in some branches of psychology to verify casual connections. Approaches to research methods have also changed over time in family studies. Quantitative methods – for example, surveys, questionnaires, statistical analyses of large-scale datasets – have been particularly prominent in some contexts, but qualitative methods – for example narrative approaches, life history interviews, ethnographies – are also now recognized as significant and robust research methods relevant to family studies. Both qualitative and quantitative methods may use longitudinal or retrospective designs to explore how family lives change over time. And many family researchers also stress the importance of working reflexively with their own understandings of family lives, and consider how they may be relevant to the research approach and findings (Allen, 2000; Ribbens and Edwards, 1998).

A further aspect of family studies is that the 'level' and context of analysis, as well as the types of conclusion and the extent to which these are generalized, may vary among disciplines. Even within sociology, some family scholars work at the level of broad generalizations, perhaps examining how family as *an institution* is organized within and across different societies, while others may focus more on the detailed minutiae of everyday lived *experiences* and how these are understood by the participants, and perhaps shaped by opportunities and constraints in their circumstances and localities. Part of the interest of family studies is precisely that it can straddle different forms of analysis, although this then raises questions about whether or how these different levels may be linked. Indeed, sometimes families are seen as a key feature of how individuals and small groups are linked into wider social patterns. Family studies thus covers a range of issues, for example: the intricacies of personal experiences and close relationships, even interior psychic life;

the ways in which international economic systems relate to global patterns of migration, employment and caring; relationships between individual parents and children living in particular localities; and how national and international legal systems define citizenship rights by reference to family ties. These, then, are some of the complexities, as well as the fascinations, of studying families.

EVALUATIONS, AMBIGUITIES AND PRACTICAL INTERVENTIONS

The term 'family' is not only used by academics, but it also features strongly in people's emotions (Ribbens McCarthy, 2010), as well as in political rhetoric. Attachments to the term can evoke deeply held desires and longings, such that some writers describe 'family' as a 'fantasy' (Mackinnon, 2006) or 'an overwrought object of desire' (Walkover, 1992). Nevertheless it can be considered a 'well-founded illusion', since it is strongly institutionalized by the state (Bourdieu, 1996) and the subject of ideological manipulation by politicians (Bernardes, 1985), with family studies as a scholarly pursuit in many societies succumbing to this ideological partisanship (Zvinkliene, 1996).

It is hard for family scholars to deal adequately with the emotional features of family lives and relationships, when these encompass variations from love to hate, and kindness and altruism to violence and abuse. Part of this difficulty is that actual family experiences may be equivocal and shifting, involving deep paradoxes around such issues as power and love, or care and oppression, and the related feelings may hold much ambivalence. The same act, say of cooking a meal, may feel like a practical expression of caring for someone on one occasion (or even at one moment), a form of sociable leisure activity on another occasion and an exploitative form of labour on yet another.

These issues are also crucial for professionals working with families, including social workers, health professionals, public health workers, educationists and also sometimes human resources professionals. Important questions are raised about how family studies as an academic field relates to professional interventions and policy decisions. Since the 1920s, some have advocated that the social sciences should contribute to the understanding of family relations and therefore to the quality of family lives and society (Karraker and Grochowski, 2006). But views may vary on how close this relationship should be, for example should family scholars and family professionals act as collaborators, or is academic study compromised by too close an association? Much will depend on the purpose of the particular research project. Interwoven with these questions is the issue (raised above) about how professionals as well as researchers may deal with personal experiences and feelings about family lives.

Some family researchers seek to describe family lives and relationships in unambiguous terms, as if it is possible for academics to stand outside such issues. This risks imposing implicit evaluations and value judgements on to the experiences of others – as we illuminate through many of the discussions in this book. Family lives may be (perhaps increasingly) an area in which people feel that their moral identities are at stake, and thus a need to defend any potential threat to their moral standing. Even where family scholars seek to be non-evaluative and to understand the experiences of family members on their own terms, the concepts being deployed may unwittingly convey all kinds of implicit assumptions and judgements. Terms such as 'dysfunctional' or 'healthy' families, or 'children's developmental needs', can all appear to be objective terms, but are actually underpinned by value judgements that are rooted in particular cultural assumptions. In this book, we have unpicked these assumptions.

This is not to say that family scholars and practitioners have to adopt a relativist position in which all family practices and patterns are treated as equally valid within their cultural contexts (Hollinger, 2007). It is to suggest, though, that researchers and practitioners need to be clear about how and where to take a particular value stance. Professionals deciding on difficult interventions with family members may find this an uncomfortable stance. Nevertheless, this is a respectful and realistic approach to take, made possible by paying careful attention to the concepts used and the theories in which they are embedded. We very much hope that this book will contribute to such an endeavour.

SELECTION AND ORGANIZATION OF CONCEPTS

This book lays out the ways in which key concepts in family studies are understood and the primary debates to which they relate. One difficulty encountered in studying families is that the topics are so 'familiar' that the terms and the underlying issues are taken as unremarkable and unproblematic in general social conversation. Throughout the book we have sought to make these familiar terms strange, unpicking assumptions to make it clear how much variability there can be in their meanings. Much of this may be difficult to see, not only because family relationships may be understood as 'natural', but because they may also be regarded as part of the ways in which things have 'always been'. Indeed, the history of family studies has been shaped by feminist arguments that family lives are not 'natural', and thus somehow outside of 'society', but are deeply social and linked to political concerns.

Deciding which concepts to prioritize in this book has been a difficult task, particularly when so many of the issues are closely related. We have dealt with this by identifying clusters of linked terms or sub-concepts and addressing them under one major key concept. Such terms are then identified in **bold** in the discussion within that heading. These **bolded sub-concepts** can also be traced across the various entries by using the index at the end of the book. At the same time, there are many cross-cutting links among the main key concept entries themselves, and the most significant of these are listed as cross-references at the end of each entry.

Besides the difficulties of selecting which concepts are key for family studies, we have also been aware that there are some important ideas, or themes, which are not included among our main key concepts entries. There are a number of reasons for this:

- We simply could not include all the concepts that we would have wished within this particular volume (but readers may like to consult publications such as Crompton et al. (2010), Kamerman and Moss (2009) and S. Lewis et al. (2009) on families and work–life balance; Crozier and Reay (2005) and Lareau (2003) for families and education; and Bianchi et al. (2005) and Broome et al. (1998) for families and health).
- Some terms have not been included as key concepts because they represent recurring themes across many aspects of family lives. **Time**, for example, is a core feature of family experiences in all sorts of ways, and is an area of academic study in itself, as are **work**, **consumerism**, **food** and **money** (see Morgan, D.H.J., 1996). Instead, these are raised in relevant entries in this book, which the reader can locate through the index.
- Some terms stand at the margins between family studies and related areas of study, for example concepts that are central to the study of personal experience in social contexts, such as the **self**, **subjectivity**, **identity**, **emotions** or the **psycho-social**. Again, the reader can find reference to these terms as sub-concepts.

As we noted earlier, different national and cultural contexts are important in understanding the significance and meaning of families and family life.

We use the phrase 'European and New World' (drawing on Therborn, 2004) as our primary way of referring to countries in continental Europe along with English-speaking developed societies around the world, that is, including the UK, the USA, Canada, Australia and New Zealand. Occasionally we also refer to 'Western' or 'Westernized' as alternative, familiar terms to avoid repetition.

HOW TO USE THIS BOOK

As a general guide to how you can make the best use of this book, the most obvious place to start is the contents list. Depending on your purposes, you may find that a particular key concept entry may provide all that you need.

If you cannot see what you want in the main contents list, go to the index to see whether your term of interest is there, and then follow it up where it appears in the key concept entries.

If you want to trace connections between a term and others across other key concepts, you can follow up the cross-references that are listed at the end of each entry and/or you can look up the bolded sub-concepts in the index to see where they appear in other entries.

Sub-concepts may not always be explicitly defined, and may be used in somewhat different ways in various entries – but the meaning should be understandable from the context of the discussion, or you can follow it up in the further reading given at the end of the main entry in which it appears.

At the end of each main entry you will find some recommendations for further reading. These will provide you with more in-depth discussions. Family studies is a very dynamic field so to study particular topics and issues in-depth you may well want to look at recent journal and book publications.

We hope you will enjoy your explorations of family studies.

Attachment and Loss

DEFINITION

The theory of attachment suggests babies and young children need to create satisfactory emotional bonds with their caretakers if they are to develop as healthy children and adults, and make adequate relationships throughout life. Attachment theory is also the basis for some theories of loss.

DISCUSSION

Attachment theory is a form of developmental psychology emphasizing the baby and young child's primary attachment figure(s), including experiences of **separation** and reunion. Attachment is seen as an innate and thus universal need, but the ways in which this need is met and its implications for child development vary considerably (van Ijzendoorn et al., 2007). Childhood relationships are seen as the foundation on which a complex set of developmental processes are built, with consequences for emotional and social outcomes in adult life. The word 'attachment' is used in preference to '**love**' because some regard the latter as too emotional and ambiguous (Parkes, 2006).

How attachments develop may also be theorized from the point of view of psychoanalytic **object relations theory**, but attachment theory as a framework in its own right was based on studies of the ways in which some newborn animals make strong attachments to their initial caretakers, theorized to be functional for their survival. Attachment theory was elaborated initially by John Bowlby, who argued that an infant's primary attachment is vitally important, persistent and monotropic; that is, it is an attachment to the particular caretaker and cannot be transferred to another person, since each relationship is unique. Bowlby's original work was based largely on his experiences of working with children with social and emotional difficulties or those who had experienced institutional care or displacement and separation through war, rather than those living in everyday families. He developed the theory of **maternal**

deprivation, which explained childhood difficulties in terms of traumas resulting from separation from the mother (or mother substitute).

There is now a body of literature on attachment theory. Some of this supports Bowlby's original theory (Lamb, 2007), while some elaborates or modifies it. Ainsworth (Oates, 2007) developed a standardized 'Strange Situation' test. In this test, an infant is approached by someone unknown to them; sometimes the parent is present, sometimes not. How the infant responds is observed, and analysed in terms of their responses to separation from their parent. Four major and definitive categories of attachment are proposed: *secure* attachments that are optimal for subsequent development, *insecure-resistant* and *insecure-avoidant* behaviour, and *disorganized* or *disoriented* attachments (Oates, 2007).

A key feature of attachment theory is that young children are only able to explore the world, and tolerate some degree of separation from their primary caretaker (often understood to be the mother), if they feel secure in the original attachment. It is attentive, responsive, stimulating and affectionate care that is seen as key to the infant's level of security. If infants experience unresponsive, frightening and/or chaotic care they are likely to have a reduced capacity for dealing with everyday stress, which may have long-term implications for their development. Families living in poverty and situations of deprivation are the most likely to be compromised in their ability to provide the care appropriate for secure attachments (Belsky, 2007).

Politically, aspects of attachment theory have been drawn on to make inferences about the roles of mothers, particularly in terms of whether babies and young children can develop satisfactorily without more or less continuous maternal care in the early years of life, a point which can feature in discussions about working mothers. A mother is seen as having the potential for an automatic attachment to her new baby, although attachment can also be nurtured through contact after birth.

Attachment theory has been expanded to include the development of attachments throughout life, as well as to take account of variable patterns of childcare around the world (van Ijzendoorn et al., 2007). Fathers, and others, may also have a significant part to play in attachment, and attachment to peers may be important for adolescent development. The term 'attachment' may therefore be used for all bonds of love, not just that between infant and primary caretaker.

Loss and **grief** are sometimes linked to theories of attachment (Parkes, 2006), but they may also be theorized within other frameworks. The theories of loss linked to Bowlby's work on attachment and Freudian theories of psychic development share the view that the appropriate (healthy) response to grief requires a process of psychological detachment from the love object that has been lost. While these views have formed the basis for much work around **bereavement** and grief, research has gradually called them into question, particularly through evidence showing that people may express a sense of **continuing bonds** with their dead loved ones, whose presence may be quite strongly felt for very many years (Klass et al., 1996). This resonates with the ways that the dead may still have a strong social presence in some cultures, particularly through their significance as **ancestors**.

Death is a key event in family lives, sometimes being theorized as a basis of transition to another stage in the family life cycle. Many theories of bereavement and grief, however, focus on the impact on the individual's psychic life (as with theories of attachment and loss discussed above). The importance of family relationships in responses to death does feature in research into the impact of disruptive childhood events on later life, which suggests that family relationships may be significant for children's responses to the death of a parent. Family bereavement has also been researched with regard to the significance of the death of a spouse or partner. Less commonly, death of a family member may be considered in terms of its implications for an individual's sense of family and ethnic identity (e.g. Ribbens McCarthy, 2006).

As a term, 'loss' does not necessarily accompany bereavement experiences, even though the two are often linked. Death of a family member does not always represent a clear-cut loss, for example, if the person's presence is still strongly felt through continuing bonds, or if the relationship was not experienced as particularly significant in the first place. There may also be the potential for some of the consequences of death to be considered beneficial: by providing for a change of role, for example, or giving rise to a sense of self-esteem as a result of having coped with difficult events.

It is also important to consider how loss (and grief) may be used to describe a variety of experiences and disruptions, some of which may also be concerned with family relationships and transitions. Divorce, moving house or changing identity (e.g. through adolescence, the 'empty nest syndrome' when children leave the family home, or the onset of disability or chronic illness) may all be regarded as a basis for loss and grief, which may be understood as a **psycho-social transition** (Parkes, 2006). Like death of a family member, however, some of the implications of these experiences for individuals may not constitute an unequivocal loss.

SUMMARY

The term 'attachment' may be important in psychoanalytic object relations theories, but attachment theory as such is strongly linked to Bowlby's work on the significance of secure attachments for healthy child development. Attachment theory also lends itself to a particular perspective on loss, although loss may also be theorized from other perspectives. Furthermore, not all forms of death or other forms of disruption necessarily constitute a loss in any unequivocal sense.

FURTHER READING

Goldberg (2000) is an accessible introduction to attachment theory, while Parkes (2006) overviews attachment theories and discusses loss from this framework. Howe et al. (1999) look at the implications of attachment theory for social work with families and children, and Ribbens McCarthy (2006) discusses bereavement, loss and change in the lives of young people.

Related concepts *Child Development; Family Effects; Family Life Cycle and Life Course*

.... Biology ....

DEFINITION

Biological approaches to family life, and use of the terminology of blood kinship, emphasize the role of genetic inheritance and motivations in how people behave and feel towards each other.

DISCUSSION

'Biology' generally refers to the structure, function, evolution, and other aspects of living organisms. Theories that build on biological approaches vary in how far they emphasize the determining role of biology, and how far they incorporate or subsume the social aspects of human lives, including families. Theories such as eugenics, socio-biology, and neo-Darwinist evolutionary psychology are not exactly the same, but share a general view of biology as destiny, thus fore-grounding the significance of human **bodies**.

Eugenics, which came to the fore in Western Europe and the USA in the late nineteenth and early twentieth centuries, saw **genetic inherit- ance** as responsible for strengthening or undermining the capacities of nations. This view was associated with the political strategy of selective reproduction towards the goal of a superior race, and was largely dis- credited through its association with the Holocaust in Europe. During the twentieth century, first **socio-biology** and then neo-Darwinist **evolu- tionary psychology** gained attention. These approaches see social behav- iour and feelings as biological in origin, and linked to natural selection processes that are assumed to stem from the time of **hunter-gatherer societies**, such that it was those genes that enabled survival that became transmitted and established in the gene pool. The evolutionary behav- iour involved is understood to be universal across time and space because natural selection works too slowly to have updated the gene pool inherited from hunter-gatherer conditions.

These theories then attempt to explain current social lives, particu- larly in families, including: the gendered division of employment and **domestic labour**; sexual behaviours that are shaped by different bio- logical strategies for ensuring the survival of as many offspring as possi- ble between men and women; the emotional commitment of parents to their genetic children (Wilson, 1978). The idea of a **maternal instinct**, for example, is propounded as the explanation for mothers caring for, protecting and nurturing their children. Step-parents, on the other hand, are argued to be more likely to mistreat and even fatally injure their step-children (Daly and Wilson, 1998).

Concerns about the links between biological parenthood, its accom- panying social status and caring practices and emotional affinity with children, is evident in research on fathering and step-fathering. **Ascribed** (or biological) fathering is seen as rooted in the biological tie, in contrast to **achieved** (social) fathering as a close caring relationship with chil- dren, with a debate about the extent to which step-fathers can or should feel their step-children to be 'their own' (Edwards, R., et al., 2002; Marsiglio, 1995). In contrast to **non-resident** biological fathers, the biological link between mothers and children is regarded as so 'natural' in European and New World societies that mothers who abandon or leave their children are seen as *un*natural (Gustafson, 2005). Nonetheless,

biology

13

mothers can and do leave their children for a variety of reasons. Such situations support arguments that no gene can determine complex and socially situated behaviour.

Biological approaches are associated with the long-standing **nature versus nurture** debate, in which proponents of the 'nature' side of the argument believe that biology is the key causal mechanism of human behaviour, rather than environmental influences. One way of trying to resolve the debate has been through studies of (identical and fraternal) twins brought up in various circumstances. Recent work points to a complex interaction between biology and environment, rather than to the determining primacy of one or the other (Moffitt et al., 2006), and this now tends to be the focus for research, particularly through an examination of neural activities in the brain, and other physiological measures. Some research points to genetically based differences in the extent to which individuals respond to their experiences of nurture (Belsky and Pluess, 2010). Recent developments in neuroscience have been investigating neural networks in the brain as an explanation for behaviour and personality, quite often using animals. Writers take variable approaches to the ways in which such research is applied, with some extrapolating from this work as a potential basis for understanding and intervening in the upbringing of children, on the basis that poor parenting develops and embeds anti-social brain patterns in children (Wilson, 2002).

Critiques of approaches that prioritize biology focus on theories of natural selection in relation to humans, and the idea of genetic inheritance as the key determinant of society in general and family life specifically. One argument is that socio-biology and evolutionary psychology distort the rules of scientific method. Proponents of biology as destiny are said to select particular observations and functions of non-human/animal behaviour that suit their arguments and then extrapolate these to humans. Other aspects of the methods used by socio-biologists and evolutionary psychologists that are criticized include the process of hypothesizing on the basis of supposed 'facts' about hunter-gatherer societies, and the tendency to rely on uncontrolled experiments with small samples, as well as secondary interpretation of heterogeneous data. Critics argue that while innate biological tendencies may be important, focusing only on natural selection as cause, and all social life as effect, is distorted and oversimplified. In this deterministic 'world of looking glass logic' (Rose, S., 1980: 165), the complexity and diversity of family lives and human relationships are ignored.

These debates are contentious not least because they carry policy implications, and can be invoked towards particular political projects. For example, biologically based approaches can be mobilized to justify the conservative status quo of unequal power relations between genders, ethnicities and class groups. Principles of heredity and **genealogy** historically have also played a role in establishing legitimate heirs, promoting the political and economic privileges of the middle classes (Davidoff et al., 1999). The view of biological parenthood as paramount for committed relationships with children has led to family laws in many countries that institutionalize the view that bringing up and providing for children rests with biological parents even if they are not co-resident with their children.

In terms of everyday understandings in Western societies, biology can play an important part in people's constructions and understandings of the meaning of family. Family **resemblances** and traits, physical and personality likenesses and differences, are accorded significance from the birth of a child onwards: 'she has her father's eyes', 'he has his grandmother's temper'. People are also motivated to understand their own identity through genealogy, with researching family history and kinship a popular interest. Some see such activities as a search for what seem to be fixed connections in an uncertain and individualistic world.

This points to the way in which genetic understandings of descent can appear to provide a solid basis for what may be social constructions of relationships, as well as their links to racial and national formations (as in the idea of **roots**, and **fictive kin**: Chamberlain, 1999; Hackstaff, 2009). Similarly, the language of biological family relationships can be invoked more widely to symbolize close emotional connection (e.g. 'she's like a mother to me'). More formalized examples of biological kinship terminology, denoting political solidarity, include the use of the terms '**brothers**' and '**sisters**' and 'father/mother of the chapel' in the socialist and trade union movements, and 'sisters' in feminist movements.

Such issues point towards the ways in which biology is socially constructed through cultural understandings, and may be invoked to provide an apparent fixity to social relationships. Anthropologists have suggested that European and New World cultures frame biology as nature, which is seen as a dominant idea that stands outside of social life (Strathern, 1992a). Consequently, when new 'facts' are developed within a scientific paradigm, such as the possibilities of testing DNA to identify the genitor of a child, this is then considered to have been an

biology

15

underlying 'truth' that was present all along, even if the people concerned did not know it at the time (Carsten, 2004).

While most societies invoke a distinction between ties that are 'given' or ascribed and those that are 'made' or achieved, in European and New World societies such a distinction is equated with divisions between ties that are based in blood and those that are chosen (Carsten, 2004). Anthropological studies of family and kinship across the globe reveal the diversity of cultural understandings of human bodies, including biological reproduction and parenting, and whether and how biology and parenting are considered to be linked (e.g. Riviere, 1985; Shore, 1992). Ideas about the constitution, relevance and significance of biological parenthood and genetic links are not universally significant.

In contemporary affluent societies, developments in **reproductive technology** have further complicated the link between biology and parenthood by intervening in the processes of reproduction, either to prevent or to facilitate it. Methods of assisted reproduction include *in vitro* fertilization (IVF), gamete donation and surrogacy. To some extent, advances in reproductive technology have enabled the establishment of non-biologically based families, including for same-sex couples, although gendered divisions of labour and power seem to remain. This poses fundamental legal and policy questions concerning custody, care and maintenance of children, and legal definitions of motherhood and fatherhood (Shore, 1992; Strathern, 1992b). Yet, as noted above, while technological knowledge may lead to interventions in the processes of reproduction, in European and New World societies biological ties are nonetheless understood as pre-eminent.

SUMMARY

Eugenics, socio-biology and evolutionary psychology approaches regard social behaviour and feelings as essentially biological, originating in reactions and emotions that developed as adaptations for the survival of individuals and their genes in hunter-gatherer societies. Criticisms of approaches that prioritize biology focus on the unscientific methods and oversimplified conclusions underpinning such work. Biology can be invoked as part of people's understandings of family descent and relationships, and as such is embedded in family law and policy in European and New World societies, but there is a diversity of cultural understandings about the nature of genetic links and biological parenthood in other societies. Science may complicate the link between biology and family through the development of reproductive technologies, but can also reinforce the importance of genetic links (e.g. DNA testing). Recently, biosocial research has focused on interactions between physiological phenomena and socially based behaviours and feelings.

FURTHER READING

Pinker (1998) and Wilson (1975) put the case for natural selection based on innate genetic drives as the root of human nature and behaviour, while S. Rose et al. (1984) and Sahlins (1977) put forward alternative understandings with Rose (2006) particularly focusing on research on the brain. Troost and Filsinger (2004) offer an overview of biosocial perspectives on family lives. Carsten (2004) includes an anthropological discussion of reproductive technologies, gender and the social construction of science in Europe and the New World.

Related concepts   *Family Law; Kinship; Parenthood; Post-Coupledom*

care

DEFINITION

Care refers to both a set of feelings and a set of activities and resources, concerned with supportive relationships, ranging from close family members to strangers.

DISCUSSION

There is a complex connection between the concepts of 'family' and 'care', and between academic work on care and caring, and family studies. Family is often taken for granted as a key site of care, involving relationships of **love**, support and **nurture**. Feminist writers in particular have argued that family, care and **gender** are interconnected dimensions of social life that need to be disentangled. They opened up the study of

17

care as a socially constructed, rather than a 'natural', set of activities, entailing considerable **work** and effort. In European and New World societies, the issue of care has become prominent within policy developments, along with the establishment of care services and recognition of carer as a **role** in both institutional- and family-based settings, particularly in the context of an ageing population. Unpaid care has become a major issue in family policies, particularly with regard to the goal of gender equality in employment and family–work balance (Lewis, J., 2006).

The term 'care' includes both physical activities of care – **caring for** – and feelings of caring – **caring about** – which may occur in various locations (public/private) and settings (formal/informal), with differing financial implications (paid/unpaid). Care also conveys moral overtones because it entails elements of negotiation, **reciprocity** and **deservingness**, through which people's kinship identities are affirmed or undermined (Finch and Mason, 1993). The term may also be employed politically to further particular agendas. For example, the term '**foster carer**' in the UK has replaced the term 'foster parent', in order to signal that this is a professional role. Nevertheless, 'carer' in relation to children can refer to a foster carer, a day carer or a parent. Care of children can thus refer to a (semi-) professional role (involving 'work') or a supposedly natural feature of parenting. Care services, however, are generally focused on the care of older people or people with disabilities rather than children. The term 'care' can also have varying legal significance for children, positioning them as dependants needing care and **protection** or as dangerous and in need of care and **control**.

Like mothering, caring has often been assumed to be part of women's 'natural' feminine character. In theorizing care, feminists have made it visible in order to consider how it is socially shaped, and have also stressed the need to value it and consider its political ramifications. **Community care** policies, for example, may act as a euphemism for 'family care', implicitly understood as care by women. The 'caring for' and 'caring about' distinction noted above has been refined to a discussion of care as an activity and care as a disposition, with the latter including a sense of **responsibility** (Tronto, 1993). Furthermore, the intrinsically gendered meaning of care affects the support provided to carers.

Others have considered whether and how care in domestic or familial contexts differs from care as paid labour in more public settings. Care provided in the course of paid employment – whether as domiciliary care of older or disabled people, nursing care in hospitals or care of young children – contains tensions between the extent to which it is a form of paid physical work and the extent to which it carries expectations derived from ideas of personal commitment that are associated with family care, and that also contribute to the low pay and status of the caring professions. At the same time, payment for informal care may be viewed as undermining its supposed basis in **emotional** connections.

As well as gender, age status, class and ethnicity are associated with family-based care. **Age status** means that the notion of 'child carers' is seen as an anachronism in most European and New World societies. Furthermore, caring relationships between adult kin are expected to demonstrate elements of reciprocity and deservingness that do not apply to care of children. Social and material **inequalities** mean that the effort of care work may be distributed along lines of **class** and **race**; for example, through **global care chains** (Hochschild, 2000), where women from developing nations are paid to care for the children of the more affluent, while sending money home to pay other women to care for their own children in their country of origin. This draws attention to the diverse social contexts in which caring relationships occur, challenging ideas of families as self-sufficient units.

Feminist theorists have also developed philosophical thinking around care as a basis for a set of values and **ethical reasoning** (Held, 2006) and a key feature of **citizenship** (Sevenhuijsen, 1998). There is a delicate balance here between appearing to celebrate women's apparently 'natural' caring qualities and explicating qualities that are of value beyond family lives. Feminists have drawn attention not only to the drudgery of much care work in caring for people, but also to the qualities involved in caring about them. Care has been analysed as involving values of attentiveness, responsibility, trust, competence and responsiveness to human frailties, with **maternal thinking** in particular entailing attention to preservation, **nurturance** and training (Ruddick, 1990). Care can also be seen as a basis for ethical reasoning that is contextual, relational, attentive and contingent, rather than universal, abstract and formal. As such, it constitutes a legitimate basis for political theory (Sevenhuijsen, 1998) and for social life in general as well as personal lives.

Recently, however, some feminist understandings of care have been challenged from postcolonial theory (Raghuram et al., 2009). There are also debates about how an ethic of care may be in tension with an ethic of **justice**, with regard to both public and family lives, for example in terms of family members having rights to distributive justice so

care

that all have equal access to family-based resources, although the notion of **fairness** may be more relevant to family lives (Ribbens McCarthy et al., 2003).

Contributions from disability studies (Garland-Thomson, 2006) have also stressed care as a relationship in which the cared-for are as significant as the carer. This raises questions about whether the relationship is one-directional and involves power and subjugation and, indeed, whether 'care' is too problematic a concept to be useful at all. Care is centrally concerned with human frailties and, as such, carries the potential for abuse and neglect. At the same time, it points to the ways in which **vulnerability** and neediness are part of the human condition, so that there is no neat division of carer and cared-for. Consequently, ideas of dependence and independence may become refined into ideas of **interdependence**.

Particular understandings of power are embedded in the predominant notion of the independent and **autonomous self** of post-Enlightenment Western cultures, in which exercising power over someone else is posed as antithetical to caring. From this view power involves the assertion of one person's wishes over another, whereas care is understood as prioritizing the wishes or needs of another. A different understanding of the self, as intrinsically relational, leads to another notion of power, in which caring for someone else may also be experienced as caring for oneself. From this perspective, the sense of self is bound up with the cared-for, which may be understood as a prime indicator of love and sometimes as a different experience of family life in general (Kağitçibaşi, 2005).

SUMMARY

Ideas about care and family are closely connected. Highlighting care risks celebrating women's 'natural' qualities, to the extent that its ambivalences may be overlooked. Feminist writers in particular have theorized care in multifaceted ways and explored its relevance to public and family lives without losing sight of such ambiguities. Emotionally, care may be experienced as a source of both positive regard and unwelcome obligation and duty. As an activity, it may be experienced as a source both of connection and of tedious hard work and potential exploitation. The international dimensions of care have received attention with regard to their economic, political and familial implications. The applicability of an ethic of care to political systems as well as family lives has been debated.

FURTHER READING

David H.J. Morgan (1996) offers a discussion of why care and gender seem to be so interlinked. Fink (2004) introduces intersections between care, family lives and social policies. Held (2006) discusses the ethics of care in relation to moral theory and society. Yeates (2009) overviews globalization, care and the implications for family lives and social reproduction.

Related concepts   *Division of Labour; Family Policies; Feminisms; Power*

Child Development

DEFINITION

Child development is a central concept within psychology for understanding change during the early years of life. It is rooted in a biological view that sees these years in terms of maturational stages from babyhood through to adulthood.

DISCUSSION

Child development theories see the early years as laying the foundation for adult life. In European and New World societies, developmental perspectives have arguably become the dominant paradigm for thinking about children. Children are understood as being different from adults, and as having specific needs. Because care of children is central to understandings of family life, and carries a **moral evaluation** of individuals as parents, how **children's needs** are understood has significant implications for families and for social policies concerned with family lives and parenting. From this perspective, children's needs have to be met if they are to fulfil their developmental potential, and this has implications for what is regarded as appropriate parenting. Historically, the parameters for 'normal' and 'abnormal' development in children were also notably developed in association with the introduction of **compulsory schooling**, which led to a new emphasis on age as a significant social marker.

'Development' may be used in a general way to indicate that the early years are important for consequences in later years, or it may refer to a model of progressive movement towards developmental goals or attainments, so that each stage is seen as being of a higher order than the previous stages. This model depends on the goals of coherent and mature adulthood.

Developmental psychology is generally divided into key areas of development, such as physical, social, cognitive, moral, emotional and linguistic. Major theorists within these different areas, such as Piaget on cognitive development and Kohlberg on moral development, have been highly influential, not only for the academic subject, but also for the training of professionals, such as teachers, health visitors and social workers. Consequently, while academic and research work may have moved away from some of the earlier foundational assumptions, professionals may continue to understand and promote child development on the basis of older sets of understandings that have become institutionalized.

Within a classic developmental framework, the infant is understood to be born with innate reflexes and predispositions towards **developmental progression**. Developmental progression and potential is viewed as unfolding from within, but also in need of appropriate nurturing. 'Appropriate development' is posed as a set of maturational stages through which the infant, and later the child and the adolescent, has to move satisfactorily in order to become a fully functioning adult.

Arising from this paradigm is a belief that scientific knowledge can lead to predictions about children's development, which can be tested by observation and experiment. Research has produced a wealth of measurements of children's functioning at different **ages**, from which benchmarks are derived to indicate what are considered to be the parameters of normal development. These then provide professionals with a basis from which to decide where and how to intervene.

A contrast to this normative, measurement-oriented developmental psychology is **psychoanalytic psychology**. A psychoanalytic perspective sees child development as rooted in unconscious desires and conflicts in the infant, particularly in relation to the mother. Like many other developmental approaches, psychoanalytic approaches view the child as moving sequentially through developmental stages based in biology (e.g. oral, anal, oedipal), which have to be resolved before moving on satisfactorily to the next stages. Unresolved issues at each stage have implications for the formation of personality, which may continue throughout life. A rather different but important form of psychoanalytic approach involves **object relations theory**, notably developed by Donald Winnicott and Melanie Klein. From a feminist psychoanalytic perspective, for example, Chodorow (1979) has theorized gender differences by reference to infants' and young children's identification with their primary carer – generally female – as an internalized, psychic structure or 'object' from whom boys and girls then respectively separate or connect.

Criticisms of child development theories centre on their cultural assumptions. The primary focus of these theories has been upon 'the child', a concept that constructs an abstract universal subject, isolated from social attributes, rather than focusing on children's variable experiences in particular historical cultures. Rooted in the cultures of European and New World societies, research has focused on children and infants as individuals, or as part of a mother–child dyad, rather than on networks of family and other relationships, including varying social, economic and cultural contexts. In this, it is tied in with the more general psychological focus on the **individual**, with an **'internal' psychic life**, a 'being' split off from the social. Furthermore, the focus on the mother–child dyad tends to hold mothers responsible for appropriate interactions with their child, arguably leading to a culture of anxiety and blame around parenthood and a neglect of the broader circumstances of family life. Burman (1994) argues that developmental psychology arose as part of a drive towards the production of moral **citizens** needed for bourgeois democracy. The apparent scientific base of developmental psychology may thus mask relationships of power embedded within this approach.

From a global perspective, it is apparent that 'child development' is largely predicated on a culturally and historically specific notion of childhood. Furthermore, it also depends on ideas of development towards a version of **adulthood** rooted in the post-Enlightenment notion of **personhood** that underpins Western values of liberal democracy (Brooker and Woodhead, 2008). Work appearing to show that **authoritative parenting** (firm and responsive) is the most effective style for optimal child development (Baumrind, 1989) has been undertaken within value systems prizing individuality and **independence**. Particular versions of children's needs and expectations of appropriate '**outcomes**' have been produced within specific cultural paradigms. These are then presented as scientifically and biologically based universals. This has led to a critique of some of the gendered assumptions behind developmental models, such as Gilligan's critique of Kohlberg's stages of moral reasoning (Gilligan, 1982), and a questioning of how far any universal statements can be made about children's needs and development. A view of universal child development risks underestimating children's capacities in different social contexts (Boyden, 2003), or understanding their capacities through inappropriate cultural frameworks. When children are studied across different cultures, their competencies at different ages are found to vary greatly depending on what have been their experiences of different ways of living and expectations of children within their societies (Rogoff, 2003).

Important attempts have been made to modify child development theories to take account of some of these criticisms, particularly to view the developmental process as one of interaction between: significant figures in children's lives, including family members and others; children's developing competencies, including genetically based capacities and characteristics; and social contexts more broadly. Bronfenbrenner's (1979) **ecological model** places the child at the centre of concentric circles, consisting of home, school, neighbourhood, and so on, and radiating outwards towards an outermost circle representing the **macro system**. This model also tries to take account of feedback mechanisms and interaction between the individual and the contexts, and between the contexts themselves, as well as processes over time. However, it provides only a limited account of cultural and social contexts (Uttal, 2009), failing to consider how individuals and social contexts interact to the point at which they are mutually entwined.

Vygotsky's work on 'mediated action' has also been important in trying to overcome the individual/social split by theorizing thought as occurring in the interaction between individuals and cultures through joint activity, leading to an emphasis on common activities with other humans, and this approach has been taken up in some anthropological studies of child development (Rapport and Overing, 2007). Gergen's work (2009) draws on a **social constructionist** perspective to consider individual development in social context, such that **identity** and **self** are theorized as being produced through interaction. Additionally, work from societies around the world has challenged the notion of personhood (Zimba, 2002) and Western concepts of the self (Nsamenange, 2004) on which much developmental psychology is founded.

Nevertheless, these more sophisticated theories may not filter through to (global) social policy or professional training. As noted above, classic developmental psychology has become heavily institutionalized, for example through international law and aid agencies, the United Nations Committee on the Rights of the Child, UNESCO, national institutions such as health and education, and policies towards parents and family lives. It has also become an unremarkable form of **governance**, in which family members monitor their own behaviours through these theories (Rose, 1999). The power of the classic focus on the 'needs' of the individual but universal child can impose Western, **middle-class**, white cultural understandings and values – a form of **cultural imperialism** that fails to take account of **diversity** across global contexts and within societies, such that any differences are seen as aberrations and deficiencies.

SUMMARY

'Child development' depends on particular notions of childhood and development, but has become established as an apparently scientific and universal form of knowledge. It is heavily institutionalized to the point where it is largely taken for granted as a basis for evaluating appropriate care and family life. However, while it is a vast and important area of study, its underlying assumptions are rooted in particular cultural and social contexts. Various attempts have been made to counteract these limitations and it is still a rapidly expanding field.

FURTHER READING

Oates et al. (2005) provide an introduction to child development theories, and C. Lewis (2005) overviews debates with particular reference to parenting. Woodhead (2009) discusses child development in the light of ideas from childhood studies. Aspects of developmental psychology from cultural perspectives are discussed in Coll and Magnuson (2000) and Kağitçibaşi (2005). Rogoff (2003) builds on Vygotsky's work to provide an overview of human development in cultural contexts.

Related concepts *Attachment and Loss; Childhood/Children; Family Effects; Socialization*

child development

Childhood/Children

DEFINITION

Childhood refers to the state or time of being a child, as a phase of life that is understood both as separate from, and in preparation for, being an adult; whereas 'child/ren' refers to specific individuals or a group.

DISCUSSION

Within the context of material affluence in contemporary European and New World societies, childhood is understood as a special phase of the life course, involving the construction of 'family' and 'home' as a key space appropriate for childhood. This means that ideas of family and childhood are strongly linked. The predominant ways of thinking about children have involved seeing the family as the proper place for children's socialization into the norms and expectations of the society in which they live, with parents as responsible for children's appropriate physical, social, cognitive and behavioural development and outcomes. More recently, however, a growing body of work, commonly known as the 'New Social Studies of Childhood' (James et al., 1998) has challenged these sorts of understandings of childhood as passive, to pose children rather as social actors, exercising their agency within family life and in other settings. Additionally, theories of **modernity** also argue that life phase distinctions between childhood and **adulthood** are breaking down, with ramifications for flows of power in parent–child relationships. And although in other societies and historical periods children are, or have been understood as, physically and cognitively capable, playing a part in the economic and social life of families and communities, it is the Western-based understanding of childhood which has become internationally dominant through such organizations as the United Nations and aid agencies. This then risks the imposition of ideas, for example about the inappropriateness of child labour, which may be at odds with other cultural understandings (Boyden, 1997).

Childhood as a separate phase of life is **institutionalized** as part of European and New World societies, through, for example: compulsory **schooling** and accompanying exclusion from substantial paid work; special treatment within the judicial system; exclusion from **civic participation** (such as being able to vote); and the construction of public **spaces** in which to contain children (such as playgrounds). Children are thus compartmentalized in specifically designated, separate and protected organized settings, often supervised by professionals and structured according to age and ability. Underlying the separateness and institutionalization of this Western notion of childhood are ideas of the **dependency**, vulnerability and incompetence of children (Archard, 1993; James et al., 1998), as well as visions of their innocence, spontaneity and freedom from responsibility and moral accountability (Ribbens, 1994; Ribbens McCarthy and Edwards, 2000). In this view of childhood, children are 'becomings' rather than 'beings' – that is, they are understood to be in a phase of incomplete and dependent development rather than considered to be complete, independent and self-possessed (Qvortrup et al., 1994). Hence children are thought to require care and direction by their parents and within families, in order to provide them with resources and protection, with parents' role being to take responsibility for children's well-being, development, and control.

The construction of the historically specific form of the post-industrial family and household over the past two centuries has defined a bounded 'private sphere' of family and home, to which children are said 'naturally' to belong (James et al., 1998). For some, a privatized realm of the family home is deeply implicated in children's socialization into forms of personal regulation and independent citizenship that are compatible with liberal capitalism in particular (Rose, 1992). As we elaborate below, this raises debates about the nature of childhood in contemporary society, concerning the extent to which children are and should be dependent within families – referred to as 'familialization' – or whether they do or should have as equal a say as adults in families – referred to as 'democratization'.

Some argue there has been a rise in cultural uncertainty about the appropriate form that childhood should take, including a focus on the part that families play in children's development into adults (Lee, 2001). Children in European and New World societies are said, on the one hand, to be increasingly 'economically useless'; that is, they do not earn a living in the labour market. On the other hand, they also have become 'emotionally priceless', meaning that high levels of economic and emotional investment in them, and obligation towards them, is required from their parents (Zelitzer, 1985).

Within this context, then, two ostensibly contradictory general trends are postulated as features of post-industrialized childhood. The first is said to be a deepening trend towards **familialization** in children's lives (Edwards, 2002). This notion captures two features of contemporary children's lives. First, children are increasingly reliant on their parents for their standard of living and the basic conditions of their lives, albeit different welfare regimes vary in the extent to which provisions for children are organized collectively and socially, or individually and privately (Qvortrup et al., 1994). Second, there is an emphasis on family upbringing as shaping children's behaviour and attitudes; for example, children's educational success is seen increasingly as linked to parental involvement in their schooling. Thus children's **identities** and activities are said to be increasingly incorporated into their family, materially and conceptually. This may leave them with reduced opportunities to experience independence in other social spaces, although there may be social class variations in this (Lareau, 2003). Implicit generational contracts are said to govern relations between parents and children in families, shaping the division of labour between the **generations** concerning flows of power, provision and dependency in resources and relationships (Alanen and Bardy, 1991). Furthermore, children's lives outside of formal institutional settings, such as school, are the responsibility of their parents. Unsupervised location outside of their family life, or other institutional contexts, is regarded both as posing risks to vulnerable children's safety and well-being, and as a danger to others and a threat to the social order from unruly children (Scott et al., 1998). Additionally, in some European and New World contexts, legislation holds parents responsible for their children's misdemeanours. An alternative perspective poses young people's independent access to public space as important for their participation in **citizenship** (Weller, 2007).

The second main trend in children's lives that is put forward as a feature of post-industrialized childhood concerns **democratization** in family life, and is part of wider ideas about a transformation in family life and relationships towards **equality** and individualization. The notion of phases of life is challenged in these wider ideas, with the boundaries and distinctions between childhood and adulthood becoming blurred (Beck, 1992). This has implications for parent–child relationships. Rather than exercising absolute power, parents are said increasingly to negotiate agreement with their children, treating them as equals, engaging in debate and giving them a say in domestic decision making. Giddens (1992), for example argues that, as part of the democratic management of family life, children should be treated as what he calls, 'the putative equal of the adult' (1992: 191), based on how a child would legitimate parental authority if she or he had access to adult knowledge. There are, however, different emphases here in relation to 'is' and 'ought'. Whereas some say that this is a trend in family life (Beck, 1997), others regard it as a desirable model (Giddens, 1992). Ostensibly, this trend contradicts some aspects of the familialization trend discussed above, although again, it is parents who have a duty to ensure this version of childhood.

Other commentators have criticized pictures of the democratization of contemporary European and New World childhoods, whether this is considered to be a good thing (as in individualization theories) or as bad for society (as in New Right formulations). They highlight interdependency in relationships between parents and children. Children can experience their parents' care as control, as a demonstration of connectedness, and as liberation, all at one and the same time. They can also experience their own concerns about, and responsibilities towards, other family members in the same complex ways (Brannen et al., 2000). At the same time, sociologists have drawn attention to the illusion of familial democracy for children and the persistence of power relations (Jamieson, 1998). Part of this illusion concerns the construction of childhood and adulthood, by exclusive reference to one another. Thus the other side of the coin of modern childhood discussed above, is that parents – as adults – are both posed as, and see themselves as, providers and protectors of children in their care, and can be held responsible and accountable as such for ensuring that children experience a 'good' childhood (Ribbens McCarthy et al., 2003).

SUMMARY

Childhood refers to an institutionally organized phase of life, as distinct from child/ren which refers to individuals or groups. Cultural understandings of childhood and child/ren may vary within and between societies around the world. In the Western view, the qualities associated with this phase of life, including dependency and innocence, mean that family is regarded as a key social unit for children's upbringing, with parents seen as responsible for this. Two seemingly contradictory trends have been identified in post-industrialized childhood in relation to the nature of family life: familialization and familial democratization. These ideas about the nature of modern childhood have their critics, drawing attention to enduring power relations and oversimplification of children's complex family lives.

FURTHER READING

James and James (2008) are a reference source for issues in relation to childhood, including for family life. Montgomery (2008) provides an anthropological view of childhood around the world, and Elder et al. (1994) highlight the contextual importance of time and place in studying children.

Related concepts   *Child Development; Home; Parenthood; Public and Private*

Comparative Approaches

DEFINITION

Comparative approaches study families across varying contexts, such as different societies, cultures, regions, neighbourhoods or historical periods.

DISCUSSION

Studies of family forms and lives across different time or space **contexts** may include comparing families in a contemporary society with the same society at an earlier historical period, or comparing families in different regions within one contemporary society. Or the comparisons could be broader, looking at family lives within or across continents, for example. Comparisons can also take account of diversity within a family form. For example, one study investigated **lone mothers'** uptake of paid work by comparing, firstly, the views of different social groups of lone mothers on the basis of **race**, **class** and **culture**, as well as the type of neighbourhood in which they lived; secondly, the employment available to lone mothers in different local **labour markets**; and thirdly, the policy treatment of lone mothers in different **welfare state** regimes (Duncan and Edwards, 1999).

Methodologies for comparative studies can be divided into large scale **quantitative** studies, smaller scale **qualitative** methods and analysis of **archival sources**. In order to make a comparison, it is necessary to find a way to generalize about families in each context. It can, however, be difficult to take account of the variability of family lives that occur within each context, and to construct a definition that is relevant across contexts. Another difficulty can relate to differences of language, and whether a term used in one society has a meaningful equivalent elsewhere (e.g. Mangen, 1999). Questions are also raised about the basis on which different people are grouped together (e.g. as members of a particular social class or national group) with the assumption that they have something sufficiently in common about their family lives to be compared with another group of people. In his **global** comparative analysis of family lives during the twentieth century, for example, Therborn (2004) differentiates regions of the world as demonstrating particular family patterns. Others seek to investigate the causes of family change across the world (Jayakody et al., 2008), while policy makers may be more interested in how family lives vary across **nation states**, for example in different European countries. What is appropriate for comparative purposes thus varies with the questions being asked.

A widespread view in family studies has been that 'the family' is universal, performing similar **functions** in societies all over the world. Murdock's (2003) thesis on the universality of the nuclear family was largely unquestioned for decades. Critics suggest, however, that notions of a universal family can only be sustained by imposing a particular understanding of one family form (the Western nuclear family) on a variety of social arrangements across societies and cultures, creating a sort of **cultural imperialism**. Another foundational view suggested that family change across the world follows an evolutionary, linear, model towards one particular family form as a result of development and **industrialization** – sometimes known as **convergence theory**. However, family change has been found to take many forms alongside industrialization.

Nevertheless, quantitative comparative studies of families often seek to establish universal **causal laws**, for example about how families affect individual lives or how families and households are shaped by wider features of social structure (Lee and Haas, 2004). Such approaches assume that it is possible to compare social systems and their properties, and that any variations between societies can be explained by relations among these properties. For example, the systemic properties of, on the one hand, women's labour force participation rates across different societies, and, on the other hand, **divorce** rates, can be considered to see if they co-vary in patterned and causal ways. Kiernan (2007) provides the example of a regular link between the experience of divorce in childhood and the likelihood of entering **cohabitation** rather than **marriage** in adulthood, but this may or may not be a causal association. She also discusses striking patterns of parenthood across Europe, showing similarities sometimes across Europe in comparison with both developing countries and the USA (in terms of a declining birth rate), but also variations between European countries (in terms of the much lower birth rate in Greece, Spain and Italy in comparison with France, Ireland and some Nordic countries).

As well as collecting new data, comparative studies use existing **statistical data banks**. A difficulty here is that such statistics may have been produced for varying purposes within different societies, and are not straightforwardly comparable. Furthermore, statistical approaches depend on the idea that it is possible to categorize and **measure** features of families and societies independently of the **meanings** that people give to their lives. Similarly, some argue that it is neither useful nor possible to make comparisons of families across societies because of the difficulties in comparing the complexities of social lives outside of their cultural, social and personal contexts. In response to this criticism, some quantitative researchers have sought to develop cross-national studies that take account of contexts as explanatory variables in their own right (Hantrais, 2004).

How we can understand and describe the lives of people living in other cultures and contexts is contentious. The concept of 'family' is a cultural framework that may presume a particular meaning of 'family' that is not relevant in other parts of the world. While contemporary English-speaking societies, for example tend to use 'family' to refer in an undifferentiated way to close **kin** from both the mother's and father's networks, in other societies relatives may be traced differently through the male or female line (Hendry, 2008). Indeed, Western academics may underestimate the significance of family connections across societies by imposing an ethnocentric (and class-specific) view of individualization theories (Edgar, 2007).

Despite all these methodological and conceptual difficulties, cross-cultural comparative studies can be a key source of insight into aspects of family and personal lives, and social reproduction more generally. This is particularly relevant to aspects of family lives that may otherwise be taken for granted because they are so embedded in the particular cultures in which researchers themselves live. Such differences of understanding and of values raise questions of how far it is possible to establish common standards across different societies, for example around such issues as 'good parenting' (Barlow et al., 2004). This need not necessarily lead to a position of **cultural relativism**, however: rather, it requires researchers and policy makers to be explicit about the values that underlie culturally based evaluations of family lives, including their own. The overall aim, then, of stepping outside the cultural assumptions of family studies rooted in particular societies arguably is an important and illuminating pursuit in a globalizing world. Exploring cultural assumptions is important, also, not only for understanding other societies or historical periods but also for understanding variations in family lives across social classes, ethnic, migrant, and refugee groups within any particular society.

SUMMARY

Looking at family lives across different societies, social groups and historical periods raises difficult conceptual and methodological issues. Quantitative researchers use comparative research to establish generalizable patterns or causal laws across societies in how family lives relate to features of social systems. Qualitative researchers seek insight into taken-for-granted cultural assumptions through exploring how different groups understand their lives and relationships. While this may then question some of the basis for scientific generalization, and thus raise questions of how to choose between, and evaluate, different family practices, this need not necessarily lead to a situation of total cultural relativism in family studies.

FURTHER READING

Lee and Haas (2004) introduce quantitative comparative family studies; Hantrais (2004) provides quantitative analysis of European family lives while also discussing the underlying difficulties. Carsten (2004) focuses on the comparative study of kinship, and Robertson offers an anthropological view built on the concept of 'human reproduction' rather than 'family'; Gillis (1997) provides a key historical account. Nzegwu's (2006) account of West African family changes since colonialism challenges understandings of North American society. See also Hollinger (2007) on cultural relativism.

Related concepts   *Child Development; Family Forms; Family Policies; Kinship*

comparative approaches

DEFINITION

Conflict theories share a concern with power inequalities that occur within and between families. They tend to bring into view the family as an oppressive institution.

DISCUSSION

Conflict theories offer a range of accounts of how power constitutes a key feature of family lives, and underpins the emergence of family forms and inequalities. Such frameworks may be accompanied by a commitment to bring about change. Some conflict theories focus on interpersonal dynamics. These include the theories of psychiatrist R.D. Laing (1971), who particularly emphasized the potential for tensions within families, as well as for physical and psychic violence. Laing argued that some mental illnesses, such as schizophrenia, are rooted in family relationships and communication patterns. In Laing's view, the politics or power dynamics of family lives may lead to communications that violate the truth of what is actually happening, placing individuals in an impossible 'double-bind' situation to which they respond with madness. In this context, verbal communication that at first appears unintelligible may be understood as a way of making sense of these conflictual family relationships. One criticism of this approach, however, is that it does not theorize any alternative to family life.

Most conflict theories focus on the power dynamics of society more broadly. This applies in particular to Marxist and feminist approaches, which may be criticized for sometimes paying insufficient attention to the specificities of actual family experiences. Like functionalist approaches, such theories tend to focus on how families link **micro interactions** into the **macro social order**, although (unlike functionalist views) conflict theories evaluate this process as society working systematically to the advantage of some groups and the detriment of others.

Some writers suggest that families are a key social context that underpins all forms of **inequality** and differentiation through the experience of a number of divisions in family relationships that are taken for granted as 'natural', such as those of gender, generation and age (Ribbens, 1994), and through the experience of family **boundaries**, which create a sense of 'them and us' (Bernardes, 1985). Such experiences may lead to the idea that social inequalities and hierarchical relationships (between adults and children, for example) are 'normal' and inevitable in social life more generally. In other words, these inequalities may become deeply internalized within family life and be experienced later by children in schools and workplaces. At the same time, however, families may also reconcile individual members to injustice and inequality, both by providing solace from the worlds of school and work, and by encouraging them to believe that they will be able to advance within the hierarchy – when children reach **adulthood**, for example, or when individuals achieve a higher status in terms of age.

Conflict based in **class** interests is a particular focus for Marxist theories. In this framework, in all societies there are interest groups that control the means of production for daily living, and these ruling groups are able to gain advantage over others. In particular, in **capitalist societies** the **ruling class** is able to take the products of the labouring or **working-class** without recompensing them fully for their work, and thus acquires the **surplus labour value** for itself. This **exploitation** may be masked, however, by ideologies – such as religion – which obscure such divisions of interest and 'dupe' those who are exploited into accepting the situation through what is termed '**false consciousness**'.

From this perspective, families serve to reproduce existing injustices by socializing children into false consciousness. An emphasis on **reproduction** rather than socialization also extends the analysis beyond childrearing to the ways that inequalities in society are reproduced in mundane ways in everyday family lives, through the physical maintenance of the labour force in terms of basic food and shelter. Furthermore, adults may be bound through **family ties** into roles that prevent them from seeking change in society; for example, the working-class man who is the main **breadwinner** may feel unable to challenge the inequalities of capitalist production systems without risking deprivation or further disadvantage for his family. This process may be underpinned by state policies that regulate family lives so as to reconcile reproduction with the needs of production in ways that help to perpetuate class privileges and exploitation (McIntosh, 1979).

One key element of false consciousness is argued to be **family ideology**, as a systematic set of beliefs that serve to justify power inequalities. In European and New World societies this may also mask the way in which one particular **bourgeois family form** – i.e. the private, **nuclear family household** – is prioritized, rooted in the need for the transmission of private property and the creation of economic alliances in a capitalist society. Families are thus seen as the route for passing on privilege and private property for the ruling class. Engels (1884) also argued that capitalism had led to close control over women's sexuality so that elite men could be certain of their heirs, who would **inherit** their wealth and property. Family ideology may also infuse the study of families, leading to a failure to analyse critically the ways in which family as an **institution** fits the needs of capitalist society, and reproduces ideologies of families as harmonious and natural.

Within Marxist theories, then, class interests are played out through family lives, to the detriment of working-class people. Furthermore, from this perspective, inequalities associated with 'race' and ethnicity are also perpetuated through family patterns, and these inequalities are again linked to class exploitation. Nevertheless, with regard to both working-class and black and minority ethnic family lives, ambiguities may be found in the writings of conflict theorists, since families may be regarded either as a repressive source of exploitation in a class-ridden and racist society, or a bulwark or refuge against wider societal racism and class denigration.

A further contribution to conflict theories comes from feminist writers, who stress the importance of examining the gender hierarchies and power inequalities that favour the position of men in families compared with that of women. This advantage may be seen both in terms of authority/power relationships in themselves and in terms of greater access to **resources** through paid work, along with the exploitation of women's unpaid work in the home, both **housework** and childcare. These ideas are sometimes referred to as the **domestic labour debate**, which sought to develop theories about the means by which women's family-based labour was exploited, leading to calls for wages for housework. An emphasis on the **economic transactions** that occur within households is thus a key contribution of feminist approaches. Different strands of feminist theory are relevant here, particularly Marxist feminism, which sees gender inequalities as supplementing and amplifying class inequalities, and radical feminism, which views **patriarchy** as the fundamental basis of women's exploitation in families. Feminist work has also been highly significant in drawing attention to personal experiences of family conflict in terms of violence and abuse.

SUMMARY

Conflict theories look 'behind' the everyday view of families as places of nurture and love, to show the conflicts of interest that may be masked by such language, and to make power dynamics visible. Marxist and feminist approaches analyse conflicts and power issues in terms of their links with wider societal inequalities, whether based in capitalism or patriarchy. These approaches are associated with work on abusive, violent and oppressive aspects of family lives and relationships, which might otherwise potentially be obscured by family values and ideology.

FURTHER READING

David H.J. Morgan (1975, 1985) reviews the various approaches of conflict theory. Barrett and MacIntosh (1982) offer an influential approach to families drawing on conflict theory based in gender exploitation. Recent overviews include Farrington and Chertok (2009) and White and Klein (2008).

Related concepts *Division of Labour; Feminisms; Functionalism; Power*

Coupledom: Marriage/ Partnership/Cohabitation

DEFINITION

Couple (dyadic) relationships may be termed marriage, partnership or coupledom, generally involving sexual coupling and often childbearing. They are usually expected to have some durability, and may be analysed as institutions or as personal experiences.

DISCUSSION

Durable relationships that are formed around sexual coupling, which may or may not be linked to childbearing and/or marriage, vary greatly across cultures. Some suggest that it is impossible to identify a universal definition of **marriage** (Rapport and Overing, 2007), and that marriage can be understood only in the context of the **gender order** of any particular society; that is, the overall understanding and pattern of relationships between people of different genders. How coupledom is understood, the meanings given to human **reproduction** and whether the sexual and/or childbearing couples are considered to be forming a family unit, vary greatly. In many societies, individuals forming a new couple may be seen to move from the **family of origin** to create a new **family of affinity**, acquiring a new set of family and kin relationships.

In European and New World cultures, 'a couple' denotes a particular idea of a **monogamous** entity; that is, a socially recognized pairing of two people who form an exclusive sexual relationship – generally understood through heteronormativity (Johnson, P., 2005). This notion of the couple is historically recent and culturally limited. In other global and historical contexts, marriage may be seen as **alliances** between kinship groups, rather than a decision between two individuals, and include **arranged marriages**, where the older generation find marriage partners for their children. Marriage by consent may indeed be a particularly European historical legacy (Therborn, 2004). **Forced marriages** (Heaton et al., 2009) also occur, in which individuals are compelled to marry. Multiple sexual partners and/or spouses, termed **polygamy**, may also be socially recognized in some cultures.

In many cultures, rules and social customs exist regarding the groups from which suitable marriage partners may be found, resulting in patterns of exchange and **reciprocity** (forming alliances and exchanging **dowry**) that continue over **generations**. Rules of **exogamy** require that marriage partners are found from outside the social group, while rules of **endogamy** specify the particular group(s) within which marriage partners may be found. Among some cultural groups, such as the Nuer in Africa, **same-sex marriage** between women is socially recognized, a particular male being identified as a suitable partner for the younger woman for procreation (Zonabend, 1998); marriage may also sometimes be recognized between an older and a younger man (Monaghan and Just, 2000).

The process of finding a mate or spouse is often accompanied by elaborate **rituals** around courtship, betrothal and **weddings**, with special **food**, music and dance. Religious beliefs and ceremonies may also be central. Sometimes the marriage itself may not be finalized until it has been consummated, and further rituals accompany this. In some contexts, the **birth** of a first child is a marker for the full establishment of a marriage, whereas in others the first pregnancy indicates that it is time to wed.

Changing cultural expectations in a globalizing world, and enhanced economic circumstances, means that in many countries the average age of marriage for women is rising, especially among more educated women, who may have better opportunities for paid **employment**. While increased **independence** may be welcomed, some changes in contemporary marriages may not be beneficial to women. Examples include arranged marriages that are modified towards negotiated marriages, in which young men meet and veto prospective wives, and polygamous arrangements modified towards the legal recognition of 'inside' marriages, leaving 'outside marriages' without rights (Cheal, 2002).

The long-standing emphasis on the couple in Western European family lives is connected to Christian doctrines and church interests in defining marriage and thereby legitimate offspring and **inheritance** rights, with men having **rights** over their wives and children. As a socially regulated system for the identification of heirs and the management of property, marriage developed largely as a **middle-class** institution in the nineteenth century, and it was only late in the century that the law restored any rights to married women. **Working-class** couples, on the other hand, often relied on the social conventions of 'common law marriages'. For the poor, coupledom leading to family life was as much a means of practical everyday survival as of emotional ties. As the ideology of family and domestic life spread, and the home became more comfortable with increasing affluence, however, ideas of the married relationship as central became common (Davidoff et al., 1999). Some residual earlier customs remain, as in a woman taking her husband's name on marriage.

Coupledom and marriage entail complex sets of practical and economic exchanges, **obligations** and rights, sometimes laid down in formal legal systems as well as through social custom. Couple practices and legal systems may not always work harmoniously together, however. In some societies, for example, the law may prescribe minimum ages of marriage and prohibit forced marriages, but may not be adhered to in practice, particularly in rural areas. A distinction can be drawn between marriage and coupledom as institutions, which are framed in legal and public terms, and the experience of marriage and coupledom, as personal understandings and experiences.

The significance of **romantic love** is not an expectation of marriage in many societies or historical periods. The idea of romantic love as a basis for marriage developed with the affluence of **industrialization**, but is now seen as the main socially validated reason for marriage in Western societies. Nevertheless, selection of a partner (**connubium**) often follows particular social lines of similarity (**homogamy**), around say **class** or **locality**. Researchers study patterns of partner choice because they feel that it says something about the extent of cohesion and openness of ethnic, religious or socio-economic **boundaries**, although cross-racial, ethnic and religious couple relationships cannot be taken as a straightforward indicator (Caballero and Edwards, 2008).

In mid-twentieth-century European and New World societies sex outside marriage was disapproved of, and marriage was regarded as the appropriate social arrangement for bearing and raising children. The development of ideas of a marriage based on **friendship** and love is characterized as indicating the advent of **companionate marriage**, with expectations of a special intimacy around shared **leisure** time, communication, and, in the later decades of the twentieth century, mutual **sexual fulfilment**. As the underpinnings of marriage in economic survival and social control grew weaker, the couple relationship was seen as requiring management, with the rise of marital experts and a medicalization of marriage (Morgan, D.H.J., 1985). The later twentieth century saw debates about how to characterize marital and couple relationships, from **symmetrical families**, understood as different but equal (Young and Willmott, 1973), to an egalitarian **pure relationship**, which lasts only as long as it fulfils the needs of the couple involved (Giddens, 1992). Such changes are arguably overstated since gendered roles and understandings continue to be apparent.

In many affluent developed countries, the late twentieth century saw a movement away from marriage towards **cohabitation**, referring to couples who are co-resident but not legally married. It is not clear whether cohabitation is a precursor or an alternative to marriage, and there may be diverse reasons why couples cohabit rather than marry. Cohabiting coupledom may be associated with a higher probability of separation, and also of abuse (Paetsch et al., 2007), but may also show more egalitarian attitudes (Casper and Bianchi, 2002). Nevertheless, marriage is still regarded as an ideal, especially where children are involved. In the UK the erroneous belief persists that cohabitation gives rise to similar legal rights as marriage (Barlow et al., 2008).

With the 'unhooking' of sex, marriage and childbearing in Western societies in the last decades of the twentieth century, the meanings of marriage have changed, for example the wedding has become a major event for **consumption**. Yet heterosexual marriage remains a contract with a particular legal standing and implications. The introduction of civil partnerships has meant that same-sex couples are entitled to some of the same legal rights in some countries. There are controversies about whether institutionalizing same-sex marriage represents a challenge to heteronormativity or a triumph of heterosexual norms.

Whether or not couple relationships involve co-residence, shared housekeeping and financial arrangements, and a sexual union of some sort, are all contestable and variable in contemporary European and New World countries. For example, couples may live in separate homes in close proximity, or they may work in different towns or countries (known as LATs – 'living-apart-together'). The general link between commitment and sexual relationships weakened with the advent of reliable contraception and greater economic independence available to women.

Nevertheless, ideas of romantic love leading to marriage retain a strong hold on Westernized cultures, with 'serial monogamy' as a feature of couple relationships over the life course. Some suggest that the meanings of marriage are widening rather than marriage becoming decentred (Duncan and Phillips, 2008), with a continuing emphasis on co-residential coupledom, whether or not legally constituted. Love in this context is understood as the basis for a personal fulfilment. Ideas of open marriage, non-monogamy, and/or communal living, are generally marginal in Western societies, despite challenges by analyses of polyamory (Munson and Stelbourn, 1999). The experience of adultery, however, is often a basis for divorce. Furthermore, the actual experience of the marriage or couple relationship may be a site of power struggles and violence, although issues of power may be managed in such a way that they are not obviously apparent.

SUMMARY

Most societies regulate the ways in which individuals come together as couples, whether or not this is understood as marriage. There are many arrangements around sexual relationships, childbearing and childrearing, daily living arrangements, and the development of alliances through marriage. With late industrialization, along with the availability of reliable contraception, coupledom has become less regulated by kinship expectations. It may thus be understood as an individual decision based on romantic love, in which adult coupledom has become unhooked from parenthood. Nevertheless, as with many areas of family lives, it is easy to overlook the continuities that persist alongside the changes.

Beck and Beck-Gernsheim (1995) address love, changing gender roles and links to parenthood. Casper and Bianchi (2002) discuss contemporary US trends in marriage and coupledom, while Duncan and Phillips (2008) look at attitudes and changing practices of coupledom in the UK.

Related concepts   *Family Law; Intimacy; Post-Coupledom; Power*

Demography

DEFINITION

Demography is concerned broadly with the study of populations as large groups, including population composition and trends in population change that relate to households and families, with implications for social policies.

DISCUSSION

Birth, marriage and **death** are key events in family lives, but they are also basic concerns for the demographic study of **populations** in general. Demography as a discipline was associated with the development of **nation states** and governments that wanted to develop policies and organize their citizens, whether in terms of the potential number of soldiers available, the labour force needed for economic development, the amount of tax revenue to expect, or to plan the provision of services to citizens. France, for example, has developed pro-natalist policies to encourage population growth since the late nineteenth century, when it was thought the low density of its population in relation to its land size made it more vulnerable economically and militarily (Hantrais, 2004).

Key building blocks for the analysis of populations include: **fertility** – the number being born; **mortality** – the number of deaths; and **migration** – the movement of citizens within and between nation states. Such statistics provide information about the present stock of the population and the

key concepts in
family studies

ways in which it changes over time. In order to make predictions for the future, demographic statistics are generally calculated in terms of the **rates** (of birth, marriage or death) in relation to existing population numbers. For example, fertility rates may be calculated in relation to the number of women of childbearing age, allowing average fertility rates to be calculated for particular populations or periods of history. Taking data from, say, earlier childbearing patterns and projecting them into the future is a basis for comparing the fertility patterns of different societies across the world, or for making predictions about future population changes. Predicting future population size also requires attention to mortality rates (including neonatal and infant mortality) and migration movements, including variations in mortality rates between different population groups within a nation state. The data available to calculate migration rates is generally more subject to errors than data for fertility and mortality rates, because of difficulties in tracking and predicting people's movements.

Much demographic data is derived from **census returns**. Censuses are a regular part of government activity in many industrialized societies. Other sources of information include **registrations of births and deaths**, migration records collected at national frontiers, and registrations concerning other changes in legal status, such as marriage and **divorce**. Sample **surveys** are also important sources of information, such as the Current Population Survey carried out monthly in the USA, with an annual supplement focused on families and households, and the General Lifestyle Survey (formerly GHS) carried out yearly in the UK. Countries vary with regard to the extent and reliability of information collected. **Birth registration**, for example, is not available for substantial proportions of the world population and few countries follow the UN Statistical Commission's recommendation to collect information about non-market labour (Bogenschneider, 2006).

To help governments plan services such as hospitals and schools, and develop policies towards future needs, demographers also analyse the composition of populations and the implications for future trends. The formation and dissolution of households and families is significant here. Governments may want to predict the rates of different household types based on studies of the patterns of relationships in **co-resident** households, for example, to predict lone parent households or the need for state care to supplement family care of older people. Such analyses involve demographers and researchers making decisions about how to define the **boundaries** of family and household groups, and how to

demography

43

categorize relationships. These decisions not only shape the pictures that emerge, but in turn may also affect how people think about their families and relationships.

Over time, the definitions used in collecting census data may shift, as census enumerators and people themselves have sought workable terms to describe people's living and family arrangements. While such terms may often be regarded as representing 'natural' **ties** and arrangements, the meaning of 'family relationships' – for example whether or not they included servants – has changed considerably historically (Davidoff et al., 1999). Apparently neutral terms used to classify aspects of populations can have different meanings across different countries and cultures. In current UK government statistics, distinctions are made between family and non-family households, with families being identified as **couple households** or **parent and child households** (Smallwood and Wilson, 2007). In the USA, by contrast, a cohabiting couple with children is not defined as a 'family' in government statistics, with this term being reserved for people living with others to whom they are related by **blood ties**, marriage or **adoption**.

Assessing the extent and nature of family changes and continuities requires attention to the construction and interpretation of population and household statistics. Some ways of presenting data convey a strong sense of marked change, while others give a different picture. For example, reductions in **household size** seem more significant if expressed in terms of the percentages of *households* that are single occupancy rather than in terms of the percentage of *people* living in single-occupancy households. Similarly, the *proportion* of births outside marriage may increase even if the absolute numbers of such births has not changed, since the proportion changes if the actual numbers of births to married women decreases, so that the numbers occurring outside of marriage come to represent a greater percentage of all births. *Cross-sectional* data of the proportions of individuals currently living alone may give a different impression than considering people who have lived alone over the course of their adult lives, since people's household membership changes according to their life course position. The picture thus looks different according to whether the individual **trajectory** or aggregated statistics are examined. Some people may experience **solo living** over much of their adult lives, but more experience solo living, or lone parenthood, for a particular period in their overall **life span**. An **ageing population** also has significant implications for the proportion of single adult households since there will be increased significance of widowhood in the population overall. Further, the extent of change can look different according to the **time period** in question: continuities are sometimes more apparent than changes if statistics look further back in time (Casper and Bianchi, 2002). Important differences may also be more or less visible if statistics take account of **diversity** between different groups within national populations (Baumle, 2006). Another key issue concerns how far demographic statistics can take account of family ties that are not bounded by co-residence but run across households. How family change and continuity is traced also depends on how the boundaries of spatial location involved are drawn more broadly: statistics collected within national boundaries often overlook family ties and activities that cross such spatial categories.

A further significant type of demographic analysis relates population rates to other features of social and economic patterns, referred to as **population studies** (Teachman et al., 1999). For example, it is apparent across the globe that fertility rates generally decline, and families thus become smaller, as society becomes more affluent. The reasons for this **demographic transition** are disputed, but may include such factors as reduced dependence on family labour for survival, increased investment in individual children, women's alternative employment choices and improved life expectancy rates. In the USA and the UK, for example the **nuclear** pattern of two parents with two children, only emerged as a majority family form in the mid-twentieth century, since when other family patterns have been seen. Some demographers see these rapid family changes as constituting a second demographic transition, in terms of increased divorce rates and single parenthood and generally lower levels of fertility in the 1960s and 1970s, followed by a plateau in which the rates of change stopped increasing (Casper and Bianchi, 2002). This has raised new concerns about shrinking populations in developed countries, although not all such countries exhibit the same level of declining fertility (Booth and Crouter, 2005). This second demographic transition is argued to be associated with ideas of individual **autonomy** and **gender** equality. The links between individual family-related decisions, and the opportunities and constraints that occur through wider economic patterns, provide a focus for analysis of the ways in which these may interact over time to influence each other in a reciprocal relationship.

SUMMARY

Demographers are concerned with features of current and projected populations. They are interested in family and household patterns in themselves as well as drawing on family and household data to feed into calculations about future population trends. Population studies extend demographic analyses to examine the social processes and implications of these patterns and trends.

FURTHER READING

Davidoff et al. (1999) discuss historical changes in population statistics. Hantrais (2004) overviews family demographics across Europe, while Casper and Bianchi (2002) address family demographics in the USA. See the Office for National Statistics webpage 'Focus on families' (http://www.statistics.gov.uk/focuson/families) for recent UK statistics, and the US Census Bureau webpage 'Families and Living Arrangements' (http://www.census.gov/population/www/socdemo/hh-fam.html) for US statistics.

Related concepts   *Comparative Approaches; Family Change and Continuity; Family Forms; Family Policies*

Division of Labour

DEFINITION

Broadly, 'division of labour' refers to the way in which different kinds of work, or parts of tasks, are divided up and allocated to (categories of) people who undertake them on a regular basis. Within families and households, labour is often divided up according to gender as well as age.

DISCUSSION

Ideas about a division of labour have their roots in broader, nineteenth and early twentieth century sociological analyses of the move from **pre-industrial** to **industrial society**. In pre-industrial societies, it was argued, there was less of a division of different sorts of labour between people, economic production was organized around the household, and social solidarity was rooted in similar lives. During industrialization, however, people became much more specialized in particular types of work, production largely moved out of the household and into the workplace, and solidarity was based more on **interdependence** (Crow, 2002). The ideal and widespread daily experience of a public sphere of employment and a separate private sphere of family and domesticity became established – albeit this varied by social class. Within this notion of different spheres, a gendered division of labour took hold, in which men were active in the public sphere, including as **breadwinners** earning a **family wage**, while women were active in the private sphere as unpaid **homemakers**, **wives** and mothers. While men were still associated with productive work, in terms of the economic value and status of what they did, women were associated with the reproductive work of family and household, including housework and caring for and about **husband** and children, which had no publicly recognized economic value or status. Similarly, the institutionalization of education as a period of compulsory **schooling**, and the legal regulation of **child labour** that accompanied industrialization, meant that children were removed from economic production within and outside of the home.

In mid-twentieth century analyses, a version of **exchange theory** was one of the main ways of understanding the gendered division of labour. This poses men's role as breadwinners and women's as homemakers as a reciprocal exchange, drawing on notions of **instrumental** and **expressive roles** contained in functionalist ideas, and ideas about **rational economic choice**. Women thus exchange their domestic labour and sexual favours for economic provision from their male partner because they are more suited for housework and caring, while men, who are more suited to the world of paid work, exchange their economic contribution to the family for their female partner's domestic maintenance and care. This theory suggests that both partners receive something in return for what they do, and they each benefit. A similar rational choice perspective on the gendered division of labour was provided by **resource theory** (e.g. Blood and Wolfe, 1960) in relation to considerations of sources of power in **marriage**, which suggested that tasks are best performed by whoever has the most fitting resources. Within this framework, the theory would predict that, if wives work outside the home, husbands would take on a share of the domestic labour. Indeed, ideas prevalent in the 1970s seemed to support these predictions, with an apparent shift to the **symmetrical family** (Young and Willmott, 1973), with greater sharing between husbands and wives of the hitherto segregated tasks of economic and domestic labour.

Research challenging these ideas about a rational exchange of resources in the gendered division of labour, and highlighting the continuing strength of ideas about public and private spheres and associated power differentials between men and women, came to prominence in the 1970s during **second wave feminism**. There was a reframing of what women did in the domestic sphere as '**work**' rather than as a natural vocation outside of the productive sphere. Feminist researchers treated being a **housewife** as an occupation and investigated the terms and conditions under which **housework** was performed (e.g. Lopata, 1971). Linked to the conception of what wives and mothers did in the domestic sphere as unpaid work, there has been vigorous debate about whether or not there should be **wages for housework**. Some of the conceptual advantages of seeing the roles and activities of wife and mother as 'work' include that it makes the labour visible, reminds people of its economic significance and resists treating what women do domestically as an intrinsic part of their nature. The application of such language, however, also imposes a male experience of labour from the public sphere that can reframe women's own understandings of their family-based activities and relationships (Ribbens McCarthy and Edwards, 2002).

In a challenge to the tenets of resource theory and ideas of a shift to symmetrical families, later research also showed that even where women were involved in paid employment outside the home, they spent more time than their male partners on routine housework and **childcare** in the home. Another challenge to rational choice exchange ideas was contained in the observation that it was not really rational for women to specialize in domestic work within a marriage when that relationship may end and leave them unqualified to support themselves through the labour market. Despite even mothers of young children increasing their participation in the paid labour force over the past few decades, in most industrialized countries it continues to be the case that women spend more time than men on domestic tasks. Indeed, in European countries' social policies, moves away from the male breadwinner/female homemaker model towards an **adult-worker model**, in which both men and women are full and individual participants in the labour force, arguably ignore the social reality of women's, especially mothers', greater responsibility for childcare and unpaid work in the home (Lewis, J., 2003).

Time use studies, for example, consistently show that while men have increased their involvement in childcare and housework since the 1970s (albeit there are disputes here about what is counted and measured as domestic labour), women still undertake the majority of routine domestic tasks, such as shopping, cooking and cleaning, or maintain responsibility for their management, with men 'helping' (Gray, 2006). For example, it is common to talk about fathers 'babysitting' their own children when their female partner goes out for an evening, while to talk of mothers babysitting their children sounds strange. Even where they delegate tasks to other family members, or indeed hire in domestic help such as cleaners, women tend to be the household managers who retain responsibility for ensuring that the domestic labour gets done. For example, women may write the shopping list that their male partner takes to the supermarket. Another aspect of the gendered division of labour is that men tend to do domestic tasks that occur outside the internal space of the home, such as lawn mowing, and/or involve machinery or craft tools, such as household repairs (Doucet, 2006). A division of labour can, however, also be apparent among same-sex couples, with one partner taking more responsibility for domestic work than the other (Dunne, 1997). Further, there are arguments that gendered divisions of labour and family relations are shaped by the introduction and use of various **household technologies**, and also themselves shape domestic technological developments (Silva, 2010).

The division of labour can also include emotions and affect. The **emotional labour** that women carry out within families has also received attention, ranging from kin-keeping work – where women take on responsibility for maintaining links with members of their extended family, including their male partner's 'side' of the family – to exercising the attention and thought involved in caring *about* people as well as caring *for* them. There are also arguments that emotional labour – in terms of the display of certain positive emotions – is increasingly demanded in the labour force (such as expectations of a smiling welcome from those waiting at restaurant tables or warmth and compassion from a nurse) and that the jobs to which this applies tend to be filled by women (Hochschild, 2003).

A key debate around divisions of labour in domestic tasks and emotions concerns equality. **Difference feminism**, for example, argues for the valuing of women's unpaid domestic and familial work as part of a rethinking of social organization, while **equality feminism** is concerned with the minimization of difference and the promotion of equality as sameness. Others argue that, rather than absolutist categorizations of difference or equality in divisions of labour, it is important to consider context (Doucet, 2006). Indeed, assessments of the equity or otherwise of divisions of labour are often imposed by researchers, but work that focuses on couples' own understandings has shown that they may consider a gendered division of activities and responsibilities to be 'fair' (Backett, 1982), or that they take a view of family as a 'team effort', in which each should put in what they are able and be supported according to their needs (Ribbens McCarthy et al., 2003).

There are questions over the extent to which the public and private gendered division of labour was in fact ever a reality for all men and women. It has been argued that the male breadwinner and father, and the female homemaker and mother, model, only really ever applied to white middle-class women in industrialized societies. Working-class and minority ethnic women, even as mothers, had to earn a living in order for their family to survive. Working-class women continued in employment in the Lancashire cotton mills after childbirth, for example (Lewis, J., 1989), and, historically, black women serviced some middle-class white women's families at the expense of their own (Glenn, 1985). Contemporarily, women from developing countries are crossing the globe to work in Western families.

Within the 'new' childhood studies (James et al., 1998), research has shown that, while industrialization saw new labour laws limiting children's involvement in paid employment, children and young people have continued to be involved in various forms of work both inside and outside the home. There is mounting evidence that children contribute to family life and domestic tasks, undertaking routine cleaning as well as caring for siblings and other emotional labour, for example, and also undertaking paid work where they can. In **family businesses**, moreover, children and young people can play a substantial but unacknowledged part in economic production (e.g. Seymour, 2005). Children's schooling may also arguably be reframed as their productive work.

SUMMARY

Gendered divisions of labour, with men as breadwinners and women as homemakers, are associated with a distinction between public and private spheres. Exchange theory argues that women provide domestic labour and men provide economic support in a mutual exchange, and resource theory suggests that a division of labour is a rational distribution of resources. Feminist ideas have challenged these theories conceptually and empirically and childhood studies have revealed children's domestic contribution.

FURTHER READING

Doucet (2006) provides a review of debates around gendered divisions of domestic labour, especially in parenting, with a focus on issues of gender difference and gender equality. Tong (2009) covers different feminist arguments about the division of labour. Jacobsen (2007) overviews economic issues concerning gendered divisions of labour, including in families. Carling (1992) and Casper and Bianchi (2002) explain exchange theory.

Related concepts   *Care; Household; Power; Rationalities*

Domestic Violence and Abuse

DEFINITION

Domestic violence and abuse refer to the exertion of power over, or the controlling and demeaning of, someone in an intimate, family or kinship relationship, especially within the home setting. The extent to which the terms cover verbal, sexual, emotional and psychological, as well as physical, threat, intimidation or harm, is debated.

DISCUSSION

A number of debates are associated with the definition and meaning of the terms 'domestic violence' and 'domestic abuse'. Some commentators argue for a limited description that is restricted to actions that result in physical injury, whereas others prefer a broader definition that includes psychological and emotional harm, and sexual harassment as well as **sexual abuse**. There are also discussions about whether definitions or forms of domestic violence and abuse, of whatever form, are inevitably culturally variable (Agathonos-Georgopoulou, 2006) (discussed further below).

Which definition is used is important for studies that measure the incidence of domestic violence and abuse, since higher and more frequent levels of violence and abuse will be found using the broader rather than the narrower definition. There are also debates about whether statistics that show a rise in violence and abuse within families represent an increase in reporting rather than of frequency of abuse itself.

Associated with the inclusiveness or limits of the violence and abuse being referred to, some researchers who prefer a wide definition argue that the term 'violence' does not convey psychological intimidation and harm, whereas 'abuse' is able to capture this aspect; those who take a narrow approach prefer the descriptor 'violence'. There are also questions about whether or not the preface term 'domestic' should be used, since some commentators feel that it obscures more general **gendered** inequalities with regard to who actually initiates or perpetrates the violence.

A range of explanations has been put forward concerning the causes of domestic violence and abuse. In play throughout these accounts are key issues about whether such actions are: (a) brought about by individual circumstances in particular families, such as the pathology of parents or children, malfunctioning systems within families, cycles of abuse or environmental stressors; or (b) related to structural gender and generational **inequalities** embedded in society more broadly. Additionally, some argue that there are different patterns of domestic violence (Johnson, M.P., 1992) that require different explanations.

Abbott and Wallace (1997) thus review three main explanations for male perpetration: traditionalist, liberal/psychiatric and feminist. According to these authors, 'traditionalist' accounts see violence and abuse by men as infrequent and sometimes incited by women themselves. 'Liberal/psychiatric' accounts also regard violence and abuse by men as rare, but, where it occurs, regard it as resulting from dysfunctions in a family or from individual mental illness. Finally, 'feminist' accounts (favoured by Abbott and Wallace) see the other explanations as rooted in a masculine view. In contrast, feminist explanations for domestic violence and abuse perpetuated by men see them as rooted in wider **patriarchal** social relations. From this perspective, family is the site of power relationships that reflect gendered inequalities in society, so that **husbands** and fathers see themselves as having authority over wives or partners and children (Delphy and Leonard, 1992). From a **rational economic choice** perspective, some suggest that improved economic opportunities for women will decrease the level of violence in abusive relationships (Farmer and Tiefenthaler, 1997).

Research shows that those on the receiving end of violence and abuse are primarily female or children in a family and that the perpetrators are male (Hearn and Pringle, 2003) – although, as discussed below, this is not always the case. A key message from campaigners is that women and children are at higher risk of violent assault and sexual abuse from people with whom they have intimate domestic relationships than they are in danger from strangers; this is in contrast to men, especially young men, who are more at risk of violence outside the home. Studies also show that it can be difficult for women who are abused by their male partner to leave a violent relationship, with many remaining or returning to their partner out of fear or **love**, or due to lack of **resources**, or a belief in promises that things will change. Children who are subject to physical violence and/or sexual abuse within domestic and family settings are often afraid to speak out. They keep silent either in response to threats from the perpetrator or from a sense of loyalty and because they worry about family break-up should they be taken into care by social workers and the perpetrator sent to prison. Both women and children may also individualize the violence and abuse, and see it in some way as their own fault.

The prevalence of male violence towards, and abuse of, women and children does not preclude men and older people also being subject to domestic assault. Debates exist about the extent of gender symmetry: whether women and girls perpetrate violence and abuse in the same way as men and boys, and for similar reasons, or whether the cause, extent and meaning of the violence or abuse is different (Dutton, 2007). Violence and abuse also occur in same-sex intimate relationships (Renzetti, 1992). Older people with dementia in particular, or in need of care for other reasons, can also be at risk of violence and abuse from family carers (Cooper et al., 2009). Arguably, the categories of abuse that are recognized are expanding – for example, to include **marital rape** and **elder abuse** – although interestingly there is no term for violence against their parents by dependent children and young people, and little discussion of the topic.

Violence and abuse cut across contemporary societal ideals and expectations about the nature of family as providing emotional intimacy and caring for **dependency** needs, such that it is hard for people to understand or accept that the violence or abuse is happening. But these expectations can be part of the exercise of power that allows for domestic violence and abuse to occur, with dependency, care, **vulnerability** and power being tightly connected. Many commentators say that domestic violence and abuse remained hidden, or were seen as a **natural** or inevitable aspect of family life, until feminist campaigners brought them to public attention. State and other agencies were said to see the issue as essentially a 'private' matter, because what happened in the family was regarded ideally as outside of the remit of state and other interventions. People themselves may also regard what goes on in family life as essentially private, and, by and large, the work of protecting children from sexual and other abuse is done by their mothers (Hooper, 1992). The exposure of what used to be called '**wife battering**' resulted, in the 1970s, in women's refuges being opened to provide 'safe houses' where women and children could escape domestic violence and abuse. In recent years in the UK, however, government has increasingly treated domestic violence and abuse, and children's upbringing in families generally, as issues of public concern requiring intervention. Children who witness domestic violence, for example, are now considered to be 'at risk' and in need of protection. Some argue that shifting ideas and policy debates around the construction of '**risk**', and which children are subject to it, are a struggle for power over how to define poor and minority **ethnic** families and communities, deflecting attention away from institutionalized inequalities and racism.

The line between physical affection and sexual abuse, and between **discipline** and violence, can be a fine one, and depend on the context of who is carrying out an act and who is assessing it. For example, while it is commonly accepted that parents and other carers can physically restrain and dress/undress their recalcitrant young children, other people doing the same thing to those children may well be regarded as assault or abuse. And fathers' indulging in rough 'horseplay' with their children, particularly **sons**, can be regarded as either a demonstration of paternal affection or the perpetration of violence, depending on the perspective adopted.

As indicated earlier, domestic violence is also subject to questions about the extent to which it is a cultural construction. Key examples of these sorts of judgements, about what is and is not acceptable at different points in time in different **social contexts**, include that rape within marriage was not considered an offence in British law until 1991; indications that parents in **working-class** and minority ethnic families are more likely than middle-class and white families to be investigated as potential 'child abusers' (Taylor, 1992); and the vigorous debate in the social work field about whether the use of corporal punishment of children among some minority ethnic groups should be understood as an acceptable cultural norm (a **cultural relativist** position) or treated as **child abuse** (Gopaul-McNicol, 1999), or whether evaluations of **child neglect** are dependent on material context (Scheper-Hughes, 1993).

Such questions about how behaviour is understood in different cultural circumstances also raise the issue of whether domestic child abuse is a continuum that shades through into child neglect or whether abuse and neglect are qualitatively distinct and different. Assessments of whether or not a child is being neglected are made in the light of what are considered to be appropriate developmental goals, and ideas about children achieving their full potential. Again though, it is important to bear in mind that there can be cultural differences in what are regarded as appropriate levels of competence and developmental outcomes for children. For example, children looking after toddlers unsupervised for periods of time, within and outside the home setting, is quite acceptable in areas of Norway (Kjørholt and Lidén, 2004), but likely to be considered as parental neglect in the UK.

SUMMARY

Domestic violence and abuse are contentious issues. Debates about limited or more inclusive definitions of the terms are important not only practically, with regard to what gets measured and recorded as incidences of violence and abuse, but also conceptually. A range of explanations is put forward for the existence of domestic violence and abuse, notably involving disputes between those who focus on reasons associated with characteristics of individual people and families, and those who regard pervasive and structurally embedded gender and generational inequalities as central. Domestic violence and abuse cut across contemporary ideals concerning the intimate and caring nature of family, but interventions can in turn cut across another family ideal of privacy. Poor, working-class and minority ethnic families are said to be more subject to having members' behaviour judged as violent and abusive, and indeed acceptable norms can vary between societies and cultures.

FURTHER READING

Mooney (2000) provides a useful introduction to the range of explanations for violence and abuse, in particular against women, while Luseke et al. (2005) focus on some key controversies in family violence.

Related concepts *Family Policies; Feminisms; Problem Families; Social Divisions*

Families of Choice

DEFINITION

The concept of 'families of choice' is intended to capture the commitment of chosen, rather than fixed, relationships and ties of intimacy, care and support. The 'non-heterosexual' form of families of choice is often seen as the clearest example of this phenomenon.

DISCUSSION

The idea of 'families of choice' was framed as a form of political affirmation towards rights for homosexual ways of life, particularly in the USA (Weston, 1991). The context of the HIV/AIDS crisis was also significant, with the emergence of friends as providers of care for lesbian, gay and bisexual people, and the perceived failure of **families of origin** and the state to respond adequately to the situation. In this sense the term has its roots in a political project. The term is also sometimes used to refer to adoptive families (Benavente and Gains, 2008). Families of choice are argued to be based on values of **love** and intimacy and a '**friendship** ethic', which stretch beyond the conventional couple. Outside of legal adoption, however, these bonds do not have recognition as kin, although gay and lesbian partnership rights are recognized increasingly (albeit patchily) in various national and federal states through **civil partnership** measures and provision for **same-sex marriage**.

The trends associated with individualization and **detraditionalization** also place a stress on choice and **agency** in varying forms of intimate relationships, providing another context for the development of families of choice, sometimes drawing also on related terms such as **elective kin** and **affectional communities**. Families of choice in this broad sense can include partners, lovers, ex-partners/lovers, and friends, as well as children and selected members of a person's family of origin, and the people concerned regard such relationships as constituting 'family' (Spencer and Pahl, 2006). The term 'families of choice' thus emphasizes **achieved** rather than **ascribed** sets of relationships, that is, relationships are acquired personally and socially through choice and effort, in contrast to a relational status assigned at birth or through law. For example, the familial position of **daughter** is ascribed through biology, at birth, or through law, as in **adoption**. But this position can also be achieved socially as part of people's understandings of the qualities of their relationship, as in the phrase 'she's like a daughter to me'.

There are debates about the appropriateness of 'families of choice' terminology, particularly for lesbian, gay and bisexual people, raising questions as to whether it fails to challenge **heteronormativity.** For some, the concept thus invokes an imitation of 'traditional' heterosexual nuclear families, implying a substitute for families of origin, reinforcing the primacy of the terminology of 'family', and taking the blood family as the basic point of reference. Even a liberal definition of 'family' is felt to risk confusing sets of relationships built on different values and to dismiss the creative interpersonal processes involved in 'non-heterosexual' connections and ties, especially given that lesbian, gay and bisexual people can have ambiguous relationships with their family of origin (e.g. Bersani, 1995).

For others, the appropriation and use of 'family' conveys feelings of connectedness and commitment in ways that other terms, such as 'friendship networks', do not. In the circumstances of coping with HIV/AIDS, 'families of choice' can signal the sense of survival, community identity and responsibility involved. 'Families of choice' can be invoked to affirm a sense of belonging and the validity of homosexual ways of life, with its members providing emotional, social, material and physical care and support (e.g. Weeks et al., 2001).

Nonetheless, it is important not to over-romanticize families of choice. As with any human relationship, sadness, pain and conflict can accompany lesbian, gay and bisexual people's attempts to develop alternative family bonds in the absence of other choices, and relations of power and unequal divisions of labour can infuse same-sex families of choice in much the same way as they do heterosexual families (e.g. Dunne, 1997).

SUMMARY

Families of choice are regarded as exemplars of trends associated with individualization, with their stress on chosen closeness, and commitments based on alternatives to traditional biological and legal ties. Some regard the concept as privileging traditional heterosexual relationships. Others argue that it conveys feelings of commitment and belonging, and affirms the validity of non-heterosexual relationships, as well as being an increasing feature of heterosexual relationships.

FURTHER READING

Weeks et al. (2001) overview arguments about 'families of choice'. R. Pahl (2000) discusses the growth of 'friend-like' relationships of choice more generally in the late twentieth century.

Related concepts   *Individualization; Intimacy; Kinship*

key concepts in
family studies

············· Family as Discourse ···············

DEFINITION

Family as discourse draws on a social scientific approach that emphasizes the importance of language and meaning in understanding social lives. This focus on meanings and their implications may thus be theorized as creating 'family' and (variable) family identities.

DISCUSSION

58

The idea of family as discourse draws attention to the importance of language and meaning in understanding family lives. Related bodies of work that draw on a notion of **family discourse**, include, firstly, research on child language acquisition, and the ways in which parents and children together construct a sense of shared family values; and, secondly, studies of interactions between family members as sites where discourses occur, with implications for other social processes such as gender, power, connection, solidarity, beliefs and values. Here, however, we focus on work that considers how family, as a meaningful social object, is constructed through discourse. This is a central issue for family studies – which is itself part of the process of constructing family as discourse.

In some respects, the concept of family as discourse has overtaken a longer-standing discussion of **family ideology**, as a system of beliefs that idealizes family in often unrealistic ways. By contrast, family as discourse suggests sets of meanings and images that are fluid and contingent, even though some discourses may be more extensive than others, and be associated with structural or institutional power. The concept of discourse also differs from family ideology in that it does not indicate that it is overlaid on, or distorts, an underlying 'reality'. Rather, it highlights how talk is organized, and its implications. Every discourse – including the discourse of family studies – represents a view *from somewhere*, understood as a standpoint that then implicates issues of power and inequality. Family as discourse is thus a complex set of interrelationships between daily experience, materiality, (structural) power and language.

As a theoretical framework, discourse analysis developed as part of **post-structuralist** approaches in the social sciences, which in turn developed from **social constructionist** and **symbolic interactionist** perspectives. These approaches argue that we cannot understand social actions and social lives without attending to the meanings by which people make sense of them. Beyond a shared emphasis on language and meaning, however, there is a variety of distinctive approaches within discourse analysis, including, for example, **conversation analysis, discursive psychology, Foucauldian approaches, critical discourse analysis** and **interactional sociolinguistics**. As noted, some of these approaches are concerned with studying discursive activity in itself, which in relation to families might involve, for example, negotiating, quarrelling, solidarity and divisions of labour.

From the general perspective of family as discourse, it is not helpful to study family as a concrete physical object. Instead the focus is on how people use the **language** of family (whether spoken or written down) in order to understand what family means to them, what it refers to in different contexts, and what its significance is for how people conduct their relationships and for the organization of social lives (Gubrium and Holstein, 1990).

An emphasis on the language of family, however, does not mean that the framework of family as discourse treats family merely as a word, since words are themselves very powerful. Family is more than just a word in several senses. Firstly, families are discussed by people as concrete objects in their everyday lives. They may refer to family as 'it', as something solid that exists outside themselves, with clear **boundaries**. The notion of 'the' family stresses this sense of an identifiable concrete object, with implications for social actions – whether by policy makers, professionals or family members.

Secondly, family as discourse is significant for how people live their lives – as when, for example, someone says, 'I could never move away from here, my family would never allow it', suggesting that this understanding of family has powerful practical consequences. Sometimes the power of family as discourse is a form of moral or political rhetoric (akin to family ideology). This makes it difficult for family researchers to avoid making **evaluations** of family lives, since their own academic discourses of family may also be imbued with moral and political judgements.

Discourses of family vary in content, and in terms of how they are contingent and localized, or systematically embedded in wider power structures. Some family discourses have greater dominance in society if they are associated with the power of governmental or institutional bodies. Power is thus exerted through discourses, but discourses also help to constitute power. While some discourses of family may be embedded in, and expressed through, professional expertise and power, various discourses may also be in conflict, and individuals may resist discourses, or find they can make creative choices between them. Family as discourse may thus be experienced as a constraint in some circumstances or contexts, or as a creative production in others.

Since issues of power are intertwined with discourses, they are the site of struggles as some groups seek to ensure their discourses are so powerful (**hegemonic**) that it is difficult to think any other way (akin to family ideology). Ideas about the importance of meeting children's needs, for example, construct a discourse that is hard to question, as are those about parental involvement in education, in European and New World societies.

Family as discourse should not be seen just as involving language. Discourses are significant for concrete practices, shaping and expressing the meanings that material objects, **bodies**, physical spaces, and **technologies** hold for people, as well as vice versa. Family as discourse emphasizes how family life is not fixed or 'natural', but located in socio-cultural and historical contexts, and socially produced – while **materiality** means that family as discourse is not infinitely malleable.

The concept of 'family as discourse' provides not only a theoretical perspective on families, but also a methodology for research. The study of family becomes one of gaining insight into people's own meanings, often through attention to how they describe their own and others' lives, which then become the basis for the researcher's description of other people's descriptions. Family as discourse also highlights the ways in which family is constituted in a variety of social interactions and textual representations, not just those that occur in the 'privacy of the home', including medical consultations, educational processes, social services meetings, government policy documents, etc.

SUMMARY

Family as discourse centres 'family' as a set of meanings, representations, images or ideas, which may occur through spoken language, written text or material practices. Family is not viewed as a solid object; rather the focus shifts to an exploration and interpretation of how family as discourse is expressed and understood, the ways in which it is intertwined with issues of power, and the implications for how social lives occur.

FURTHER READING

Wetherell (2001) overviews discourse analytic approaches and related debates in general terms, while Gubrium and Holstein (1990, 2009) provide an extensive analysis of how family is produced and enacted through discourse. N. Rose (1999) shows how powerful expert discourses of family regulate and shape people's lives.

Related concepts   *Family Practices, Phenomenological Approaches, Power*

family as discourse

Family Change and Continuity

DEFINITION

Issues of family change and continuity draw attention to major debates about trends and patterns in the nature of family lives and relationships.

DISCUSSION

Much of the contemporary debate about family in European and New World societies centres on the idea that there has been unprecedented change in families since industrialization and into the twenty-first century. One perspective on family change is that it is a response to the changing needs of wider social systems, most notably the needs of economies. From this approach, families are positioned between **micro** and **macro** levels of society, with family change being driven by broader change at the macro level. An alternative possibility is that the accumulation of individual- and family-based decisions has effects on wider social processes, including economic change. This perspective is more apparent in historical studies of family change (e.g. Davidoff and Hall, 2002); historians have also suggested that attention to processes over time illuminates the interactive nature of the links between shifts in family lives and other forms of social change (Scott and Tilly, 1980). Other writers focus on the impact of 'ideational forces' of ideas and beliefs – often based on a perception of Western family forms as favourable for **economic development** – in bringing about family change around the world. Such ideational forces may be shaped through **education**, urbanization, **religion** or **mass media** (Jayakody et al., 2008). At the same time long-standing and persistent 'geocultures' of family systems in the different regions of the world (Therborn, 2004) show increasing divergence as much as convergence across the globe, through changes that are uneven in time and space. Additionally, shifts in political power and legal frameworks can have major impacts on family change (Abbasi-Shavazi and McDonald, 2008; Therborn, 2004).

Within European and New World societies, historians suggest that change has been a recurrent feature of family lives for many centuries, alongside persistent continuities – including the long history of public anxiety about family change itself. A preoccupation with documenting change may lead to **cyclical change** being mistaken for linear progression, with older patterns and divisions being re-embedded in different formats (Edwards, R., 2008). The meaning of the term 'family' may itself be part of what has changed historically, and past lives are defined in retrospect as going through a form of **historical arc**, linking past virtues to present troubles and necessary developments for a better future (Clarke and Fink, 2008). Discussions of family change commonly posit a shift from **tradition** to modernity, although what is 'traditional' is often left undefined. Furthermore, empirical evidence does not necessarily support what is asserted to be happening to families under modernity. For example, kinship networks continue to be important – contrary to the supposed shift to isolated **nuclear families** with advancing **industrialization**. Similarly, the persistent generalization that early industrialization led to a change from extended families in **agrarian societies** to urbanized nuclear families, has been contradicted by detailed historical evidence.

Contemporary sociological debates about family change often 'periodize' previous times, particularly **modernity, late or high modernity**, and **postmodernity**. Modernity is the term used to characterize post-Enlightenment **industrialized societies**, with capitalist economic systems and a belief in rational progress. The processes of industrialization and modernization are described as a move away from traditional agrarian society – in which economic production and family lives were closely intertwined – leading to the ideological and physical separation of home and work, and ideals of the family home as the proper site for motherhood and childhood.

As industrialization has become more internationalized, the character of modernity is also argued to have changed. Some describe a 'high modernity', whereby late twentieth- and early twenty-first-century industrialized societies are in the grip of global capitalism, with widespread surveillance and control of citizens. Others, however, characterize such societies as postmodern, characterized by uncertainty, destabilization and a loss of belief in progress. In such societies individuals are argued to have much less certainty about who they are, or what is the nature of the world. Within these frameworks, then, modernity is characterized by the nuclear family with a clear and gendered division of labour; and postmodernity is associated with a fluid set of arrangements, characterized by **diversity** in terms of patterns of partnering and parenting, as part of individualized lifestyle projects. However, some writers suggest that, instead of indicating freedom of choice and individualization, this plurality of family lives points rather to the needs of multinational capitalism for a cheap and flexible workforce, characterized by the underemployment of men while women are engaged in vulnerable and poorly paid employment.

In the broader public political debates, there are three main interpretations of the changes that have happened since the mid-twentieth century in many European and New World societies:

1   large changes have happened and this is a bad thing (with family breakdown and loss of wider family support causing insecurity and disorder)
2   large changes have happened and this is a good thing (people are free to develop individual lifestyles)
3   there is much continuity as well as change (moral panics about family change repeat the same stories as in the past, and racial, classed and gendered familial and social divisions persist).

Besides responding to these debates, social policies may shape family change in unanticipated ways. For example, variations in the decline in fertility rates between different European countries may be associated with different policies towards the support available for working mothers, and the recent shift towards an **adult-worker model** of family life and support might have the unintended consequence of undermining community life and family care (Lewis, J., 2003).

Quantitative studies suggest that aspects of family change are apparent across a number of European and New World societies, including falling **marriage rates**, rising **age of marriage** and **childbearing**, decline in **family and household size**, rising **divorce** rates, the unhooking of marriage and childbearing, rising proportions of **lone mother households** and fewer **multigenerational households** (Hantrais, 2004). At the same time, while change was rapid in the second half of the twentieth century for many affluent Western countries, more recent evidence suggests that the rate of change has subsided, if not levelled out altogether. At the same time, it is also possible to see variations in family change between different European and New World countries, with some experiencing more change and different patterns from others. In the USA, for example, marriage continues to be the overwhelming choice in adult life, albeit at a later age than in the mid-twentieth century (Casper and Bianchi, 2002).

However, such generalizations about family change face difficult questions of their methodological underpinnings, including the basis for drawing up the categories within which such generalizations are made, and identifying their meanings and significance to people themselves. Furthermore, such data focuses on household patterns, while family patterns may continue across time. More broadly, variable cultural value systems and family patterns may persist alongside other family changes associated with the **demographic transition** and increasing affluence (Kağitçibaşi, 2007). Assessing the extent and nature of family change and continuities thus requires very careful attention to the construction and interpretation of population and household statistics.

Beyond changing statistical patterns, other debates about the meanings of relationships and family ties are significant for interpretations of family change and continuity. Giddens (1991, 1992) and Beck and Beck-Gernsheim (1995, 2002) suggest radical shifts in people's ideas of how to manage their sexual and gendered relationships, and how to relate to their children, leading to increased choice and self-determination, sometimes seen in terms of increased **individualism** or individualization.

Yet there is evidence of the continuing importance of 'family' events and relationships, kinship ties, desires for a lifelong intimate partnership, and commitment to the needs of children (Williams, 2004). Even where household formations change, patterns of family practices may well continue unchanged, but, alongside this, parents' responsibilities for their children's lives have arguably become more entrenched and extended.

Family lives are dynamic and multifaceted, adding to the methodological and theoretical difficulties in reaching an agreed view of family change and continuities. Different pictures emerge depending on which questions are asked, what areas of change are examined, and at what level of analysis, and all are interwoven with social, economic, political and personal processes. **Gender** – itself linked into **heteronormativity** – is a key element in many of the debates about change, since it is often gendered power relations, and changes in women's roles, which are seen to be particularly at stake here. Strong moral views, value judgements and political stances may underpin the arguments that are put forward, and cultural assumptions may underlie apparently neutral discussions (e.g. around the needs of children). If change is occurring, further complex questions concern how to determine which changes matter, for what reasons and in what ways.

SUMMARY

Theories of social change in European and New World industrialized societies suggest that early industrialization can be characterized as modernity and later industrialization as high or postmodernity, with changes in family lives and forms linked to these different characterizations. Disentangling the extent and nature of family change and continuities is extremely complex however, linking to value judgements and political debates. While some stress the extent of changes, which they consider to be either beneficial or harmful for society and individuals, others point to the extent of the continuities in family lives over time.

FURTHER READING

Charles et al. (2008), Gillies (2003), J. Lewis (2003) and Williams (2004) each provide reviews of issues of family change and continuity; Cheal (1991) discusses postmodern families. Davidoff et al. (1999) provide a historical discussion, while Hantrais (2004) offers an overview of recent European demographic changes, and Casper and Bianchi (2002) do the same for the USA. Therborn (2004) reviews change in family behaviour across the world during the twentieth century, and Jayakody et al. (2008) do likewise from an ideational perspective.

Related concepts *Comparative Approaches; Demography; Family Forms; Individualization*

Family Effects

DEFINITION

'Family effects' is a broad term generally used to indicate how family membership and experiences may have consequences for individuals.

DISCUSSION

Some social scientists consider the ways in which general patterns of family lives – including individual decisions by family members – affect wider processes, such as economic development. However, contemporary research on family effects is largely preoccupied with how various aspects of family experiences affect individuals, with such questions being related to political and policy issues.

Studies of family effects generally assume that events and processes in early life help to shape the individual life trajectory, often strongly linked to theories of child development and attachment. Various perspectives are invoked to explain such effects, including economic resources, family patterns, stressful life events, and individual characteristics. The significance of particular family forms (Golombok, 2000) and aspects of parental relationships and **parenting styles** have received particular attention, and family effects have also been a focus of studies of siblings. Which perspective is adopted carries implications for how it is thought best to shape policies to improve individual **life chances**.

The idea that the (very early) parenting and care experienced in childhood shapes, or resonates throughout, the individual's subsequent life experiences has been an important feature of psychological research. Nevertheless, some have contested the inevitability of such links. Clarke and Clarke (1976, 2000) cite evidence that shows how early childhood adversity can be reversed by later compensatory care. Furthermore, they argue that adverse experiences in adulthood can have significant effects on individuals, perhaps even more so than in childhood. Others argue for the importance of **genetic inheritance**, which may limit the extent of family effects (Belsky and Pleuss, 2010). Some stress the importance of children's own **agency** and active participation in shaping how their family experiences affect their lives (Brooker and Woodhead, 2008).

Unravelling the complexity of family effects poses major challenges. Relevant research approaches include **quantitative** studies – such as statistical analyses of large-scale datasets; or **qualitative** studies – for example, in-depth analyses of individual **life histories** or **clinical case studies**. Some studies use mixed methods, as in the US Fragile Families and Child Well-Being study (http://www.fragilefamilies.princeton.edu/), or the international Young Lives study (http://www.younglives.org.uk/). Studies using any of these methods can also be based in one point in time – for example, presenting **cross-sectional** statistical data about people's characteristics and current circumstances, or inviting **retrospective** life stories. Or they may be **longitudinal**, with the data (whether qualitative or quantitative) being collected from the same individuals over varying periods of time. **Cohort studies** generally involve large-scale quantitative studies of people born at a particular time, who are then followed up over many years, for example see www.cls.ioe.ac.uk/.

family effects

The use of individual life histories or biographies enables the tracing of interacting events and circumstances as these occur over the individual life course. Such methods provide insight into the meanings that family relationships and events hold for the individual concerned, while also providing the opportunity to consider wider historical and social contexts and their interweaving with individual biographies. It is possible, however, that only certain types of people are willing to be interviewed about their individual life histories in this in-depth way. There are also questions about how to interpret the resulting accounts and, although insights may be gained into the individual impact of particular family circumstances, such methodologies cannot substantiate 'family effects' in any straightforward way.

In large-scale outcome studies quantitative measures are used to study different aspects (or variables) of people's lives. Such studies depend on being able to develop appropriate and unequivocal measurements of such experiences. Analyses are then undertaken to see whether there is a **statistical association** between particular childhood experiences and an increased probability of particular family effects in later life – generally termed '**outcomes**' in such approaches. Yet some outcomes may vary considerably over time, or show up only in the longer term.

Most of the outcomes studied in this way concern aspects of life that are considered undesirable or unwelcome. Some suggest that a search for more 'positive' outcomes would almost certainly reveal other patterns, potentially highlighting beneficial, as well as problematic, family effects. Furthermore, outcomes might hold variable meanings and be evaluated in different ways by different individuals, and in variable cultural contexts.

Studies of outcomes have established some broad trends or patterns when large numbers of children are researched, but these findings cannot be extrapolated to individual children. Furthermore, often the size of the statistical association involved means that only a small part of the adult outcomes can be 'explained' by reference to that single childhood event. In other words, there may be so much variation *within* the groups, showing different adult outcomes, that the identification of an association with a particular childhood event may be of little practical use. Indeed, it is possible that different children might react in quite opposite ways to similar events (e.g. parental death might lead some children to strive harder at school, whereas others lower their expectations), which are lost from view when individual measures are aggregated for statistical analysis. Additionally, simple associations of this sort may not always take account of other relevant factors. Notably, what are called **selection effects** mean, for example, that people living in social disadvantage may be more likely to exhibit particular family forms and outcomes, rather than the family form creating the outcome of social disadvantage.

Where a particular childhood experience is found to be associated with an increased probability of unwelcome outcomes, it is viewed as a **risk factor**, perhaps in terms of medical difficulties (Garmezy, 1994) or social policy concerns (e.g. aspects of social exclusion) (Bynner, 2001). It is now generally accepted that it is the constellation of such risk factors – rather than any single variable – that is important. Studies therefore seek to calculate and **predict** outcomes on the basis of such risk factors, against which the rest of the population are presumed to be 'on target' for appropriate positive outcomes. Furthermore, inferences are made to suggest that such childhood experiences have 'caused' these outcomes; indeed, the term 'outcome' itself implicitly infers that such **causality** is present but what is meant by 'causality' is complex. Furthermore, statistical tests can suggest only that particular childhood experiences are associated with particular outcomes to an extent that is not likely to be attributable to random effects occurring in the sampling of the populations being studied.

Difficulties in establishing causality may lead to a preference for cohort and other longitudinal studies rather than cross-sectional research. **Multivariate statistical analyses** have been developed that can take account of several variables at once, along with more sophisticated **models** of how events may occur and interrelate over the life course (e.g. Schoon and Parsons, 2002). These models include a range of individual, family, social and structural factors, which may interact over time in ways that put children at greater risk of particular deleterious outcomes. Models also seek to establish features of children's lives or personalities that have a protective effect, such that children who are considered at increased risk of adversity do not in fact show negative outcomes. This is sometimes called '**resilience**', although the term is criticized for lack of clarity about whether it refers to a quality in the child or family.

Large-scale quantitative studies are influential for social policy, since policy makers are concerned with developing strategies to deal with the behaviours and experiences of populations overall. Evidence of some groups being at increased risk of social exclusion may be used, for example, to target resources in particular neighbourhoods or towards particular populations. It may also be used to develop policies to encourage citizens to make particular decisions about their lives (e.g. to support marriage).

SUMMARY

The effects of particular family experiences on the lives of individuals are important for researchers and policy makers, but such effects are very difficult to establish conclusively. Studies may draw upon multivariate statistical analyses to establish broad trends showing links between particular events and subsequent outcomes. Researchers using these approaches have developed complex models of processes over time. Extrapolation from large-scale data, however, may oversimplify processes of causality and risk. Other approaches involve the interpretation of clinical case studies, or the exploration of individual biographies over time.

FURTHER READING

Schoon (2006) introduces the concepts of risk and resilience, and overviews the impact of early family adversity for long-term consequences, drawing on UK data. Luthar et al. (2000) discuss the concept of resilience, and associated questions, more generally. Amato (2004) discusses US evidence on the effects of divorce on children; Karraker and Grochowski (2006) offer a general discussion of risk and resilience in the US context.

Phelps et al. (2002) overview longitudinal studies in the USA. McLeod and Thomson (2009) address researching changes in relationships over time using qualitative methods.

Related concepts   Attachment and Loss; Child Development; Family Change and Continuity; Parenthood

Family Forms

DEFINITION

'Family forms' concerns the variety of patterned, or structured, ways in which people live and relate together as family members, sometimes raising technical issues of how to describe individuals' relationships to each other.

DISCUSSION

Family forms are mapped by academics and policy makers, using specialist terms that may or may not correspond to how family members themselves feel about their particular families. People are more likely to think in individual terms of the various family members they know and relate to. Over time, however, the specialist terms of academics may become part of people's accustomed language, particularly when family change has become an aspect of media, public and policy debates. The differences between nuclear families and step-families, for example, are now widely understood by the general public in contemporary European and New World societies, although the term 'nuclear' family was originally used by social scientists rather than being part of everyday language. This is an example of the way that social scientific perspectives are not just a matter of detached and objective observation, but themselves have an impact on the ways in which the objects of study – in this case, family members – think about themselves, which can in itself be a source of further change in how people live their lives.

The idea that families may be mapped according to certain patterns rests on the presumption that 'the family' exists as a structure in its own right. This view of family as an objective structure may be important for policy makers who want to gain an overview of statistical patterns and trends. Such family structure may be determined through various features such as **residence**, kinship links, distribution of resources and responsibilities, regular contact and interactions. Where these features are found together the structure may seem easy to identify, and uncontroversial. In contexts where the various features give rise to different patterns, it may be more difficult to decide how family forms may be labelled and described. Such controversies may also centre on issues of whether family necessarily implies the presence of children, or a co-residential couple, for example do **LATs** (couples 'living apart together') or **same-sex** (gay and lesbian) **couples** constitute a family form?

Several terms are used by Western-based social scientists to describe various family forms, including nuclear, extended, lone parent and step. Some anthropologists (e.g. Hendry, 1999) have criticized these terms for using the nuclear family as an assumed benchmark, with other forms then described as differing from this norm. Yet the concept of the nuclear family may be irrelevant to a range of societies and periods of

family forms

history. This benchmark approach has also been challenged for ignoring the family lives of people who have a history of international **migration** and diaspora.

Nonetheless, the term '**nuclear family**' has a powerful impact, both in its widespread usage in academic contexts, and in terms of ideology. It is understood to refer to a particular residential arrangement, of a married (or perhaps cohabiting) heterosexual couple with their dependent biological children. The nuclear family is often associated with the idea of **traditional family**. It is unhelpful to join the terms in this way, however, since this closes down questions about the particular periods of history and social contexts in which the nuclear family form has occurred. 'Nuclear' in itself carries the assumption that this family form is the fundamental building block on which wider family ties are built – which may be an assumption that is relevant primarily to white middle-class European and New World societies at a particular point in history.

Some family historians (e.g. Goldthorpe, 1987) suggest that the nuclear family has a long-standing relevance in the history of north-western European societies. The emphasis here is on a **monogamous** marital tie as a basis for household formation and childrearing. For other European societies, however, a history of extended families is more apparent, in which the tie between parent and child continues to have primary significance into adult life, as a basis for residence and also economic arrangements. The **extended family** refers to a family form in which intergenerational, and other wider family relationships, are an important feature of residence, contact, and/or various forms of support and control. In some cultures, the term **joint family** may also be used, since households and everyday family relationships may centre on sibling ties into adulthood, along with their partners and children, as well as ties across generations.

There is often a misconception that extended families were more a feature of pre-industrial societies, being replaced by nuclear families as **industrialization** and urbanization took hold. This trend is often assumed to be continuing, with a concern that we have 'lost' the contact and support of wider family members. In fact, historical demographers in the UK (e.g. Anderson, 1971) have shown that pre-industrial households were often based on a nuclear family (but sometimes with others present, such as apprentices or servants), while extended families were an important part of people's lives as they moved into towns from the countryside. Indeed, historians have shown how the term 'family' had a variety of meanings for people in times past in the UK, some of which are very different from contemporary usage (Tadmor, 1996). Extended families continue to be a central part of many people's lives, albeit in different ways across the social classes. For working-class families, geographical mobility may be less significant, and frequent contact across households and generations (especially between women) may be part of everyday life. For middle-class families, geographical mobility may be more usual. Extended family ties may be mediated by various forms of regular contact (including electronically), and form an important source of support and obligations.

Step-families are often assumed to be a feature of contemporary Western family lives, but, historically in the UK, this family form was as common in the nineteenth century as in the late twentieth century (Haskey, 1994). The difference is that in the nineteenth century step-families were generally formed following **widowhood** rather than **divorce**. Step-family, as a concept, is premised on a comparison with the nuclear family, and refers to a family in which there is a (heterosexual) couple with children, but one of the adults who constitute this couple is not the biological parent of at least one of the children in the family. The label 'step-family' is often resisted by people as a way of describing their own family relationships (Ribbens McCarthy et al., 2003), being understood as a deviation from the ideal of the traditional, nuclear family. Other terms for step-family include **blended family** or **reconstituted family**. The term **step-cluster** has also been used to avoid assumptions of where and how family **boundaries** are drawn within complex residential, financial and childcare arrangements.

A historical perspective also challenges some misconceptions about **lone parent families**. In the UK, for example, while the proportion of lone parent households can be shown to have increased greatly (from a very low starting point) from the mid to the later part of the twentieth century, tracing statistics back further to the early part of the twentieth century shows much more continuity with earlier patterns (McRae, 1999). 'Lone parent' family is an umbrella term for a residential unit of a single parent – overwhelmingly the mother – caring for a dependent child or children. Under this umbrella are different routes into and out of lone parenthood. For example, it may result from a child being born to a **single mother** who has never been married nor cohabited with the father, or from divorce or widowhood. Furthermore, lone parents may have relationships with partners, even if they do not identify them as part of the family unit and/or live with them full time.

In many European countries and the New World, children growing up in lone mother families are more likely to be living in poverty than children growing up in a household with two adults. This economic disadvantage, combined with long-standing debates about potential links between 'broken homes' and socially undesirable outcomes such as truancy or delinquency, has led to a negative perception of lone mother families. Again, the concern with the implications of a **non-resident father** (**'absent'**) is based on an assumption of the nuclear family as the norm. Some writers (e.g. Wilson and Pahl, 1988) contend that the focus on the significance of the residential unit (or household) obscures the fact that the term lone parent family is a misconception, since all children do have two parents whether or not they live with them or have contact with them. Nevertheless, lone mother families have become the focus of 'moral panics' at times (Duncan and Edwards, 1999).

The issue of lone mother families raises a more general point concerning the relevance of categorizing families in terms of particular forms or structures, with regard to their usefulness in shedding light on major debates around contemporary families. Is it more useful to identify them as lone parent families or as mothers? Which of these categories or identities is most significant in shaping their experiences and those of their children? Similarly, for people from minority ethnic or working-class backgrounds, it may be that ethnicity or class are more significant factors in terms of their family experiences, rather than the particular family form to which they belong.

A cross-cultural perspective provides another basis for different understandings of family forms, including a consideration of the family lives of minority ethnic groups currently living in European and New World countries who have originated from other parts of the world. From this alternative viewpoint, household residence may not be a key feature of what defines family form at all, while family patterns may be understood more broadly by reference to fluid kinship links. Some family scholars argue for the importance for family research generally to consider networks that go beyond the boundaries of the family-household (Widmer and Jallinoja, 2008).

SUMMARY

A focus on family forms and their measurement is useful in mapping patterns and their distinguishing features, including changes in the predominance of particular family structures over time. This approach can, however, be subject to, and perpetuate, assumptions about the nuclear family as the norm, as well as obscuring features such as class, gender and ethnicity that cut across family form and shape what 'family' means in everyday lives. It may also overestimate the significance of co-residence for family relationships.

FURTHER READING

Goldthorpe (1987) provides an overview of the history of Western families, including the relevance of the nuclear family. Duncan and Edwards (1999) discuss issues concerning lone mother families, Ribbens McCarthy et al. (2003) do so for step-families, and Finch (1989) for extended families. Scanzoni (2004) discusses the indicators and implications of family diversity.

Related concepts Demography; Family as Discourse; Family Change and Continuity; Household

Family Law

DEFINITION

Family law comprises the legal rules that govern the formation, functioning and dissolution of families, and personal and proprietary rights and obligations existing between its members.

DISCUSSION

Traditionally, and in a narrow sense, family law has been concerned with questions of **status**, such as wife, father, child, legitimate, adopted and so on. It deals with how these statuses are created, carried out and terminated, and governs and protects the rights, **responsibilities** and duties that flow from them, between adults, and between parents and children. These laws can be secular in nature – applied through the state judicial system – or based in **religion**. Halaka (Jewish) and Sharia (Islamic) law, for example, regulate not only religious practices but also daily life generally, including issues of status and behaviour in family life. In some nation states, religious laws are incorporated (fully or partially) into state judicial laws (as in India, Israel and Lebanon). In secular states, such religious laws governing family life and followed by religious adherents can be in tension with that country's family laws. There may also be difficult tensions between traditional customs (which may have been codified by male judges through case law) and the constitutional and international rights of individuals, for example for women (Nzegwu, 2006). Indeed, the field of family law is an arena for a variety of political, religious and ethnic struggles (Jayakody et al., 2008). In European and New World societies, state legal systems and religious legal systems (largely) are independent of each other.

Most commentators agree that family law is dynamic, continually influenced by social, demographic and economic concerns, and changing public norms and scientific possibilities. At the same time, family law is also embedded in the legal traditions from which it springs. In the UK and USA, the focus on status in family law can be understood as stemming from the long-standing central role of the ownership and transference of **property** and wealth in common law, particularly through **inheritance**. In the UK **common law** evolved over centuries and is based on decisions made by judges, also referred to as case law. Family law is part of 'private' or civil law; that is, it is concerned with **rights** and **obligations**, and actions or claims, between people. Where the law is concerned with relationships between family members and the state, however, it is part of '**public law**', based on regulations issued by government or statutes emanating from UK Acts of Parliament, and can involve prosecution under criminal law. In addition, child law concerns the protection of children from abusive parents.

Broader definitions of family law cover any area of law that has an impact on family life and the relationship between families and the state, and, in this sense, there may not be consistency between public and private family law. For example, a cohabitant is treated as a spouse in the context of **welfare benefits** but – as noted below – is not necessarily treated so in terms of provision at the end of a relationship.

It is important to bear in mind that the rules and distinctions of family law and people's own understandings of family and behaviour do not always coincide. Furthermore, family law can run counter to – lagging behind or running ahead of – people's own ways of doing family. For example, when it comes to relationships between (heterosexual) adults, traditionally **marriage** has formed the centre of UK family law, with

divorce now of equal importance. At the time of writing, important legal distinctions between cohabiting and married families remain, in terms of rights and responsibilities on partnership breakdown. Nonetheless, in the UK, there is a deeply embedded folk belief in the existence of a status of 'common law' marriage, even though there has been no legal recognition of 'informal marriage' since the mid-eighteenth century (Barlow et al., 2005). Conversely, in the USA, it is argued that private 'contract cohabitation' laid the groundwork for same-sex civil union legislation in some states (Katz, 2007).

For relationships between parents and children, marriage confers **legitimacy**, although with the rise in **births outside marriage** the considerable legal privilege this used to bestow has not been sustainable, and legitimacy is no longer a dominant legal concept. In most European and New World states, biological parentage *per se* now brings legal rights and obligations in relation to children. Here, the law's focus on maintaining obligations and relationships between **biological parents** and their children can cut across everyday understandings of the significance of **social parenting** and the importance of a clear-cut family unit for **step-families** (Edwards, R., et al., 1999).

The term 'family' itself is not always legally defined in family law systems (as distinct from 'marriage', 'parenthood' and other terms that *are* defined). This means that questions of whether family status should be determined by marriage, **blood ties**, household, self-definition or function, are left open. There are different perspectives on this situation. Some argue that the lack of definition of 'family' in the law allows a subtext of values to operate that are gendered and heterosexual, reinforcing ideologies of family life as private and outside of state control, and ignoring inequalities of power within families (Land, 1995). In contrast, others argue that the lack of definition means that, increasingly, family law can accept a variety of family forms as falling within its remit and as being of legitimate consideration (Eekelaar and Nhlapo, 1998).

There are strong arguments that Western family law systems are heading towards convergence, with national differences diminishing steadily (Glendon, 1997). The trends identified include, on the one hand, changes in the law concerning status (divorce, inheritance, legitimacy, etc.) to reflect changes in society. This includes decreasing regulation of marriage formation, dissolutions and conduct of family life, for example the adoption of no-fault divorce. On the other hand, however, another cross-national trend is increased regulation of economic- and child-related consequences of marriage or cohabitation. Additionally other areas of law (such as social security, employment) are increasingly impinging on family life.

Despite convergence, there are also continuing fundamental distinctions in different countries' family laws that stem from their divergent histories (Land, 1995). Those based on Germanic law (such as in England and the USA) are shaped around the rights, obligations and remedies accorded to individual family members. Those systems rooted in Roman law include a notion of communal property and principles of **reciprocity** (with an extended sense of **liable relatives** with an obligation to maintain each other). Such considerations of property inheritance, and obligations to maintain other family members, raise issues about which families the law has been designed to address and serve, bearing in mind that poor families are unlikely to own property either individually or in common, for example.

Even *within* nation states, however, there can be differences in laws regulating family rights and obligations. Notably, in the USA there may be differences between family law at the state and federal levels, and in the UK, Scottish law differs from English and Welsh law. Nonetheless, family law is increasingly shaped by and operates in an international dimension. International law and conventions, as with national family law, set normative standards but also encourage international co-operation and the harmonization of different approaches to family-related issues. For example, the European Convention on Human Rights and the United Nations Convention on the Rights of the Child lay down principles of respect for, and rights to, a private and family life for adults and children, although there may be no clear definition of 'family' across societies and cultures.

SUMMARY

Family law is concerned with the status of relationships between people in families, and the rights and responsibilities that flow from these. More broadly, it can also refer to any area of law that has an impact on family life. National differences in family law systems in Europe and the New World are said to be converging, but family laws and people's own family practices do not always coincide. Family law is dynamic and subject to swings or shifts in emphasis on upholding rights or responsibilities, but is also embedded in divergent legal traditions that mean that there may still be distinctions in different countries' family laws, albeit that family law is increasingly shaped by international law and conventions.

FURTHER READING

Textbooks covering aspects of family law are regularly issued in new editions to take account of changes. Pearl (2000) addresses family law in relation to the (religious) implications for minority ethnic families, while Bailey-Harris (2000) discusses the law in relation to same-sex families. Masson et al. (2008) provide authoritative text on many aspects of UK family law, Mason et al. (2004) discuss family law in the USA, while Glendon (1997) surveys legal developments affecting family life in the USA and Western Europe. De Cruz (2010) offers a comparative global discussion of family law.

Related concepts   *Coupledom; Domestic Violence and Abuse; Family Policies; Post-Coupledom*

Family Life Cycle and Life Course

DEFINITION

The notion of the family life cycle suggests that the ways in which families change over time are characterized by a cyclical pattern, while the concept of the life course pays particular attention to the individual life trajectory as a person moves through different roles and experiences.

DISCUSSION

Concepts of the family life cycle and the life course both draw on the interweaving of embodied and cultural categorizations, but each involve quite different perspectives on how to understand family and **time**. Overall, this field lends itself to multidisciplinary work, including sociology, anthropology, psychology and history.

'Family life cycle' denotes the idea that families pass through clearly demarcated stages in a circular process, with new families forming in place of the original unit. It assumes a recurrent pattern in how families change over time. A family is seen to commence with the union of two adults: **marriage** or coupledom is therefore the first stage of the process. Subsequent stages include new parenthood; the raising of a new generation through early childhood and the teenage years; the movement of the younger generation out of the family home, leaving the parents as a couple unit again; and retirement and old age, culminating in death. Alongside this, the younger generation move into new couple relationships and become parents in turn, and the cycle starts over again. Each of these stages is understood as a 'natural' part of the playing out of individual lives. As an idea, family life cycle was used particularly in the mid to late twentieth-century family sociology, since this was a time when there seemed to be a regular pattern in **family formation**, understood largely in terms of the **nuclear family**.

Anthropologists use a related concept of household or domestic **developmental cycle** to refer to how a household moves through different forms over time as members arrive and depart, and new households begin, which can be culturally specific (Fortes, 1958). When the family life cycle is understood in such developmental terms, transitions between life cycle stages are framed in terms of particular developmental tasks that have to be completed in order to move on satisfactorily to the next stage.

As family patterns and forms changed in European and New World societies in the late twentieth century, the notion of the family life cycle was challenged as misleading (Cheal, 1991). The cycle of family life denoted was criticized as setting up its stages as somehow 'normal and natural' (including through implications of a biological developmental basis) such that deviations from this pattern might be seen as aberrations or an indication of **dysfunction**. Furthermore, it seemed to emphasize biological, age-related stages rather than the interweaving of social processes within and beyond families. Additionally, the notion was linked to the idea that particular families passed attitudes and behaviours down the generations that might lead to an underclass trapped in a **cycle of poverty**.

The idea of a life cycle can also be applied to individuals, but the more widely used term is that of 'life course'. This enables a flexible analysis of the interactions between biological change and social role and status, within the context of family and historical changes, without assuming any cyclical pattern. The life course approach suggests age-related life stages with associated roles, through which individuals pass and which include **birth**, childhood, **youth** or **adolescence, adulthood, old age** and **death**. Here again, though, there is a risk of assuming a fixed biological sequence (e.g. what of death during childhood?), particularly if a developmental perspective is adopted. There is also a risk of focusing on static **age status** categories, rather than considering how individuals and families experience historically mediated transitions. Furthermore, some age statuses (e.g. childhood) have received much more research attention than others (e.g. adulthood). A focus on **individual biographies** may help obviate some of these difficulties, enabling analysis of the interweaving of the individual biography with transitions between different age status categories in social, historical, cultural and political contexts. Such trajectories are composed of 'bundles of decisions' (Casper and Bianchi, 2002: xxiv) that are also interlocked with other trajectories. The individual's understanding of their own life events, and the choices they have made in their lives, can thus be analysed alongside the social contexts and historical time period in which these events occur and choices were made (Elder et al., 2003). Such biographies may be investigated through retrospective **life history** approaches or through repeated interviews with individuals over time in **qualitative longitudinal research**.

Life course approaches thus draw attention both to the social significance of chronological **age** and the social construction of associated age statuses. A related concept is that of the **life span**, which focuses on the individual life, often with particular reference to stages in the later years. Age statuses may vary considerably in duration and structure across different cultures. Furthermore, each status is likely to be associated with different roles, including different benefits and responsibilities with regard to family relationships as well as other social ties. These roles are likely to be structured and understood in variable ways according to **gender, class, ethnicity**, as well as by spatial location and historical time.

As noted earlier, the term '**transition**' captures people's movements between age statuses. For some this idea includes changes in a person's life that they consider to be significant, while others restrict its use to changes that are widely shared and recognized, persist over some period of time and carry implications for the individual's identity (Teachman et al., 1999). Normative ideas are implied if a transition is supposed to occur at a certain age. Transitions between age statuses may be more or less clearly demarcated and may occur over relatively shorter or longer periods of time. Life markers, such as starting or leaving school, moving out of the childhood home, setting up an independent household, retiring from the workforce, are usually recognized as significant moments of transition in European and New World societies. Some transitions, however – for example from youth to adulthood – have arguably become more protracted and ambiguous with more recent changes in the workforce and the educational and benefits systems. Furthermore, youth itself may be understood as a protracted phase of transition from childhood to adulthood.

Some cultures mark life transitions clearly, including movement into and out of particular residential sites along with the practice of customary rituals. There are also variations in how such transitions are evaluated, as sources of increased advantage or loss, or more neutrally as markers of change. Nevertheless, there are concerns that the notion of life course may also seem too fixed with regard to the transitions and statuses through which individuals are expected to pass. Another concept is that of the **trajectory**, which refers to the sequence or sets of roles that are experienced over the life course, while the notion of **turning point** refers to subjective or objective changes in the direction of a person's life (Elder et al., 2003).

Benefits of a life course approach include attention to different aspects of the individual's life experience, through social pathways such as **work**, **education** and family, and an analysis of how these interweave. The focus on individual lives may include detailed attention to their family-related experiences, relationships and transitions. An extension of this approach entails tracing the life course of several related individuals over time using the notion of '**linked lives**', as well as a consideration of how different 'levels' of analysis, such as **macro** and **micro** social contexts, may be interlinked in and over time.

A focus on the interlinking of lives provides a flexible sense of family, with individuals moving in and out of the group over time. Analysis of **multidimensional developmental pathways**, exploring the interweaving of individual and family transitions over time, permits greater attention to fluidity and diversity than in studying 'families' (Bernardes, 1986). From this perspective, families consist of a series of interlocking individual trajectories in particular social contexts over time. Indeed, time is a key feature of the life course approach, distinguishing between **individual time** (changes in individual biography), **family time** (transitions in the family or household unit) and **historical time** (the general historical period during which individual and family time occur) (Elder, 1999).

The issue of time points to the significance of **generation** for understanding family, focusing on relationships across life courses, and across individual and historical time. The meaning of generation may also be close to that of a **cohort** (a group of people born in a specific historical period of time). This further reveals the implications of linked lives within families, as when parents' family trajectories changed during the Depression in the 1930s in the USA, which then affected the trajectories of their children's later life transitions. Some age cohorts or generations may experience greater diversity than others with regard to family-related transitions in their life course, with arguments that conditions of **postmodernity** mean people feel greater uncertainty than previous generations about their future life course or trajectory and how far they may shape or are responsible for their own life course.

SUMMARY

'Family life cycle' and 'life course' are terms that emphasize how family and individual lives occur over time. Family life cycle conveys a sense of socially shaped patterns of family formation and dissolution, while life course draws attention to individual trajectories through socially constructed age and family statuses. The life course perspective in particular enables attention to individual movement or transitions between status positions, interwoven with the life trajectories of other family members and located in social and historical time.

FURTHER READING

Cheal (1991) and David H.J. Morgan (1985, 1996) discuss life course and family life cycle. Elder et al. (2003) give an overview of some aspects of the life course approach, while Gubrium and Holstein (2000) cover a constructionist approach to life course.

Related concepts Family Change and Continuity; Family Forms; Family Systems

DEFINITION

Family policies refer usually to government statements, goals and courses of action concerning the provision of welfare and distribution of goods that affect family lives, family resources and family forms, but can also be implicated in a very wide range of policy areas.

DISCUSSION

The relationship between family life and the social policies drawn up by government (whether at the level of a single nation state or the level of unions or federations of states) is a complex and contested one, encompassing debates about causal relationships and the appropriate extent of **state intervention**. For some commentators it is social policies that drive developments in family life and shape family members' attitudes. This relationship is often discussed in negative ways, with arguments that family life is undermined if there is anything more than minimal welfare provision. For example, welfare benefits are said to encourage young women to have illegitimate babies without a father to support them, and laws enabling 'easy' no-fault divorce are said to lead to increasing rates of **marital breakdown**. Thus, in this view, family policies need to impose family responsibility, rather than state reliance, and bolster what are regarded as 'traditional' self-sufficient family forms and lifestyles.

For others, as part of the modernization process, wider social change is driven by family members' choice of values and lifestyles (Giddens, 1992). In turn, policy is seen to be responding to these changes, although often lagging behind them. For example, extensions of formal **childcare** provision often follow mothers' increasing uptake of paid **employment,** rather than leading it, and thus are somewhat lacking in both extent and accessibility. Some suggest, however, that since contemporary family lives are diverse, state interventions to support a clearly defined normative model of family life can only do harm rather than good. Apart from the regulation of destructive elements, such as partner, child and elder abuse, government attempts to socially engineer family forms and lifestyles inevitably, it is argued, cut across family members' own values (Cunningham-Burley and Jamieson, 2003; Duncan and Edwards, 1999).

Still others argue that the relationship between family life and values and social policy runs in both directions and that they mutually affect each other (Hantrais, 2004).

There are many differing histories and ideas between different nation states, concerning what is seen to be the optimum relationship between families, government, and economic market forces. Countries also vary in the extent to which they have explicit family policies, but many other areas of government – including **education, health** and social care, **housing,** employment, **income** maintenance and taxation, immigration and **citizenship** – all have significant assumptions about, and/or implications for, how family lives are envisaged and shaped. Differing stances towards family policies largely concern the extent to which the state can or should intervene in family life, and the balance between state and family responsibility for its members. Typologies have been developed that categorize **welfare state regimes** in this respect, with Esping-Anderson's (1990) three-fold model being particularly influential.

In broadly 'liberal' regimes the relationship between families and the state has historically been one in which the state does not intervene to offer support, other than in a limited and imposed way to stigmatized and/or 'dysfunctional' families and groups. Indeed, some argue that a privatized realm of the 'traditional' **nuclear family** is crucial to socialization into notions of personal regulation that are compatible with liberal capitalism (N. Rose, 1999). Mothers can 'choose' to be in the home, caring for children, through dependency on their male partner (or, minimally, through state support in the absence of a male partner, as for lone mothers), or they can be involved in paid labour. Traditionally, the state takes a background role, aside from a regulatory one, and relies on markets or the voluntary sector to provide family services and supports. The USA and the UK are often seen to exemplify this welfare regime category. Policy analysts in the USA, for example, suggest that there is a void in policy making towards families, partly because of the strong cultural emphasis on individualism, which has led to calls for policies to be analysed in terms of their 'family impact' (Bogenschneider, 2006). In some aspects, however, the USA has seen a tendency to frame families as less of an institution in a legal sense, and more as personal relationships like other private contractual arrangements.

In broadly 'conservative' regimes the state acts to support traditional male breadwinner and female homemaker families and extended family **obligations**. Institutionalized care for children, including the school system in terms of the length of the school day, assumes that mothers are not engaged in paid work. As with liberal regimes, historically the emphasis is more on dependent family members – such as children and older people – being the responsibility of their family; there is far less emphasis on state-promoted or market provision. Germany is often pointed to as an example here.

In 'social democratic' regimes the state takes a far more active role in supporting and shaping the nature of family life, through a focus on individuals rather than on families. Mothers, with or without male partners, are expected to be in paid employment, with the state providing widespread day and after-school childcare. At the same time, they are also supported independently of, and alongside, any male partner through extensive state benefits providing **parental leave** when children are young. Children also tend to have stronger citizenship rights in such regimes. Overall, material and cultural responsibility for dependent family members is shared between families (of no preferred form) and the state. The country that is most often identified as exemplifying the social democratic welfare regime is Sweden.

Others have added the 'rudimentary' welfare state regime to this classification. In this regime there is little right to support from the state; rather, there is an emphasis on families and religious charities to provide welfare (e.g. Liebfried, 1993). Countries in southern Europe, such as Greece, are examples here. It needs to be remembered, however, that nation states rarely present a pure case that falls precisely into one welfare regime type, and may also change over time. Further typologies have been produced to highlight gender inequality and unpaid caring more strongly, or children's position (e.g. Pfau-Effinger, 1998).

For the UK, Hendricks (1994) has charted the ways in which images of childhood and children's needs are inseparable from social policy developments. Such images are seen as linked to the economic and moral future of society. Arguably, as a sense of risk and uncertainty spreads through the general social climate, the policy emphasis is intensifying concerning children's upbringing as a means of shaping and controlling the future fabric of society (Prout, 2000). In the UK, for example, government has significantly increased its involvement with, support for, and surveillance of, parenting practices and relationships.

One area in which the family/state/market balance is highlighted particularly starkly is in relation to **lone mother** families: should family policy ensure that lone mothers and their children are supported by the **absent parent**, or should the state support lone mothers and their children through welfare benefits, or should lone mothers go out to work and support themselves and their children? Different countries have varying approaches. In the UK, as a largely liberal welfare regime, the state has long regarded this as a dilemma, latterly moving from state support (albeit minimal) to an increasing emphasis on both the financial responsibilities of absent parents (through the Child Support Agency) and lone mothers' own responsibilities to take up employment (Duncan and Edwards, 1999).

Another particularly marked dilemma for family policy concerns the general move away from assumptions of a gendered division of labour, in which fathers are breadwinners and mothers are homemakers, towards mothers' increasing uptake of paid work. This has resulted in a growing focus on how parents can achieve a reconciliation of family life with employment – often termed '**work–life balance**' (Hantrais, 2004). 'Family-friendly' policies associated with these concerns include maternity and parental leave, the extensive provision of formal childcare, and flexible working time. The extent to which family policies have developed to deal with such issues again varies in different national contexts and welfare state regimes.

SUMMARY

The relationship between family policy and family lifestyles is subject to much debate. Some see welfare state policies as driving developments in family life, whereas others argue that changes in family relationships are driving the development of family policies, and still others regard the relationship as an iterative one. Another key area of debate is the extent to which it is appropriate for the state to intervene in family lives. Family policies, in different national contexts, contain normative assumptions not only about the balance of responsibilities between families, the state and markets, but also about relationships between family members within and across the generations.

FURTHER READING

Cunningham-Burley and Jamieson's edited collection (2003) lays out many of the debates about the extent to which the state should intervene in family life through family policies. Hantrais (2004) gives a detailed account of changing family living arrangements and policy debates across Europe, while Strach (2007) debates the significance of family for a range of policies in the USA in both federal and state contexts.

Related concepts   Family Law; New Right; Problem Families; Public and Private

family policies

DEFINITION

The concept of family practices is intended to direct attention to the 'doing' of family as an activity, in contrast to a focus on family as a form or institution to which individuals belong. As such, it is a broad orientation rather than a firmly defined notion.

DISCUSSION

The concept of 'family practices' has been developed by the family sociologist David H.J. Morgan (1996, 1999) to highlight how 'family' is not a static category or structure defined by residence, **blood ties** and the legal system. Rather, he says, because we live in a complex and fluid society, family has to be actively created by its members; family is something that individuals 'do' rather than something that people 'are'. As a term, 'family practices' is broad because it covers everything concerning 'those relationships and activities that are constructed as being to do with family matters' (Morgan, D.H.J., 1996: 192). These can be identified as 'roughly, those practices to do with marriage or partnering and with parenting and generations' (Morgan, D.H.J., 2003: 2). It encompasses people's identifications, understandings, feelings, values, interactions and activities that draw on ideas about kinship relations, **marriage** and partnership, parenthood and parenting, and so on, as well as the expectations and **responsibilities** that stem from these. It covers actual practices on the part of family members, accounts or **evaluations** of these practices by others, and aggregations or statistical summaries of them.

These relationships and activities, which are often thought of as **natural** or given, have an emotional and **moral** significance for individuals and for society generally. They may be perceived as good or as oppressive or **dysfunctional**. Such evaluations may be made by and about the individuals involved, as well as by and about society as a whole. Debates about the nature of families are a form of family practice in themselves. In this way, family practices provide a link between **self** and society.

David Morgan emphasizes issues of multifaceted process in understanding family in contemporary society and identifies six key features underpinning his conception of family practices. As will become clear in discussing these below, Morgan's use of the term 'practices' (as he himself notes: 1999: 21) has some overlaps with Bourdieu's (1990) theory of 'practice'. They both see practices as fluid, negotiated and cross-cut with other practices (with Bourdieu emphasizing **class** practices) and highlight the societal and historical dimensions of lived practices, although, in Morgan's view, his own concept is more open than Bourdieu's, encompassing challenges and reformulations rather than, solely, reproduction of existing practices.

Within David Morgan's discussion, the first key feature of 'family practices' is that it alerts us to the perspectives of both actors and observers (such as other family members, social workers or social researchers) and the interaction between these viewpoints. Secondly, the concept focuses on activity rather than an object. As Morgan (1996: 189) says, 'If we compare the terms "family structures" and "family practices" … the former is static and carries a sense of something thing-like and concrete … The latter carries with it a sense of doing and action'. Thirdly, the idea conveys a sense of the daily and unremarkable nature of people's family existence; the mundane small activities – everyday care such as bathing the children or preparing **food**, **leisure** activities such as taking them swimming – that link into what Morgan refers to as wider systems of **meaning** about family life. In other words, the concept of family practices locates parts of everyday family experience within wider discourses about family in society. Fourthly, linked to the '**dailiness**' of family life, the term invokes regularity and repetition rather than unusual events (e.g. the children are bathed every evening at 7pm).

Fifthly, as indicated earlier, David Morgan stresses the sense of fluidity that the concept carries. While family practices are, as we have seen, everyday and regular, they are also open-ended. Family practices are not discrete but connect with and relate to values, sites and practices more broadly. For example, they may be related to and/or understood as **ethnic** or **religious** practices (e.g. how people from particular ethnic or religious groups live their family lives), as **gendered** practices (e.g. expectations about mothering or fathering), as **age** practices (e.g. parents taking responsibility for children) or as **body** practices (e.g. who may or may not touch whom, when and where). This means that practices can be understand in more than one way or in different ways, as noted above in relation to actor and observer having shared or different perspectives.

The sixth and final feature of family practices identified by Morgan is their constitution as a major link between **history** and **biography**. The historical context in which family life takes place has a bearing on family practices, and this is subject to shifts and change while, at the same time, family practices are also rooted and created in an individual's **life history** and experiences.

David Morgan's concept of family practices has had a strong influence on UK family sociology, especially empirical research. As illustrated below, developments and critiques around the idea include, firstly, whether the idea of family practices can form the basis for attempts to pin down aspects of how people 'do' their family lives, especially maintaining more of a sense of family as a unit over and above individual actors; and, secondly, attempts to adopt alternative and broader concepts in an effort to centre the individual actor still further.

Finch has developed the notion of **displaying families** to bring into view how meanings are intertwined with family practices. She draws on and strengthens David Morgan's identification of practices as fundamentally social in nature, involving interaction between actors and observers and keying into wider systems of meaning. Finch argues that, if activities are to be effective as family practices, their meaning – as constituting and being about family – has to be conveyed to and understood by others. As Finch (2007: 79) neatly puts it, family 'must not only be "done" it must be "seen to be done"'.

Smart's extension of Morgan's ideas provides some contrast to Finch's attempts to delineate a key aspect of family practices, but shares with them both a desire to bring a firmer orientation towards meaning into view. Smart does this through the concept of **personal life** (Smart, 2007), which is even broader than the concept of family practices. She sees the radical shift in understanding associated with Morgan's identification of family practices as vital, but, for Smart, the focus on activities at the heart of family practices does not touch upon the individual imaginings, memories and desires associated with family life and with intimacy more broadly. Indeed, she argues that family is only one of many forms of personal relationship in contemporary society, which need to be explored and understood. In this way, the idea of personal life both adds inner **emotions** into and subsumes David Morgan's concept of family practices.

SUMMARY

'Family practices' provide a conceptual link between family lives as lived and understood by individuals, and the evaluations and nature of family in wider society. As well as the perspectives of both actor and observer, 'family practices' emphasizes a sense of everyday, regular activity. It suggests that the way in which family relationships and activities are understood and carried out is shaped both by an individual's biography and by social and historical context. Family practices also involve fluidity, in that they can overlap with other 'practices' invoking gender, age, ethnicity and so on. The idea of family practices has been developed further, both through a more defined notion of 'displaying' families and by a looser orientation to 'personal life' more widely.

FURTHER READING

Empirical examples of family practices include: Smart and Neale (1998) on parenthood after separation or divorce; Ribbens McCarthy et al. (2003) on step-parenting; and R. Edwards et al. (2006) on sibling identity and relationships.

Related concepts   *Family as Discourse; Intimacy; Personal*

Family Systems

DEFINITION

The notion of family systems draws on the idea of system as used in engineering, to describe the family as a whole entity, in which all the parts are seen as closely interconnected.

DISCUSSION

In family systems theory, a family is seen as an interconnecting unit. Family members are understood to influence each other continuously and in a reciprocal manner, even if they may subjectively experience themselves as distant from their families. This makes their behaviours and functioning **interdependent**, such that a change in one person's functioning will necessarily lead to changes in the functioning of others.

Although families may differ with regard to the degree to which they are interdependent, such interdependence is always seen to be present.

This approach to looking at families was derived from systems theory more generally, as applied to organisms or to machines. A system consists of elements and their characteristics, and the relationships between these. These different elements exhibit comparatively stable relationships, so can be seen as a structure, in which the different parts of the system are linked causally to each other (see Tufnell et al., 1998).

Systems theory is the primary basis for a variety of forms of **family therapy**. It is an applied theory that is intended to identify and explain where things are going 'wrong' in families, and to help put them 'right'. In this regard, some family systems are seen as more healthy, or functional, than other more dysfunctional family systems. A basic premise here is that the treatment of one individual for a (mental) health problem, or other difficulty in their lives, will not be successful unless the rest of the family is also part of the treatment, because the individual's behaviour, beliefs and mental state are an integral part of the family system.

One important aspect of family systems theory is that every aspect of the family is seen to fulfil a particular function for the system as a whole, with the result that each individual's part cannot be changed without also effecting change in the rest of the system. For example, one individual may be treated as the family 'scapegoat' and thus 'carry' much of the blame for things that are considered by other family members to be 'going wrong'. Among siblings, one might play out the part of the 'naughty' child, while another is the 'good' child. If the behaviour of the naughty child starts to change, the whole system will be affected and the good child might start to show more naughty behaviours. In this regard, individuals work out particular 'family scripts' (Byng-Hall, 1985) since their individual behaviour can be understood only in the context of the part they play in the whole. Additionally, each individual receives attention and a part in the family system, by contributing their particular piece of the 'jigsaw', which goes towards making up the whole family, even if the part they play results in disapproval or negative sanctions.

This notion of the family system can be extended and elaborated, for example, in terms of sub-systems within the family system as a whole (e.g. a sibling sub-system or a couple sub-system), or in terms of each individual themselves being composed of a set of 'internal' sub-systems. There is also the notion of the **external environment**, sometimes understood as a **meta-system**, with which the family system has **feedback mechanisms** that lead to changes being accommodated and a new 'homoeostasis' reached, that is, an equilibrium or steady state. Some argue, however, that it is more useful to see families through a dialectical approach, recognizing that any balance reached is fleeting, since there are always variable tensions around changes, connections and contradictions in families (Chandler Sabourin, 2003). Family systems theory is also attentive to **time**, regarding the family processes of previous generations as still affecting current systems.

Bronfenbrenner's (1979) elaboration of families as nested within a series of interacting systems exemplifies a multilayered systemic model that is influential in psychological work on families. Responding to changes in the family environment, or to changes in the family system itself (e.g. through the illness or death of a family member), is understood to pose adaptational challenges that must be met if the family system is not to dissolve. While this **ecological model** is drawn upon as a way of paying attention to the environments of family systems, others suggest that a more complex and interactional understanding of contexts is needed (Uttal, 2009).

In the early years of family systems theory, the notion of 'family' was often limited and ethnocentric, that is, the **nuclear family**. Over time, 'the system' has come to include supportive long-term relationships, regardless of how these are constituted and whether or not they are regarded as 'family'. Nonetheless, there may still be underpinning assumptions of **heteronormativity** (Leslie and Southard, 2009). It is necessary of course to take some view about which individuals are members of the family system under examination, and thus where to draw the **boundaries** between who is inside and who is outside of that system. Some argue that systems theory is applied inappropriately to family lives. Families are not equivalent to mechanical or biological systems, which have clear physical boundaries between an internal set of interconnected parts and an external environment. Family boundaries arguably are more fluid and contingent, dependent on the perceptions and understandings of people involved.

Furthermore, the criteria for what is considered to be 'healthy' functioning within a family system is culturally specific even though systems theory often discusses such criteria as if they are universal. The concept of family 'enmeshment', for example, refers to the ways in which family members may be over-involved in each others' lives without a clear sense of their own individual boundaries. However, cultures vary in what they consider to be the appropriate balance between individual **autonomy** and family **connectedness** (Dilworth-Anderson et al., 1993) and may not see the two as being in conflict (Kağitçibaşi, 2005). Indeed,

family systems

93

in recent years, the notion of '**dysfunction**' in families has itself been interrogated (Levner, 1998). The implicit values that frame different approaches within family therapy have been the subject of debate (Melito, 2003), with attention paid to the significance of the therapist and how he or she also shapes the therapeutic encounter.

Another major criticism levelled against family systems theory is that it struggles to account for structurally patterned dimensions of power that originate from outside the system – such as **gender, class** and **ethnicity** – which influence the dynamics of interaction within the family system (Miller and Perelberg, 1990).

The main contribution of family systems theory as a therapeutic base is that it draws attention to an individual's behaviour and functioning in the context of the web of relationships in which they are implicated. Family therapists are interested in what goes on between people as much as within individuals, and solutions to problems are seen to lie in the treatment of people in relationships rather than of individuals. Nevertheless, practitioners vary in how far they emphasize individual rather than family issues.

SUMMARY

Family systems theory is the basis for a therapeutic approach that views families as comprising interconnected parts (individual family members) with the behaviour of individuals understood only in the context of their web of family relationships. Systems theorizing posits that family systems develop a form of internal balance in order to survive in the face of environmental or other adaptational challenges. Systemic therapy is subject to criticisms regarding how to evaluate healthy functioning, and how to define the family system, as well as lack of consideration of differentials of power derived from wider social processes.

FURTHER READING

Horne and Ohlsen (2002) introduce different approaches to family therapy. Sutcliffe et al. (1998) exemplify systemic approaches to family crisis. Leslie and Southard (2009) discuss the impact of feminism on family therapy.

Related concepts   *Child Development; Functionalism; Problem Families*

Fatherhood/Fathers/ Fathering

DEFINITION

Fatherhood refers to the processes associated with designating specific men as fathers, thereby holding a gendered parental relationship with individual child/ren.

DISCUSSION

Distinctions between fatherhood, fathers and fathering have recently become a focus of social scientific discussion (Morgan, 2004), with *fatherhood* referring to broad institutional structures, while *fathers* refers to specific individuals who occupy the position of male parent. However, unlike mothering, '*fathering*' as a verb (in English usage) can mean either to beget a child or to engage in a set of activities around the care of children. This may or may not link closely to ideas about biological paternity, which are culturally variable. What constitutes fathering has thus been a source of academic debate.

For many men, historically and cross-culturally, the experience of fatherhood is a source of **adulthood** and social power. Historically in the UK, for example, fathers were assumed to be the **head of the household** for census purposes, with other household residents subject to their authority. The term '**patriarchy**' refers to 'the rule of the father' which has been a widespread and historical social phenomenon providing men with both paternal and conjugal power (Therborn, 2004), although it may also be used to refer to systematic structures of male power more generally (Walby, 1990). In many cultures, connection to the male adult provides a child with their **identity** within the society in terms of kinship links and wider political position. In **patrilineal** societies this adult will most often be the person who is recognized as the father of the child, but this is not necessarily so, and sometimes males from the mother's kin group – particularly her brothers – provide a child with a wider social identity.

Uncertainty around who is the father of a child arguably is linked to widespread, if variable, cultural practices to determine the child's legitimate social position in terms of the connection with the father. Such **legitimation** is a basis for the institutionalization of **marriage**, and relevant to rules about the transmission of **property** rights. While some feminist writers argue that this is a key foundation for the patriarchal oppression of women across societies, in circumstances where men have few **resources** to provide for women and children, they may be marginalized as fathers (Pine, 1998). The law is changing in some Western societies to give automatic legal recognition to fathers of children born outside of marriage (Sheldon, 2009) – a move that may be associated with increased expectation of **financial support** from men as fathers outside of marriage or cohabitation. Identification of the man who is considered to have 'fathered' a child thus carries implications for responsibility and support.

In most English-speaking cultures, the concern with biological fatherhood is of long standing, traceable to Latin terminology. The Romans identified the **biological father** as the *genitor*, a term that was reserved for use with only one individual. In contrast, the word *pater* was used to refer to other individuals acting as a **social father.** In recent years in the UK, the law has changed to make it possible legally to recognize more than one man as having connections as a father with a child. This development, however, is occurring alongside a tenacious hold on legal understanding of what is seen as a biological link. Challenges to legal definitions of fathers are apparent in relation to new **reproductive technologies** (Collier and Sheldon, 2008), raising difficult legal questions. For example, while it was thought previously that children's interests were best served if it was assumed that they were the biological children of their mother's husband – thus affirming the family unit – genetic testing now provides men with a new route to determining children's paternity. At the same time, assertion of a child's right to know the identity of their genetic father risks a reduction in the number of donors available for assisted conceptions, while other deliberations may cut across delicate balances between biological fatherhood and legal fatherhood (Fortin, 2009; Smart, 2007).

Across time and place, social fathering has been more relevant than biological fathering for less affluent groups, for whom the struggle to survive is more central than the transmission of property and social status. The shift in Western societies towards industrial production and paid employment away from the home, and the ideal of the **family wage**, positioned men-as-fathers as important sources of economic support: as

breadwinners. At the same time, being away from home for long hours could restrict fathers' relationships with their children. In the twentieth century, fathers' marginalization from daily childcare, along with an emphasis on the attachment needs of children, became the basis for divorce courts to prioritize mothers as the **primary carers**, giving fathers fewer rights to custody. The late twentieth century then saw the establishment of fathers' rights groups campaigning for greater rights for fathers after divorce or separation. Such groups have received much publicity but there are questions about how representative they are (Collier and Sheldon, 2006).

Issues of responsibility and support have been identified as key issues in contemporary fatherhood. Some writers argue that two contrasting trends can be identified: 'good' 'new fathers' who are both providers and carers, and 'bad' 'deadbeat dads' who take no financial or emotional responsibility (Furstenberg, 1988). Indeed, a recurring theme in research on fatherhood is that it is undergoing a transition from **ascribed** to **achieved**, which has left fathers and fathering in a state of uncertainty. On the one hand, the lack of clarity in quite what fathering consists of is felt to affect certain types of fathers in particular, with **step-fathers** subject to even less clear norms about the role they should play (discussed in Ribbens McCarthy et al., 2002). On the other hand, lack of clarity means that men have more latitude about how to undertake fathering, and may thus be less subject to **moral** scrutiny than mothers (Ribbens McCarthy et al., 2000; Miller, 2010).

Since childcare is understood largely as falling within women's sphere of activities, it is difficult to perceive the activities of fathers with their children as a form of parenting in its own terms. Fathering has been differentiated into **paternal engagement** (direct time with children), **accessibility** (presence in the home) and **responsibility** (ensuring availability of care and resources) (Lamb et al., 1987). The consideration of fathering as a set of activities beyond the provider role raises questions about whether there is something distinctive about fathers' activities with their children in comparison with mothers'. Research into fathers' involvement in their children's daily lives suggests, for example, that fathers are more likely than mothers to engage in 'rough and tumble' play and to take children on outings, such as sports activities, whereas they are less likely to be closely involved as someone to talk to and act as a confidante. In recent years psychologists have also looked at the part fathering plays in children's development (Pleck and Masciadrelli, 2004). This research indicates the varying significance of different types of parental involvement over the shorter or longer term, with play, for example, linked to longer-term development (Lewis, C. and Lamb, 2003).

The increased emphasis on fathers' involvement in children's lives in European and New World societies generally seems to find **middle-class** couples espousing egalitarian ideals of childrearing, although in practice it may be **working-class** fathers who have more time for involved fathering (Lewis, C., 2000). While there is evidence of changing attitudes favouring greater paternal involvement, and in the USA **lone father** households are showing a significant increase as a proportion of lone parent households (Casper and Bianchi, 2002), nonetheless there are strong cultural and structural processes that continue to shape fathering as secondary to that of mothering.

SUMMARY

Fathers are often key to a child's general social positioning. Distinctions are drawn between the institution and the experience of fatherhood. Fathering as a verb denotes ambiguous meanings, which in themselves highlight paradoxes around how the role of fathers is changing in contemporary European and New World societies. While there is evidence of changing attitudes that encourage fathers' increased involvement in their children's lives, there are also persistent patterns and processes that place fathers as the secondary parent.

FURTHER READING

C. Lewis and Lamb (2003) and Lamb (2010) contain general discussions of fathers from psychological perspectives; Dermott (2008) and Miller (2010) provide sociological discussions; and Featherstone (2009) overviews fathers in policy and professional practice.

Related concepts   *Division of Labour; Family Law; Motherhood; Parenthood*

DEFINITION

There are a number of schools of feminist thought with varying interpretations of family and its implications. Nonetheless, all feminisms, in
making women visible, draw attention to gender politics and see family,
and mothering in particular, as a key site of power.

DISCUSSION

Feminism is often divided into waves, with the first wave occurring
mainly in the nineteenth century in European and New World societies,
the second wave from the mid to late twentieth century, and the third
wave beginning in the twenty-first century. Intellectually, feminist work
has challenged ideas about 'natural' **gender roles** by arguing that families
as social institutions play a particular part in the way in which society is
organized. Key feminist contributions include new questions about
motherhood and housework, and making visible **violence** in families.
Feminist theorizing is also often divided into different perspectives, such
as liberal, socialist and radical – and hence 'feminisms' in the plural are
spoken of, rather than 'feminism' in the singular. Feminist approaches
each have somewhat different emphases in what they have to say – both
bad and good – about family and family relationships as a social institution. As well as being a collection of intellectual approaches, feminism
has a political activist dimension, sometimes referred to as the 'women's
liberation movement', and is a force for women's rights around the
world. While feminist work and activism has had a major impact on family studies, some writers suggest that the relevance of feminist thinking
to family studies is a 'stalled revolution' (Allen, 2009: 9).

   A common assumption about feminism, of whatever sort, is that it is
'anti-family'. Indeed, some commentators regard the rise of 'second-
wave' feminism as responsible for the so-called breakdown of the
'traditional' two-parent, **male breadwinner family** (e.g. Dench, 1997).
Certainly, feminisms can see family and family relationships as repressive, but there are also perspectives that identify strengths. A recurring
debate cross-cutting various schools of thought is whether family forms

a source of women's subordination or a site of resistance and empowerment. It is also important to remember that women themselves can experience family lives in ambiguous ways.

Looking first at feminist critiques of family, a liberal feminism perspective regards the restriction of women to being full-time wives and mothers as suppressing their potential and capacities, which would otherwise find expression in the public sphere of education, employment and politics. This restriction is also said to be what lies behind the feminization of **poverty**, where mothers' responsibility for bringing up children means that divorced and single mothers, and elderly women in later life, exist on minimal state benefits rather than having established themselves in a career with good wages.

Marxist- and socialist-informed feminisms are also concerned with women being able to enter the public sphere, and equally emphasize the division of labour in the private sphere. They differ, however, in their conception of the oppressive systems at the root of women's unequal positioning in family. For Marxist feminists, women's subordination emanates from **capitalism**, where they provide free care for the current workforce (husbands, fathers, brothers) and reproduce and bring up the future workers and carers (sons and daughters). In turn, women are economically dependent on men in exchange for the provision of care and of their **sexuality**; hence Engels' famous description of **marriage** as a form of prostitution (1884). From a related materialist feminist perspective, Delphy and Leonard (1992) regard marriage as a 'class-like' relationship between men and women, in which wives and mothers are entrapped in an exploitative domestic mode of production in the same way that workers are caught in the capitalist mode of production. Commentators in these Marxist and materialist veins might advocate either the collectivization of the family responsibilities and tasks that are posed as '**women's work**', notably childcare and housework, or the payment of **wages for housework** and care, making their work-like nature evident and providing women with a self-generated income.

Socialist feminists, however, make a distinction between capitalism and **patriarchy** as oppressive systems, and might regard women as oppressed by both (albeit that the interests of each do not always coincide) (Hartmann, 1979). Patriarchy literally means 'rule by the father', where authority and resources are passed from father to son, but the term is also used to refer to the institutionalized domination of men over women in status and power. The gendered division of labour is argued to position family as a primary site for the perpetuation of gendered inequality and of the differential socialization of children by gender. The construction of feminine and masculine **identities**, of self and Other, and of domination and subordination, through the gendered and patriarchal structures of family has also been a concern of **psychoanalytic feminism** (e.g. Dinnerstein, 1987). In this vein, feminists are often concerned with promoting an equal division of domestic labour and caring between the sexes in families.

Radical feminism also focuses on patriarchy, posing sexism as the original and most pervasive form of oppression, with biology at the root of men's power. The dominant patriarchal **heterosexual** family structure is said to oppress women through fathers' and husbands' (sometimes violent) control and exploitation of women's sexuality and unpaid domestic labour, and through their childbearing and childrearing destinies. Firestone (1979) argued that only the replacement of biological with **reproductive technology** will free women. Separatist ideas also stem from this analysis, seeking to exclude men, reject heterosexuality and establish woman-centred sexuality and family life. In this vein, Rich (1977) argued that men attempt to control women because they fear their power to give life, and that women need to reclaim control of **childbirth** and **childrearing** from its institutionalization by men in developed societies. Pivotal to Rich's argument is an important distinction between mother*hood* as an institution that oppresses women and mother*ing* as an individual experience, which is much more ambiguous in being a source of emotions and activities that simultaneously hold the possibility of empowerment and being shaped by broader societal patriarchy.

Indeed, some strands of feminism regard family in all its forms as playing a more positive role in women's lives and in society. Black feminists, for example, have drawn attention to the way in which much feminist thinking about family marginalizes minority **ethnic** perspectives. While white middle- and upper-**class** women may experience family as a source of oppression, for minority ethnic and working-class women it can be a place of refuge and resistance in a racist and unequal society (Hill Collins, 1990/2008). Some argue that work from feminist family studies is only just beginning to address issues of **intersectionality** and **transnationalism** (Allen, 2009).

Other feminists argue that family relationships in general, rather than subordinating women, form a model for the creation of a more moral and just society. For example, Elshtain (1981) poses family as providing love and care separate from the competitive profit motive of capitalist society. Family, and the practice of mothering in particular, allows people to learn and experience **obligations**, intimacy and compassion – all qualities that, if placed at the centre of public civic life, would radically reframe society for the better. Similarly, Ruddick (1990) argues that '**maternal thinking**' is characterized by nurture and protection and that the expansion of such thinking to wider society would be beneficial. Critics of these sorts of arguments, however, argue that families can be dysfunctional, that mothers can be abusive, violent and neglectful, and that mothers also need an autonomous life (Flax, 1984).

The feminist movement, broadly defined, is often either lauded or blamed for its impact on women's family lives. As noted earlier, higher rates of motherhood outside of marriage and higher rates of divorce have been attributed to the rise of feminism. While some characterize such trends as demonstrating the breakdown of society, others see it as part of its **democratization.** On a more specific level, following on from feminist campaigns, rape in marriage, and violence and abuse in family relationships, have been made offences in most European and New World societies, while childcare provision and parental leave have become a state concern in many such countries.

SUMMARY

Feminisms have provided important challenges to assumptions about the way in which family lives are organized. A number of different perspectives comprise feminism, cross-cut by debates about whether family is a source of women's subordination or a site of their resistance and empowerment. A feminist critique of family emphasizes the suppression of women's educational, employment and political potential, and their oppression through unequal gender divisions of labour, power and authority. There is some ambiguity, however, around family and motherhood as social institutions, and family lives and mothering as individually experienced by women. Another feminist view can see family as providing a respite from societal inequalities, and family relationships as empowering women and providing a template for a more moral and just society.

FURTHER READING

Budig (2007) provides a good introductory review of several different schools of feminism and their ideas about family. Sommerville (2000) charts how family became a public concern in the UK and the USA in the late twentieth century, and how this history links with feminism.

Related concepts   *Conflict Theories; Division of Labour; Motherhood; Power*

Functionalism

DEFINITION

As a theory, functionalism sees 'the family' as an institution constituting a basic building block of society, performing certain functions that must be fulfilled for social order to be possible and for society to continue.

DISCUSSION

When people refer to the functions that family fulfils, their meaning may be quite uncertain. They may simply mean that family lives have certain effects or consequences (such as care of children), or they may be implicating functionalism as a sociological theory about the purposes family fulfils for society.

Functionalism was influential in family sociology for many decades. As a sociological theory it is sometimes particularly traced back to the work of the nineteenth-century French sociologist, Durkheim, who wanted to demonstrate that society is more than just the sum of the actions of individuals, and displays systematic features and patterns that can only be understood at the macro societal level. These ideas were taken up in North American sociology, particularly by Talcott Parsons in the middle of the twentieth century, whose influential writings are often seen as developing functionalism fully as a theoretical model (Parsons, 1964). Parsons argued that, for societies to continue to exist, there are certain 'functions' that have to be fulfilled, and this occurs through the key institutions of society, of which the family is one. This treats 'the family' as a solid object that exists in its own right, with characteristics and effects beyond the actions of the individuals who comprise it.

Parsons argued that the family fulfils two key functions for society. The first is the socialization of the next generation so that they are equipped to become fully functioning members of society, in terms of their orderly containment and their potential to contribute to society in the future. This comprises two aspects in functionalist theory: children's general learning and **internalization** of social norms and expectations (**cultural transmission**), and the allocation of particular roles that they will play in society as adults (**role allocation**). The second major function of the family concerns the **stabilization of adult personalities** through the development of close relationships, and provision of a role to play that will give them a sense of fulfilment and also help to create harmonious social order. These functions were said to be most appropriately met – particularly in industrialized societies – through the **nuclear family**. Men were argued to have the adult **instrumental role** of providing for their families and dealing with the public world, particularly paid labour, while women have the adult **expressive role** of caring for children and other dependents, and maintaining the **domestic sphere**. This picture might be said to be a simple, if idealized, description of the prevalent family form in the USA of the mid-1950s. This was not meant just as a description of what was happening, however, but as a theoretical framework implying that this family form was the optimum one for society at large – a view that loosely continues to underpin fears of the consequences of the supposed 'breakdown' of the family. From this point of view, if families fail to fulfil these 'functions', social order will not be achieved. Within this social theory, then, families serve to link **micro interactions** to the **macro social level** in response to the needs of the wider social order, creating security for both individuals and the wider society, to the benefit of all. Thus Parson's descriptive accounts of contemporary American, white, middle-class, family life, need to be considered separately from his theoretical model of how society functions as a harmonious whole.

The suggestion that all societies need families in order to function may also be linked to Murdock's (2003) argument that the family is to be found universally across all societies. One of the difficulties of the functionalist approach however, is to explain how social change occurs, if existing institutional arrangements are always seen as functional. When families are changing as they have done in some significant respects in contemporary developed societies, is this an indication that something is breaking down in the functioning of society, or are families changing in response to the changing needs of other aspects of society, such as changes in the economy – which leads to a form of **economic determinism** in which families are shaped in straightforward ways by economic systems.

Either way, functionalist approaches have to find some way of describing and accounting for family change. One such account is to say that industrialization has seen a decline in the functions that the family has to fulfil, particularly with production moving from domestic sites to large-scale factory sites, and the establishment of compulsory educational systems. From this perspective, the family has been declining in importance for society, although a further strand to the argument suggests that its remaining functions (notably socialization and the stabilization of adult personalities) have intensified in importance. Furthermore it may be argued that the family has acquired new functions, most notably as a major institution for **consumerism**.

Overall, functionalism as a grand social theory has been robustly criticized on many grounds, such that by the late twentieth century it had largely fallen into disfavour. Besides its limitations in accounting for social change, such critiques included its failure to deal with power relationships and its neglect of antagonistic interest groups in society – resulting in an unrealistic view of society as harmonious, with social processes working to the benefit of all, rather than to the benefit of certain groups over others. It was also criticized for 'reifying' society, and mistakenly regarding it as analogous to a machine that could stop 'working', or an organism that might cease to 'exist'. A final major strand of criticism was that it treated individuals as passive recipients of social forces, failing to allow for human **agency**.

Nevertheless, some features of functionalist theory may be pertinent to contemporary family studies. These include the possibility that family interactions produce a social arrangement that cannot just be reduced to individual processes; that different individuals may take particular roles or parts within the family group; and that family lives have effects on wider social processes and are integrally bound up with varied social institutions. Indeed, much political debate about families continues to be preoccupied with the view that families are, or should be, a key building block for **social order**.

SUMMARY

Functionalism is a complex social theory that explains how societies work as interconnected systems. From this perspective, the family is an institution forming part of the overall social system, and fulfilling necessary functions on behalf of society through the socialization of children and the stabilization of adult personalities and roles. As a theory, functionalism has been criticized, but may still have some value in terms of its emphasis on how family lives interrelate with other broad features of society.

FURTHER READING

Parsons and Bales (1955) provide the most complete account of functionalist theory of the family. See David H.J. Morgan (1975) for a comprehensive discussion of such theories in their heyday, and Kingsbury and Scanzoni (2009) for the continuing relevance of functionalist approaches.

Related concepts *Family Change and Continuity; Role Theory; Socialization*

Grandparents

DEFINITION

Grandparent/s is a term denoting the parent/s of a person's mother or father, invoking a relationship across three generations of a family.

DISCUSSION

The increase in life expectancy in affluent European and New World societies means that children are now likely to have living grandparents into their adult lives, although smaller families mean that grandparents are likely to have fewer grandchildren in their lives (Casper and Bianchi, 2002; Dench and Ogg, 2002). Reference is often made to **bean pole families**, which stretch across several generations while having few members in any one. Grandparents rarely feature in books in family studies, yet the topic highlights issues of family lineage and assumptions about the nature of family relationships and kinship, within particular families and broader society. Nonetheless, the form and quality of grandparent–grandchild relationships has received research attention, most extensively in the USA.

In the contemporary context, much empirical attention has been paid to the amount of childcare and **financial support** that grandparents provide, or the care and financial support they themselves require. A main feature of this work is that, although some grandparents may be reluctant to take on a caring role, or be unable to because of their own paid work commitments, for the most part grandparents see providing material and practical support as part of their relationship with and commitment to their children (their grandchildren's parents) and grandchildren, rather than as requiring repayment (Ferguson et al., 2004). This highlights expectations of altruistic **obligation** down the generations in families, rather than a transactional exchange. Indeed, grandparenting falls within Finch's (1989) description of a kin relationship as **asymmetrical**, where feelings of affection flow more strongly down the generations than back up them.

Research in different cultural contexts consistently finds that grandchildren's relationship with their grandparents changes with age (Van Der Geest, 2004). In European and New World societies, decreasing contact over time is attributed to children's growing independence from family life and influence. In other cultural contexts such as Africa, with different understandings of childhood, shifting relationships may be seen through a framework that highlights different pasts and futures within a shared present. Grandparents' own ageing process and the social status of older people in a society generally, are also likely to be of relevance. In the European and New World context, some suggest that ageing on both sides does not necessarily mean that grandparents and grandchildren feel less close to each other emotionally (Ross et al., 2006), whereas in the Ghanaian context, for example, the opposite is argued – with respect for grandparents in public still demonstrated even when the emotional content of the relationship is said to have dwindled (Van Der Geest, 2004).

The strength of relationships between grandparents and their own adult children is often identified as determining the quality of grandparent–grandchild relationships, highlighting how relationships across three generations are mediated by or derived from parent–child relationships. Indeed, work on young, white working-class mothers points to the way in which their relationship with their own mothers in particular is closely interwoven with the young mothers' sense of themselves as caring and capable (Duncan et al., 2010). Work on grandparenting after parents'

divorce, focusing on amount and quality of contact between grandparents and grandchildren, usually remarks on how this is largely a continuation or intensification of the nature of grandparent–grandchild relationships before the family break-up.

Lineage and gender are other key features of research on grandparenting. A grandparenting hierarchy has been developed by researchers in European and New World contexts, in which grandparents are 'ranked' by gender and kin status according to the amount of contact and involvement they have with their grandchildren (gender of grandchildren is not noted, however). In this hierarchy, grandmothers are ranked more highly than grandfathers as having most contact with their grandchildren, alongside a marked **matrifocal** tendency for maternal, rather than paternal, grandparents to be more involved, thus placing maternal grandmothers at the top of the ranking. The lineage and gender hierarchy is explained variously as stemming from grandmothers' relationships, as mothers, with their daughters (Aldous, 1995) or tied to investment in genetically more certain kin (Laham et al., 2005). The priority accorded to paternal grandfathers in some cultural contexts, however, would question such grand statements (Szinovacz,1998).

The matrilineal hierarchy is also said to apply to **step-grandparenting**, with step-grandfathers more involved than step-grandmothers because of their links through their relationship with the grandchildren's grandmother (Dench and Ogg, 2002). While generally grandparents can provide a bridge to the past as sources of family history and heritage (Ross et al., 2006), grandmothers are also said to be involved in their grandchildren's lives in domestic ways, while grandfathers undertake more physical and public activities. Such findings result largely from studies of grandparents in European and New World societies. In distinction, there is reduced access to maternal grandparents in **patrifocal** families and societies, albeit grandparenting hierarchies are not a feature of research in these contexts (Szinovacz, 1998).

Other studies have drawn up typologies and classifications of grandparenting styles – often as part of psychology's interest in child development (Ferguson et al., 2004) – highlighting the closeness or distance of the relationship, its active or passive nature and who is the main focus. The terms used in these typologies and classifications can carry implicit evaluations (compare the descriptors 'remote' and 'passive' with 'companionate' and 'supportive') and involve value judgements on the part of the researchers constructing them. These may well be based on the understandings of those who are dominant and powerful in society, marginalizing or problematizing the grandparenting practices of minority ethnic and/or working-class grandparents and ignoring the styles of grandparenting in other cultures (Szinovacz, 1998).

Some researchers have also identified general norms or guidelines in grandparenting. These include obligations to 'be there' for their family, and the requirement to treat grandchildren fairly and ensure that any favouritism is not obvious (Ferguson et al., 2004). A norm of **autonomy** and **privacy** for the nuclear family is also often identified, with grandparents adhering to a delicate balance between providing support and help and observing implicit rules about non-interference (Ross et al., 2006).

It is important to note, though, that such norms are cultural and thus variable within a society over time and by social class, ethnicity and so on (Casper and Bianchi, 2002), as well as between kinship patterns of different societies. Research on working-class (UK) or blue-collar (USA) grandparenting in the post-Second World War years shows that strongly participative rather than detached grandparenting was the accepted practice, despite some researchers' ideas that this comprised a grandparent syndrome in which the adult parents were infantilized by grandparental involvement (Szinovacz, 1998). The small amount of research that has been carried out on African-Caribbean grandparents in the USA, for example, rather than the dominant white majority, has also noted that they often adopt more authoritative and 'parent-like' relationships with their grandchildren. Minority ethnic grandparents can also see themselves as having responsibility for handing down religious and cultural traditions and **rituals**, while, as noted earlier, their grandchildren can place an emphasis on respect towards grandparents (Ross et al., 2006).

As well as the focus on investigating grandparents themselves, some attention has also been paid to the grandparent–grandchild relationship by researching **grandchildren**. Much of this work replicates the main preoccupations of grandparenting studies, notably the influence of gender and kinship status on amount of contact in European and New World societies. Nonetheless, along with the interest in children as agents in society generally and in families specifically, attention is starting to be paid to how children and young people themselves understand the importance and quality of their relationship with their grandparents, and the reciprocal nature of care and support between them (Ross et al., 2006).

The legal status of grandparents has also been a feature of attention. There is some variety in the extent to which grandparents have statutory obligations to maintain, or are given statutory rights to, contact with their grandchildren in family law systems (Ferguson et al., 2004). Under the jurisprudence of European and US institutions, it is clear that even if grandparents have **right** of access, these will always be superseded by prevailing constructions of a child's welfare that place them firmly within the nuclear family model, under parental control. In contrast to the potential broader understandings of family in, say, South African and Macedonian jurisdictions, European and New World grandparents are positioned within a model of extended family that sees them primarily as a practical resource and contributor to the socialization of children, supporting and prioritizing the parent–child family core. The dominant societal norm of non-interference on the part of grandparents in these nation states means that grandparents are unlikely to be granted contact if parents feel that this is not in the child's best interests.

SUMMARY

Research on grandparenting is shaped by the society in which it takes place as much as by grandparenting itself. In the European and New World context, research on grandparenting draws attention to generational obligations, mediation through parent–child relations, and the influence of lineage and gender. Various styles of grandparenting have been constructed by researchers, and implicit norms shape not only how grandparenting is understood within families themselves, but also grandparents' legal standing in European and New World institutions. Kinship structures and grandparenting styles and norms vary between cultures, as well as over time.

FURTHER READING

Casper and Bianchi (2002) offer a discussion of grandparents in the US context; Ferguson et al. (2004) overview grandparenting in European and New World societies generally. Szinovacz (1998) looks at research on grandparenting. A special issue of the journal *Africa* (71.1: 2004) is concerned with grandparents and grandchildren in a range of African contexts.

Related concepts   Care; Kinship; Social Divisions; Socialization

Home

DEFINITION

Home is both a physical space and, specifically in terms of family, a place carrying social and emotional ideals of kinship relations, such as intimacy, rootedness, belonging, solidarity, security and privacy.

DISCUSSION

The idea of 'home' in European and New World societies, is often conceived of as a physical, spatial location, but more than this, it is a conceptual or interpretive construct or symbol that informs people's understanding of who they are and their relations with others (Dawson and Rapport, 1998). Cieraad (1999: 11) describes home as 'the emotionalisation of **domestic space**'. Home as the location of a kinship household can be a physical and emotional site of people's sense of themselves as part of a family. Indeed, the terms 'family' and 'home' are often intrinsically linked and used as synonymous with one another, symbolizing togetherness and **belonging**. For example, adult children living in their own households can refer to visiting their parent/s as 'going home', and the phrase 'a broken home' denotes **divorce** or separation in a family. Conversely, a family group may have accommodation but not think of it as being their home (such as placement in bed and breakfast accommodation). From this perspective, 'home' can comprise an **identity** for people who see themselves as part of a collective group which calls a particular location 'home' (for example, Jamaican/Jamaica, Londoner/London), as well as migrant engagement in making a 'home away from home'.

It is often argued that processes of **industrialization** have created a separation of the workplace from the home as a household not only in the West but also spreading across China and South Asia (Thornton and Fricke, 1987). In Europe and the New World at least, this led to a view of home as the key physical and emotional setting for people's family and personal lives – a refuge or haven from a competitive public world, alongside a shifting of the meaning of 'home' away from referring to birthplace, village or country to meaning family dwelling and house (Janeway, 1971). Nevertheless, for some families, the home may also be a workplace, as in family-run hotels or paid home-working. Such examples highlight how far this understanding of the home as a haven is constructed through particular beliefs and ideals among certain groups at a particular period. For instance, for working-class families, home has historically been open to many functions – rather than a retreat, it has been regarded as a resource for generating income (Hareven, 1993). There seems to have been little attention to non-Western cultural meanings of 'home' outside of European and New World societies in relation to family in the mainstream literature, however, as opposed to reference to the household or the significance of ancestral homeland.

The withdrawal of manufacturing production from the home, noted above, is also associated with normative ideas about the **privacy** of what goes on within the walls of the home. Such privacy in many contemporary north European societies is built around a family living independently in their own household. Moving out of the parental home and into one's own accommodation is regarded as a symbolic marker of reaching the independence and **autonomy** of **adulthood**. Ideas about the privacy of family life at home can cover a range of social and emotional **meanings**, such as secrets about parentage and lifestyle, and can mean that researchers find it hard to gain access and build up a picture of home life. There are also concerns about the protection of home and family life from interference by the state and, conversely, about the downside of privacy, where the home can be the site for abuse and **violence** 'behind closed doors', away from sources of protection.

Home can mean different things to different members of a family, notably according to **gender** and **generation**. For example, home is argued to be a site of gendered work and potential **inequality** and oppression across a range of societies and cultures (Low and Lawrence-Zúñiga, 2003), since the creation and maintenance of home as a domestic family space is associated with women's unpaid labour as **homemakers** for **husbands** and children. Women can feel especially responsible for the appearance of their home. Yet, the surface mundane character of the home as the site for the everyday experience of domestic life belies the energy, **resources**, **time** and **emotions** that have to be put into its management. This effort has historically been the sphere and responsibility of women, albeit men are thought to have become more home-centred since the mid-twentieth century.

The material and emotional idea of home is also said to shape family members' activities, such as through communal eating of **food**, the division of labour, and so on. In this view, the routines of home life produce a sense of solidarity at the same time as they involve the exertion of power by some family members over others. Furthermore, the organization and condition of the home can act as an implicit sign of the state of the family who inhabit it. In **welfare state** societies, welfare professionals, such as social workers or health visitors, for example, can interpret tidiness or shabbiness, and so on, as a reflection of family life and relationships.

It is easier for some groups than others in society to create a family home, however. Marginalized families can find it difficult to keep their home lives private in the face of possible surveillance and intervention from welfare professionals. The idea of home as a haven from a hostile world rather than a site of (gendered) oppression can have particular significance, for instance, for **working-class** and minority **ethnic** mothers and children in European and New World societies (e.g. Gillies, 2007; hooks, 1991). Children can also want the home to be a bounded family space, free from the requirements of **schooling** (Edwards and Alldred, 2000). Furthermore, the family home may be a place where women experience creativity and power as well as a site of their labour (Pink, 2004), and they may thus experience complex and ambiguous feelings about it. Furthermore, their work in the home can also impose obligations on others, and can carry important symbolic meanings as well as material significance (Martin, 1984). It is also the case that women and men can challenge the dominant gendering of activities within the home, sharing or reversing **responsibility** for home-making (e.g. Van Every, 1995), but nonetheless it seems that home continues to be regarded as the most appropriate place in which care between family members takes place.

Home as a normative site for family caring to take place has ramifications not only for those members who are undertaking care, but also for those in receipt of it. Within childhood studies, home is often discussed in terms of arguments that, in European and New World societies, childhood has been increasingly domesticated physically and ideologically. Not only are children spending increasing amounts of time actually in their home, but there is also a sense in which home is understood as the 'proper' place where children should spend their time outside of school, in the care of their parents rather than 'home alone'. Some children also

home

spend time in two homes, the emphasis being on the importance of retaining links between children and their **biological parent/s** after divorce or separation and leading to shared care. Home as the best place for the care of young children in particular is said to influence some employed mothers' preference for **childcare** arrangements that reproduce home-style environments for their children. The normative link between children and family home also underpins studies of homeless children; residential accommodation for 'looked after' children in state care is also often referred to as 'a home' – as, indeed, is collective residential care for older people.

SUMMARY

As well as a physical space, home carries social and emotional meanings concerning people's sense of who they are and their family relationships. Industrialization has been associated with the separation of home from the workplace and other aspects of the public world. In European and New World societies, this separation is argued to have several consequences, particularly for normative ideas of privacy, and gendered inequality. The spatial organization and routines of home life are said to produce a sense of family solidarity at the same time as they are cut through with inequalities. Some social groups can find it easier than others to create a family home, however. Home is also argued to be increasingly regarded as the place where children should be located when not at school.

FURTHER READING

In relation to European and New World societies, Mallett (2004) reviews the literature on home across a range of disciplines. David H.J. Morgan (1996) raises interpretive issues to do with the location of the family home in space.

Related concepts   *Childhood; Division of Labour; Household; Public and Private*

key concepts in
family studies

DEFINITION

A household is a physical structure that can contain an individual or a social group that may or may not be considered a family, who co-reside, usually involving sleeping under the same roof and typically sharing a range of domestic activities. Thus, the concept of household directs attention towards everyday practical living arrangements.

DISCUSSION

The term 'household' commonly refers to a physical structure that houses or provides shelter for people. Household is also strongly linked to the notion of home in popular ideas, and the place where families are likely to be located, and yet the terms 'family' and 'household' each raise quite different conceptual and analytic questions. In the UK and the USA today, the majority of households contain family members who are living together, and contemporary everyday understandings often take 'families' and 'households' to mean the same thing. Nevertheless, conceptually these terms refer to different social entities or processes, and are distinct. A household can contain an individual, for example, who does not share **residence** as part of a family unit, but still maintains family relationships with people who live elsewhere. Indeed, what is now often referred to as '**solo living**' – that is, single person households – has risen considerably in many affluent societies over recent decades, including the USA and the UK. In the USA, however, the categories used for national **surveys** link families and households in particular ways, with a specific category of 'family-household'. This term refers only to co-residents who are related by **blood ties**, **marriage** or **adoption**, thus excluding cohabiting couples from the category of a family-household.

Apart from the question of how families and households link to each other, in multi-occupancy houses where people are not related by blood, marriage or adoption, there is also the question of how to decide whether such a group of co-resident people constitute one household or separate households. The sharing of cooked **food**, or other domestic activities such as **housework**, or sharing a budget, have all been used at times as relevant criteria for defining households, for example, in the context of a group of students living in one house. Where research data is obtained at the household level, it is thus necessary to establish the relationships between the people at the same address. In the past, this focused around the contentious idea of a '**head of household**', with an automatic assumption that a husband or male partner was the head of the household. A more common contemporary research strategy is to avoid the notion of a 'head', instead designating someone as the **household reference person** or identifying the householder owning or renting the accommodation (Thomas, 1999).

Whether or not they overlap with families, households can vary considerably in the character, form and size of the social group involved, and in how they organize their daily lives together, as well as in the structure and **boundaries** of the living space in which they reside. Households are also fluid as people alter their daily living arrangements and move in and out of families, kinship groups and co-residence. This makes what constitutes a household subject to meanings that change over time and in different contexts, and also subject to question. How much of a shared division of domestic activities is necessary to be counted as a household, or how frequently does someone need to sleep overnight in a household in order to be a member of it? Are children whose parents have divorced or separated, and who, for example, live with their mother during the week and their father at weekends, a member of two households? Official definitions of household also change over time (e.g. Celsius, 2010), but even within one country, as well as across different European countries, population surveys may use varying definitions of household, making comparative work difficult.

As noted earlier, another issue is the extent to which a household overlaps with the notion of a home. People living in unsatisfactory household accommodation may feel themselves to be housed but not living in a place that they consider to be a home, for example. In many European and New World societies, moving out of the family household and setting up 'a home of one's own' is now considered a demonstration of **autonomy** and a desirable goal. It is generally assumed that a couple, and parents and children, will form their own household. Yet in the UK, for example, into the mid-twentieth century, young **working-class** couples co-residing with her or his parents was quite a common phenomenon, although generally it would last only for a year or so after the marriage (Gittins, 1989). Contemporary challenges to the straightforward equation of coupledom and family with a household include **living-apart-together (LAT)** arrangements.

Moreover, anthropological studies show how other arrangements apply in cultures around the world. Mead's (1971) study of Samoa, for example, showed how children chose the household in which they wanted to reside. In other societies and historical periods, people may reside in clusters of dwellings that make up a compound or be situated within an enclosure, rather than in a single demarcated household as such. Boundaries between household, home and economic activity can also be blurred in situations such as this, in farming economies and where the household home is also a place of work.

Consequently, while in some cultures the overlap between family and household typically involves a **nuclear family**, in others it is more typically a merger between household and an **extended family** or other form of kinship grouping. Anthropologists have classically explored the **lineage** patterns shaping the formation of households, in particular whether households are organized around the male or female line of descent. Such household structures may be seen as indicative of the cultural principles and socioeconomic processes of a society. Anthropologists debate whether these different arrangements are rooted in economic and **property** interests or whether other factors are (also) at play, and the extent to which structural organization overlaps with lines of power (Lowie, 2004). In the UK and the USA, **matrifocal** households are often posed as a defining feature of black family life, comprising mother-headed households, and the supposed displacement of black men from the household is said to be a cause of **poverty**. There are, however, challenges to this picture of black matriarchal households, identifying and demonstrating the range and fluidity of black African-Caribbean family lives and household composition (Reynolds, 2002).

A focus on the concept of household tends to emphasize the distribution of **resources** and division of labour among co-residents, whereas the concept of family brings to the fore issues such as solidarity and care between **generations**. Research in this vein has shown how, rather than equal sharing between members of a family household, income and other resources, including household space, are unequally distributed, often on the basis of **gender** and **age** (e.g. Himmelweit, 2000). This analytic framework, which is particularly favoured by economists, has thus opened up research and debate concerning the ways in which income and other resources are obtained and distributed in households, and how **labour** is organized and divided.

household

SUMMARY

The concept of household draws attention to basic issues of provisioning and resourcing the everyday lives of people who are co-resident. Key questions concern the criteria by which to determine whether a co-resident group constitutes a household, while contemporary language often equates households with 'families' and 'homes'. Government censuses and surveys tend to focus more on 'households' than 'families', on the presumption that households can be more clearly defined, but even these administrative definitions have changed over time in response to the shifting patterns of people's everyday lives and relationships. Around the world, households may concern more complex arrangements, with several kinship or household groups being organized around one physical site, such as a compound, which may be structured by reference to particular lines of descent, or lineage.

FURTHER READING

Gubrium and Holstein (1990) discuss how families, homes and household are conceptually related. Allan and Crow (2001) review debates on households and families. Himmelweit (2000) contains perspectives from economics. Reynolds (2002) and Casper and Bianchi (2002) discuss black family households in the UK and the USA, respectively, while Lowie (2004) focuses on household structures cross-culturally.

Related concepts   *Division of Labour; Home; Kinship; Power*

Individualization

DEFINITION

The individualization thesis suggests a radical transformation in family life and relationship aspirations and choices. Contentiously, it argues that nowadays 'family' has become a set of associations between people who choose to be bound together for as long as being so feels fulfilling to all involved. In turn, ideas about predetermined family obligations and a sense of permanent ties are said to have lost their dominance and relevance.

DISCUSSION

The individualization thesis is one of the most influential and debated in contemporary family studies. It is part of a body of social science theory that makes overarching statements about high or late 'reflexive' modernity as a social process with implications for people's personal motivation. Individualization is also said to produce the **democratization** of contemporary family life, exemplified in contemporary European and New World societies, characterized by values of **autonomy**, **equality**, mutual respect and communication – or at least a desire for these values. Wider kinship ties are also supposed to have followed this trajectory (Bauman, 2003).

The idea of reflexive **modernity** refers to the way in which education, economic prosperity, the welfare state and **contraception** are supposed to have freed people from traditional obligations and standard life pathways, so that they now have greater choices in the types of family that they can form and the sorts of lifestyle they can pursue. People are said to be constantly creating, considering and assessing their lives without reference to the customs of past generations, which have become irrelevant as guidance for the conduct of personal relationships – a process referred to as **detraditionalization**. 'The family' and other structural formations, such as **gender**, social **class**, **generation** and **religion**, are said to be losing their relevance. Individualization theorists thus refer to them variously as zombie categories that are 'dead and still alive' (Beck and Beck-Gernsheim, 2002) or **shell institutions** in which a form exists but its content has changed and opened up (Giddens, 1999).

Terms such as '**plastic sexuality**' (Giddens, 1992) and '**liquid love**' (Bauman, 2003) are used by individualization theorists to capture the way in which, in contemporary society, they understand people to be free from the requirements of **reproduction** and assumed **heterosexuality**. These writers argue that, because women increasingly are employed in the **labour market** and thus are no longer so materially dependent on their husbands, the structural framing of heterosexual partnership is shifting away from prescribed gender roles and divisions of labour that place men and women in asymmetrical power relations to each other. Instead, who does what within a partnership is open to negotiation

individualization

between equals. People are now said to be reflexive authors of their own biographies, pursuing the project of the **self** and creating their own **identities**, values and commitments, rather than following structurally predetermined pathways (Giddens, 1992). The pursuit of individual self-fulfilment is said to have replaced the previous emphasis on collective solidarity as part of family life, with a shift from families as a **community of need** to ties based on **elective affinities** (Beck and Beck-Gernsheim, 2002). The arguably growing diversity of family forms in Western societies is put forward as evidence that previously taken-for-granted ideas about structures of family life and shared norms have fragmented and been replaced by more individualistic responses to lifestyle construction. Now, 'brave new' family relationships are 'undecided' (Stacey, 1990) and there are 'families of choice' rather than prescription and obligation (Weeks et al., 2001).

Beck and Beck-Gernsheim (1995: 73) point to the significance of children as a profound and durable 'anchor for one's life'. They say that this is because the individualization process and its contingent intimate relationships prompt longings for a return to the security of apparently stable family norms. Giddens (1998) additionally says that biological parents have lifetime responsibilities that continue whether or not the relationship that begat them continues. Thus individualization, while mainly progressive for adults, has to have some limits placed upon it when it comes to relationships with children. Nevertheless, parental authority is recast as part of the democratization of family life.

Other writers, from different political and value positions, have a more negative view of the same processes described by the individualization thesis. New Right and revisionist perspectives tend to use the term '**individualism**' to capture what, for them, is the rise of a hedonistic, self-absorbed and atomized approach to personal lifestyle, family life and wider kin relations. In their terms, 'appetitive individualism' (where people pursue their own desires) has produced 'families without fathers … mothers without husbands, men without children, marriages without permanence, love without fidelity, self-interest without self-denial' (Davies, 1993: 2). From this conservative perspective, the lack of concrete norms and values to structure relationships and family life is bringing social fragmentation and disorder (e.g. Morgan, P., 1995), while the democratization of parent–child relationships brings a loss of control over children, with harmful consequences for social order more widely.

Some social theorists on the left retain the concept of individualization to make similar points, this time laying blame on the encroachment of the capitalist logic and **consumerism** into family life. They highlight the **moral** and emotional costs of individualized relationships and family life, resulting in individual alienation and social breakdown. At the same time, the discourse of individualization is argued to prevent people from understanding the structural constraints that shape their resources and possibilities (Bauman, 2001). This is said to chime with dominant neo-liberal political rhetoric's emphasis on markets, choice and individual responsibility (e.g. Fevre, 2000).

The individualization thesis has been criticized on several fronts, conceptually and empirically. Notably, it is said to highlight the idea of generalized independent choice devoid of social or historical context. **Agency** is unhooked from structure, and social conditions and disparities of gender and social class are obscured. As part of this, there are arguments that proponents of individualization ignore important and systematic variations in **welfare state** provision and local cultural contexts, which are important for how people are able to live their lives (Brannen and Nilsen, 2005).

The nature of 'the individual' constructed under the thesis has also been criticized as reflecting an autonomous, 'stand-alone' and instrumental view of the self and **individuality**. This is as opposed to a relational understanding of individuality as embedded in webs of interconnected and **interdependent** relationships (Sevenhuijsen, 1998). The idea of the separate and independent individual in the individualization thesis is argued to reflect adult masculine experience and to highlight adult sexual relationships over process-oriented relationships between mothers and children in particular (Ribbens McCarthy and Edwards, 2002). Consequently, the concept of 'democracy' has been imported erroneously from the public sphere, ignoring material and power inequalities that are apparent in empirical research, particularly between parents and children. Democratic childrearing is said to be an illusion: power and inequality are not eliminated but, rather, they are suppressed (Walkerdine and Lucey, 1989).

Some argue that it is important not to confuse the concept of individualization as a social process with treating individualization as personal motivation. Indeed, the extent to which individualization has permeated people's experiences of contemporary family life in practice is debatable. Crow (2002) argues that there was far more fluidity and diversity in people's family understandings and behaviours historically than is often recognized. Moreover, he says that there is still adherence to long-standing family values and norms in contemporary society and that gender, social class, **age** and **ethnicity** remain important in shaping people's family lives. Likewise Jamieson (1998) concludes that the research base does not support the individualization thesis as a depiction of either the current state of family relationships or the direction in which they are moving.

Indeed, empirical work with families in different forms, and from different social classes and ethnic groups, often shows that the moral commitment to 'putting the family first' and 'putting children first', forgoing individual self-interest, still has a strong hold (Reynolds and Zontini, 2006; Ribbens McCarthy et al., 2003). Thus it would seem that individualism as a feature of how people live their personal and family lives is not a necessary consequence of the changes in family forms that underpin arguments about zombie categories and shell institutions.

SUMMARY

The individualization thesis argues that contemporary European and New World societies are undergoing a process in which people are progressively freed from the traditional forms and obligations of family life, which is then asserted to have consequences for the conduct of personal relationships. People are said to exercise greater choice in family lifestyle and to pursue individual self-fulfilment through contingent and democratized intimate relationships. Families as 'communities of need' are being replaced by family relationships that are characterized by 'elective affinity'. Criticisms of the individualization thesis variously highlight theoretical presumptions of autonomous rather than connected individuals; how its focus on individual choice obscures still-existing structural constraints and variations; and the abundance of empirical evidence revealing that people still demonstrate considerable adherence to values of commitment rather than self-interest in their family lives.

FURTHER READING

Beck and Beck-Gernsheim (1995, 2002) and Giddens (1992, 1999) offer largely positive views of the individualization process and Bauman (2003) a more negative position. Contributions to Davies (1993) discuss individualism in families as selfishness. Ribbens McCarthy and Edwards (2002) discuss the construction of the individual in the individualization thesis.

Related concepts   Families of Choice; Family Change and Continuity; Intimacy; Negotiation

Intimacy

DEFINITION

Intimacy refers to the meaning and expression of close family and personal relationships, as these are understood in contemporary European and New World societies, and to the qualities that they may be supposed to provide.

DISCUSSION

In a broad sense, all family and domestic life can be said to be intimate in that it involves familiarity arising from close association. A particular concept of intimacy has become important in Western social science debates, however, prompted by ideas about family change and **diversity** in the late twentieth century. The interest in the interior **emotional** quality of relationships has been referred to as the 'intimate turn' in family studies. It is said to have replaced a concern with more functional and structural analyses of relational bonds that emphasized family form, roles and outcomes, and social divisions and power (Gillies, 2003). As the economic role of the family has declined, intimacy and **love** have come to be regarded as the new lynchpin. There are arguments that mutual **self-disclosure** has emerged as the primary understanding of closeness and meaning in personal and family relationships, notably prompted by Giddens' (1991, 1992) arguments about the 'transformation of intimacy' as part of his wider discussion of the individualization thesis.

Giddens asserts that, across contemporary Western societies, a fundamental change has occurred in the nature and understanding of intimacy. Ease of access to reliable birth control means that sex has become unhooked from **reproduction**. This is said to have brought about a revolution, with women equal to men in partner relationships. Sex freed from reproduction is termed '**plastic sexuality**' (Giddens, 1992) and '**liquid love**' (Bauman, 2003) because, it is asserted, relations have to be negotiated between couples rather than determined by set ideas about appropriate gender and sexual **identity** and **roles**. There are also arguments that **heterosexual** and **homosexual** relations are increasingly becoming more like each other in their desire for a certain type of

intimacy

123

intimacy, with heterosexual relationships following the pioneering patterns of choice, **equality** and **reciprocity** laid down in homosexual relationships (Roseneil and Budgeon, 2004). Intimacy is said to have been restructured around the aspiration for, and negotiation of, **pure relationships** that are free from ties of **tradition**, necessity and **obligation**, and based on meeting personal needs.

In this view, pure relationships, based on self-realization, mutual trust and negotiation, are seen to be entered into for their own sake, and conducted from a position of self-awareness – an intimacy of the inner **self**. The quality of intimacy has to be **achieved** and recognized reflexively, rather than assumed in **ascribed** relationships. A particular sort of communication is central to this achievement, founded on the sharing of thoughts and the expression of feelings.

While Giddens and others (e.g. Weeks et al., 2001) regard these transformations towards disclosing intimacy in a largely positive light, as involving equality and mutuality, others agree that the trend is occurring, but regret it. They see the intensity of intimacy in contemporary society as reflecting a self-obsessed and competitive **individualism**, which undermines not only family life, but also cohesive communities (e.g. Sennett, 2004). Uncertainty and anxiety are said to be at the heart of contemporary Western experiences of family and personal relationships. So, while Beck and Beck-Gernsheim (1995) claim that **romantic love** has overwhelming significance as the positive **moral** guideline for relationships and new family ties, they also suggest that the association between **risk** and intimacy has led to a 'normal chaos of love'. People's reflexive awareness of their autonomy involves a loneliness that leads them to seek love, intimacy and deep connection with another, even while they know its achievement is uncertain. Being and developing oneself at the same time as seeking mutual closeness to another is an intricate balancing act that often breaks down.

In the context of frail adult sexual relationships, children are said to represent a stable and reliable source of love and affection. Relationships between parents and children, however, are also thought to be subject to the emphasis on disclosing intimacy, with parents seeking to develop an emotionally intense bond and open communication with, as well as a deep understanding of, their children. Giddens (1992) states a parent–child version of the adult-based pure relationship is replacing notions of parental **authority** and power. For Giddens, not only is parent–child intimate dialogue what *is* happening, but it is also what *should* be happening. He is careful to add, however, that although parent–child relationships may mirror the 'pure' basis for intimacy in adult relationships, they should not be contingent in the same way. Rather than ending relationships with their children if they do not provide personal fulfilment, parents have an obligation to sustain ongoing involvement.

Jamieson (1998) offers a comprehensive critique of Giddens' and others' arguments. Firstly, she argues that their accounts of the emergence of disclosing intimacy as a key organizing principle of people's family lives and personal relationships is partial, and has little empirical evidence. Reviewing the research literature on parent–child, **kin**, sexual and couple relationships, as well as **friendship**, Jamieson concludes that social divisions of **generation, gender** and **class** still shape family life and personal relationships; the same is true of **ethnicity** (Reynolds, 2005).

Secondly, Jamieson distinguishes different dimensions of full or partial intimacy, to argue that experiences and degrees of intimacy are wider and more variable than the sole ideal of the pure relationship based on disclosing intimacy. Rather, she identifies sympathy or emotional understanding as a further feature of deep insight into the inner self of others that constitutes intimacy. Through close association, people are said to gain familiarity and a privileged and detailed practical and bodily knowledge of each other. Jamieson also suggests there can also be silent intimacy, where feelings of affection and closeness are not accompanied by disclosure, and may be expressed implicitly through practical and physical as well as emotional dimensions. Further, while intimacy might have connotations of love and care, it can also be controlling and oppressive – for example, in someone's desire to know their partner's or child's every thought – or, when it comes to bodily intimacy, degrading and violent. While sexual intimacy is often idealized in conjunction with emotional intimacy, Warr and Pyett (1999) explore the difficult tensions for sex workers in any private sexual relationships, because the physical intimacy of their work is seen to be almost irreconcilable with a private relationship based on emotional or disclosing intimacy. Furthermore, there is a risk that previous basic normative ways of understanding family and personal bonds may be superseded by new but equally universal and proscriptive categorizations (Gabb, 2008).

From another perspective, Zelitzer (2007) argues that intimacy is linked to economic processes. Although she avoids attributing a purely **economic rationality** to relationships and emotions, arguing that intimacy and **money** are not only compatible but pervade each other, Zelitzer sees economic activities as underpinning the creation, maintenance and renegotiation of intimate ties, focusing especially on sex, care and household **labour**.

SUMMARY

Intimacy refers to the quality of close family and personal relationships in the cultural contexts of European and New World societies. There are arguments that contingent pure relationships, based on self-realization, mutual satisfaction and equality, have emerged as ideals in the pursuit of intimacy, with self-disclosure as an organizing principle. This sort of love and deep connection with another adult is a risk, however, since its achievement is insecure and under constant reflexive evaluation. Parent–child relationships also are and should be subject to disclosing intimacy, but should not be seen as contingent in the same way as adult relationships. Criticisms of this picture of the state of family and personal relationships contend that it is partial and selective, with social divisions and economic factors still shaping patterns of intimacy. This means that the state of contemporary close family and personal relationships is far more complex and variable than allowed for in the notion of pure relationships as the primary form of intimacy in contemporary society.

FURTHER READING

Gabb (2008) discusses methodologies of investigating intimate family relationships, and encompasses more recent literature since Jamieson's (1998) compelling overview. Hochschild (2003) explores the 'commercialization' of intimate life.

Related concepts *Coupledom; Families of Choice; Individualization; Personal*

Kinship

DEFINITION

Historically, as a concept, kinship refers to formal systems of relationships with regard to alliances of marriage and lines of descent. More recently, it is also used to refer to broad family connections in contemporary developed societies.

DISCUSSION

The term 'kin' has been used historically as a way of describing people who are considered to have particular relational connections and to refer to relationships based in blood ties. Early twentieth-century European and New World anthropologists, studying people living in societies very different from their own, took patterns of kinship to be the central organizing principle – or structure – in such societies where there was no formal government. Because some early anthropologists viewed the **nuclear family** as universal and rooted in psychological and biological factors that were constant across all societies, their interest centred instead on variations of kinship. In the process, they developed a specialist terminology, describing variable kinship patterns through theories that they thought could be applied in a universal way.

This analysis of how people in different cultures identified relationships of **birth**, **reproduction** and **death**, involved two main questions: how are **alliances** (or **marriages**) formed with regard to reproduction, and how are lines of **descent** traced according to births and deaths? While some saw alliance as the key determining principle of kinship systems, others argued that lines of descent were crucial. These issues are interconnected, however, since alliances or marriages may be a way of defining legitimate intergenerational ties. Levi-Strauss (1969) suggested that alliances as an aspect of kinship reveal the ways in which women are moved around between kin groups.

Various formal terms were developed to classify cultural variations around kinship, according to how the line of descent is traced (e.g. **patrilineal** or **matrilineal**), where the reproductive social unit is expected to live (e.g. **matrifocal** or **patrifocal**), and how groups are demarcated and bound by rules for forming alliances within or outside of such groups (**exogamy** and **endogamy**), and so on. In some cultures, where there are no separate legal, political or economic systems, networks of ties and alliances were analysed not only as the basis of personal relationships, but as having broader social and political significance for the distribution of power and **resources**. In a patrilineal system, descent is traced through the male line, and authority in society and households is likely to be **patriarchal**, with social rules and restrictions placed on female sexuality in order to establish the legitimacy of a woman's children. In a matrilineal system, descent is traced through the female line, but this does not generally make for a **matriarchal** society: rather, men take their line of support and authority from their mother's brothers.

Actual practices and sentiments are more flexible than is apparent from looking at kinship systems in an abstract way, so that the categories used by anthropologists may not provide insight into the ways that people understand their own relationships. In everyday lives, kinship might not constitute a formal system so much as a set of opportunities and constraints operating on different principles for different purposes even within one society. Furthermore, classic anthropological studies of kinship often left out the experiences of individuals within kinship systems, especially in relation to issues of power and access to resources, a neglect that meant marginalization of the study of women and children.

Although perceptions of someone as kin or non-kin may have implications for such issues as **identity** and **personhood, property** and **authority**, the distinction may be centred primarily on emotion and the moral quality of relationships, rather than on ideas of biological or 'natural' connections. Indeed, although European and New World anthropologists are steeped in cultures that take a scientific view of **nature** as fixed, predictable and the ultimate test of 'reality', this framework for understanding nature may be quite irrelevant to many other cultures (Strathern, 1992a). Many have therefore come to the view that the search for logically consistent categories through which all societies and cultures can be analysed makes it impossible to understand how people living in different cultures themselves see their kin relationships.

Indeed, European and New World ideas about biological paternity are not relevant where cultures view the act of sexual mating as a side-issue in determining social fatherhood, or where a child may be seen as having more than one 'biological' father or mother. In these contexts, genetic biological ties as Western scientists define these are not the issue for studying kinship; rather, what is significant is the ways in which different cultures give social meaning to ties that may be understood as biological. It is these kinship ties that form the basis for the transfer of property and social position after death, and for social obligations and rights, as well as what are considered to be appropriate feelings and sentiments. Similarly, while systems of alliance for the purposes of reproduction may be formed through marriage in many parts of the globe, what constitutes 'marriage' across different societies is also extremely difficult to agree.

Late twentieth-century scholars have concluded that it is not possible to produce a definition of kinship that works effectively across all cultural arrangements and belief systems. As an anthropological topic, 'kinship' has been transformed into a fluid set of themes around personhood, parenting and nurturing, through which people's everyday lives may be explored in cultures around the world. This focus gives rise to questions about how such themes are enmeshed within wider cultural frameworks of meaning, including the nature of human existence and the basis of knowledge and explanation. Some writers have suggested alternative, more open terms to that of kinship, including **relatedness** (Carsten, 2004) and **personal-kind terms** (Overing, 1985).

In the context of European and New World societies, family is the more significant focus for analysis outside of anthropology. Kinship may nevertheless constitute a key aspect of personal and family lives, although the term '**relatives**' is the more everyday term. Kinship is implied in common distinctions between 'immediate family' and 'wider family'. 'Kin', or 'relatives', are terms generally used to refer to a bio-logical or blood connection or a kinship established through marriage. These ties, however, are more complex than may first appear. For exam-ple, some kin connections may be understood as important, while others are not, and ties with unrelated individuals may be understood as **fictive kin** or **quasi kin**. In European and New World societies it is often women who undertake the **kin-keeping** work to maintain such ties (e.g. through visits, phone calls and the exchange of birthday cards). The definition and personal priorities concerning kin ties may be marked through particular **rituals** and holidays, such as **weddings** or Christmas gatherings, with shared **food** an important aspect of such social interac-tions (Etzioni and Bloom, 2004). Ties with blood or marital kin may thus be open to choices about whether they constitute permissive or obligatory ties (Allan, 1996). Maintenance of kinship ties may also be valued regardless of geographical movements; indeed, for people moving across the world, networks of wider kin may be a crucial part of life in both their place of origin and their destination.

Mason (2008) uses the term '**affinities**' as a way of exploring the underpinnings of kin ties as being bound together in some way. She delineates four different forms of affinity that may be relevant: fixed; negotiated or created; ethereal; and sensory. The first two forms have received more attention within studies of kinship and family than the last two. Fixed affinities – commonly fixed by biology – are a distinctive way of demarcating kinship, while negotiated affinities constitute a key way of determining which kinship relationships matter, and with what consequences. Mason also suggests using the term as a verb, so that people may actively 'kin' relationships that are not biologically based but about which they want to make the status and claims of kinship.

Kinship connections are often a source of fascination to people in their everyday lives, from the tracing of family trees, to working out how kinship may be understood when **reproductive technology** creates new forms of biological linkages (Mason, 2008). Indeed, kinship may be a key way in which people's ideas about their families are linked to the past and the future, constituting family projects rooted in **historical time**. Kinship also continues to be an important part of people's every-day lives, despite the often repeated – but probably misleading – belief that kin relationships are declining in importance or that **friends** may be seen to be equivalent to kin. Grandparents often continue to play sig-nificant roles in family lives, and sibling and wider kinship ties also continue to be important throughout adult lives. Generally, kinship may be the basis for expectations and negotiations of obligations and sup-port, and for (moral) identity.

SUMMARY

'Kinship' is a central term in classical social anthropology, but over the course of the twentieth century, attempts to produce formal classifica-tions and definitions of kinship that are universally relevant have been replaced by a loosely defined set of related topics, particularly around reproduction and nurturing, embedded in broad culturally variable meanings and practices. Studies of kinship in contemporary European and New World societies have focused on everyday negotiations and meanings around kinship.

FURTHER READING

Reviews of classic anthropological approaches to kinship can be found in Fox (1967) and Rapport and Overing (2007). See Mason (2008) for a sociological discussion of kinship, and Allan (2005) and Karraker and Grochowski (2006) on the continuing significance of kinship ties in the UK and USA, respectively.

Related concepts   Biology; Care; Comparative Approaches; Family Forms

key concepts in
family studies

Motherhood/
Mothers/Mothering

DEFINITION

Motherhood refers to the processes associated with designating specific women as mothers, who are understood to be the bearers and/or primary carers of, children.

DISCUSSION

Motherhood was regarded as a marginal social science topic until the work of feminist writers from the 1970s onwards made it visible as a social institution rather than a biological destiny (Thorne and Yalom, 1992). While becoming a mother may appear to be unequivocally biologically based, assisted **reproductive technologies** create new challenges, for example, as with the gestation by one woman of another woman's fertilized embryo. Furthermore, women's labour force participation means that social mothering – in the form of childcare provided by other women – is widespread. **Community mothering** is also a feature of Caribbean communities, as part of collective and political struggles (Reynolds, 2005), and work and **childcare** may be closely integrated in some circumstances, depending on how the work is organized and where it is located.

Adrienne Rich (1977) importantly distinguished between motherhood as an (oppressive) **institution** and the **everyday experience** of being a mother. Indeed, some feminists argue that women's power to reproduce and give birth is the basis for men's desire to control women and their fertility. Much second wave feminist writing regarded motherhood as the key source of women's oppression, with some arguing that women could be equal to men only if technological developments freed them from giving birth (Firestone, 1979).

Feminist philosophers have argued that the experience and practices of mothering lead to an orientation to preservation, growth and social acceptability – a set of values summarized as **maternal thinking** (Ruddick, 1990). Within this framework, 'mother' is not a noun signifying an identity, but a verb signifying a set of activities or practices that can be carried out by men as well as women. Another perspective focuses on the **psychic capacity** to provide maternal care, as distinct from the identity and institution of motherhood (Hollway, 2006). The association of mothering of young children in contemporary Western societies with particular values and orientations has been described as constituting particular 'ways of being' (Ribbens McCarthy and Edwards, 2002).

An important element in social scientific research in recent decades has been mothers' own views on their experiences and preferences (e.g. Gillies, 2007; Reynolds, 2005; Ribbens, 1994), leading to a consideration of the paradoxes and ambivalences that may be experienced by women-as-mothers in many Western societies. Nevertheless, particular discourses of motherhood continue to be pervasive, despite women's resistance to medicalized and scientific discourses on the basis of their own experiences (Miller, 2007). At the same time, some earlier feminist writing on motherhood has been criticized as failing to take account of the ways in which motherhood intersects with other key social dimensions such as **ethnicity, class, migration** and **sexuality**, leading to calls for attention to transnational **intersectionality** (Mahalingam et al., 2009). The care of young children in circumstances of poverty that threaten basic survival, for example, may be shaped by different understandings of mothering as the 'letting go' – rather than preservation – of some infants (Scheper-Hughes, 1993), while also wanting to raise enough children to be able to receive reciprocal care in old age (Schalge, 2009). And in many societies, it is only as mothers of **sons** that women gain respect and social position.

Dominant Western ideals and moral discourses of mothering are easier to attain for mothers bringing up their children in particular circumstances than it is for others. **Working-class** and black mothers can find themselves, and their mothering values and practices, marginalized and pathologized in the face of professional benchmarks (Gillies, 2007; Reynolds, 2005). **Step-mothers** are subject to the 'myth of the wicked step-mother', which places them outside of the predominant ideology of 'good' motherhood as selfless, caring responsibility for children (discussed in Ribbens McCarthy et al., 2003). **Lone motherhood**, and especially **never-married motherhood**, has led to hot debates about whether mothers need to be matched with a co-resident father for successful childrearing (Duncan and Edwards, 1999). **Teenage mothers** are (erroneously) blamed for creating poor outcomes for themselves and their children (Duncan et al., 2010). Mothers in developing societies physically leaving their own children to care for the children of other mothers in more affluent societies, so that they can provide for their children materially, may also be regarded askance. Motherhood is thus the site for powerful **moral evaluations** of women's lives.

In European and New World cultures, the processes by which motherhood became institutionalized in certain ways can be traced to **industrialization**, with both the concentration of production in large factories and the development of ideas about childhood. Changes in the law removed children from the workplace and required them to undertake **compulsory education**. This had repercussions for women's lives, along with their legal exclusion from many professions and from higher education. It led to a **domestic ideal** that saw mothers as the guardians of a morally virtuous and caring domestic sphere in which children could be protected and cared for away from the amoral and calculative practices of the **public sphere** of the workplace. In reality, this was largely a **middle-class** experience, since the ideal of the mother-at-home was unattainable for poorer women. Among working-class mothers it might be associated with economic activities that were home centred (such as laundry work or taking in lodgers) (Davidoff et al., 1999), as well as with demands for a **family wage** to enable working-class men to support a wife and children at home (Humphries, 1995). Nevertheless, in some industrialized regions, working-class mothers were engaged in factory or other work outside the home.

By the mid-twentieth century, few mothers of very young children in Western societies were engaged in paid **employment** outside the home, while many mothers of school-aged children saw part-time employment as the best option while they were caring for dependent children (Martin and Roberts, 1984). Some feminists argued that the ideal of stay-at-home motherhood masked **isolation** and depression for many women (Friedan, 1963), with researchers seeking to make visible the **work** and drudgery that could be associated with the **housewife** role (Lopata, 1971; Oakley, 1976). Others argued that this reframing of women's experiences as mothers through masculinist understandings of 'work' risked marginalizing ongoing relationships with children (Ribbens McCarthy and Edwards, 2002), as well as overlooking the social significance of mothers' **localized networks** outside the home (Bell and Ribbens, 1994). While the number of mothers of young children in paid employment has risen in Western societies since the late twentieth century, their orientations to paid work are complex and vary with regard to social dimensions such as ethnicity (Mcquillan et al., 2008). Furthermore, where mothers experience a period of full-time care of children, this may shape their identities and household divisions of labour in the longer term (Allan and Crow, 2001; Bianchi and Casper, 2002). The extent of material and emotional investment in children has also arguably increased in recent years, sometimes framed as an increasing emphasis on **intensive mothering** (Hays, 1996). There may be difficult tensions for mothers between a sense of personhood and a sense of motherhood, or between **individuality** and **intersubjectivity** (Hollway, 2006). Such issues are heightened in those (Western) societies where individuality is prized, and where mothering is not embedded in wider communities of 'blood mothers' and 'other mothers' (Hill Collins, 1990/2008).

Women's **age** of first motherhood is related to their educational and employment opportunities in early adulthood and may be seen to both reflect and perpetuate inequalities between women (Thomson et al., 2008). Timing of motherhood and who controls it is also evident in debates over abortion. And the significance of motherhood with regard to women's life trajectory has become more complex, not least because increases in life expectancy have led to a distinct phase in the **life span**, in the additional years after women have raised their children. While childlessness may be seen as a barrier to being a 'proper woman' for some women in Western societies (Edwards, J., 2000), the increasing numbers of women who choose not to have children suggests that for some at least, motherhood has become less central to ideas of femininity. At the same time, the rapid increases in births outside of marriage in European and New World societies has created some political and public anxiety about how to view women raising children without male input.

SUMMARY

Motherhood and mothering have received sustained attention in the years since second wave feminism first argued that the experience of being a mother is socially constructed rather than a biological destiny. Motherhood continues to be a core identity for many women, and closely determines their moral and social standing. Mothering may also be theorized as a particular way of thinking and being, that is nevertheless cross-cut by other dimensions of class, ethnicity and so on. At the same time, while ideas of appropriate mothering have intensified, mothers seek to optimize their work–family balance as they increase their labour force participation.

FURTHER READING

Tong (2009) overviews feminist theories of mothering. Recent scholarship tends to focus on parents rather than mothers, but see Ribbens (1994), Gillies (2007), Thomson et al. (2008) and Miller (2005) for empirical work on mothers in the UK, and Chase and Rogers (2001) in the USA. Walzer (2004) reviews motherhood scholarship in the USA. Ruddick's work is assessed in O'Reilly (2009). See also the Motherhood Initiative for Research and Community Involvement website (http://www.motherhoodinstitute.org/) for further academic resources on motherhood.

Related concepts *Division of Labour; Feminisms; Parenthood; Public and Private*

Negotiation

DEFINITION

In the specific context of family studies, the concept of negotiation concerns interactions between family members about how to understand a situation, and the courses of action that emerge from these understandings. The negotiations can be both explicit and implicit.

DISCUSSION

The concept of negotiation arises within the context of broader sociological theories about the links between individuals, social processes and social structures. In particular, some sociological perspectives see meaning as arising out of social interaction between people, with structural differences emerging from such interchanges. In relation to families, rather than adherence to less flexible **authority** structures, negotiation between family members has arguably emerged as a key motif of modern family life in European and New World societies.

Giddens (1992), for example, argues that intimate relationships have shifted away from a preordained and imposed normative order, exemplified by **marriage** and its sense of permanency. Rather, they are now shaped by a negotiated and contingent normative framework in which people decide – and constantly reflect on and renegotiate – whether they want a relationship with each other and what sort of relationship this should be. Similarly, relationships between children and their parents are argued to be undergoing a process of modernization whereby they now involve negotiation rather than the previously given situation of parents having power over children (du Bois-Reymond et al., 2001).

Most notably, the concept of negotiation has been developed analytically by Finch and Mason as part of their work on **obligations** between adult kin (Finch and Mason, 1993). These writers argue that family members' responsibilities to each other, or lack of them, are shaped by negotiated understandings and commitments over time, rather than being duty-bound by the **status** of their relationship. Analytically, Finch and Mason distinguish between explicit and implicit negotiations, but say that these often occur alongside each other in family life. Explicit negotiations comprise expressed and open discussions between family members around specific needs and events, whereas implicit negotiations are developed incrementally over long periods of time as part of family members' shared history, such that where responsibilities lie and who should be involved in deciding them are assumed and unremarked. This **time** perspective in the development and acknowledgement of family responsibilities, for Finch and Mason, is what gives the concept of negotiation its purchase in explaining family life. Rather than given, **ascribed** rules about the substance of obligations providing norms to follow, it is the negotiated creation and process of the allocation of **responsibilities** that is normative in contemporary Western societies.

The concept of negotiation as an aspect of family life is invoked in Berger and Kellner's (1964) classic phenomenological notion of '**marital conversation**'. These authors say that people bring differing understandings of the nature of family and the social world to their intimate relationships. Through their **everyday interactions**, shared history and expectation of a future life with each other, however, married couples constantly develop and negotiate a taken-for-granted mutual construction and reaffirmation of the 'reality' of their relationship, parenting and family life. Children also contribute to this interaction, with the marital conversation said to become a 'family symposium' in this respect. Berger and Kellner's ideas are sometimes referred to as the way in which 'you + me' becomes 'we'. Others have built on Berger and Kellner's work to draw out the ways in which negotiations feature in such processes.

For example, Benjamin (1998) explores the negotiation of **discourses** and **emotions** between married couples, and Smart and Neale (1999) echo Berger and Kellner in their use of the term 'moral conversation', which they say involves negotiation, in their study of post-divorce relationships between parents and children.

Berger and Kellner's work in particular has been criticized for ignoring gendered power relationships within marriage and for over-emphasizing the unity of the couple, and indeed many of the studies building on their ideas mentioned above are concerned explicitly with drawing out **gendered** and **generational** power imbalances in negotiations. In a critique of ideas about negotiation, for example, Dempsey (1997) argues that discussions between **husbands** and **wives** involve only 'token negotiation' because latent inequalities between them keep certain matters off the agenda. Giddens' ideas have come in for similar criticism about the neglect of power and social divisions, as well as the way in which his notion of negotiation invokes and involves ideas about individualization and **democratisation** that do not capture parent–child relationships in particular. Finch and Mason's advancement of the concept, and work that draws on their ideas, avoids the rebuke of neglecting such **inequalities** of power by arguing that these structural differences emerge through the process of negotiation. There are concerns, however, that the notion of negotiation is stretched so far (to include both implicit understandings and people's exclusion from negotiations, for example) that it becomes meaningless; everything is posed as negotiation and the term loses its specific.

SUMMARY

The concept of negotiation is an integral element of understandings of contemporary Western family life as fluid and active, as opposed to being prescribed by status. It captures the way in which family members' interactions over time shape their understandings of their commitments to each other, and how they understand the 'reality' of their relationships. The most developed analytic treatment of the concept in relation to family life, by Finch and Mason (1993), distinguishes between explicit and implicit negotiations. Criticism of the use and prevalence of the concept of negotiation to understand what is going on in families focuses on, firstly, the way it can sidestep wider social expectations and inequalities of power, and secondly, the heavy burden of meaning that the concept has now come to bear.

FURTHER READING

Berger and Kellner (1964) and Finch and Mason (1993) are key readings in relation to negotiation in couple and family processes. Crow (2002) and Dempsey (1997) provide critiques of ideas of negotiation.

Related concepts *Individualization; Intimacy; Phenomenological Approaches; Power*

New Right

DEFINITION

The New Right comprises sets of political and intellectual ideas about the value of self-sufficient family structures, and traditional morality and relationships, drawing on social-authoritarian and neo-liberal thought.

DISCUSSION

New Right thinking can be seen as a combination of two main political perspectives: **social authoritarianism** and **neo-liberalism**. It does not, therefore, necessarily integrate into a coherent and unified idea. The social-authoritarian strand stresses social order and the value of people taking financial and moral responsibility for themselves and their families. The neo-liberal strand espouses freedom of choice, with people making choices for themselves and their families rather than being provided for and regulated by the state. In the UK and the USA, in government contexts the New Right has been associated notably with Conservative and Republican policies, respectively.

New Right ideas have some similarity with functionalist understandings. They pose the nuclear family as a universal and key foundation of a stable society, based on **marriage** and **monogamy**. From the New Right perspective, the **nuclear family** controls the potentially destructive behaviour of men, women and children. It provides for the civilization of men, who would otherwise act promiscuously, in attaching to them a **breadwinner**/provider role and channelling their energies in a positive manner; ensures that women put the interests of family and homemaking before 'selfish individualism'; and is the foundational condition for the socialization of children into acceptable **moral values** and social behaviour. From the more authoritarian strand, for example, Roger Scruton (1986) posits an essential difference between the sexes, with marriage and gender roles institutionalizing the **heterosexual** bond. From the more liberal strand, Ferdinand Mount (1982) has argued that the nuclear family is a natural form that stands outside of historical change. It acts as a subversive bulwark against totalitarian church and state control, and as a private haven from market forces.

New Right commentators disapprove of what they regard as a contemporary breakdown of this long-standing version of family life. They see the spread of different sorts of family forms (such as cohabitating, single parent and same-sex), and rising rates of **divorce** and **births outside marriage**, as creating **moral decay** and a range of social problems. A number of causes are said to be creating these threats to what New Right proponents see as the most socially useful family unit. These include:

1 feminism, which is hostile to the family and to the role of fathers especially
2 the **welfare state**, which undermines the work ethic and underwrites 'irresponsible' family behaviour, and has taken over family responsibilities for socializing children and caring for elderly members
3 **reproductive technologies**, such as embryo fertilization, which dislocate traditional family relations.

For example, contributions to Caroline Quest's edited collection on feminism (1994) claim that feminism works against the interests of women by undermining family life. Rather than feminism providing liberation, it encourages women to pursue selfish **individualism**, erodes both the protection afforded by marriage and the **family wage**, and leaves them to cope alone with **divorce** and **childrearing**. Charles Murray (1990) regards the growth of **single mothers** having children outside of marriage, supported by state benefits, as having cut young men loose from their provider role, freeing them to indulge in criminal behaviour and leaving their children to grow up without paternal **authority** and responsible role models. Mount (1982) castigates professionals working in the fields of health, education and so on, as encroaching on the private sphere of the family.

The social-authoritarian and neo-liberal sources of New Right thinking can lead to a split on what to do about the perceived breakdown of the family in contemporary Western societies, either advocating state intervention to strengthen family ties and **responsibilities** or recommending the withdrawal of state regulation so that the family can regain its independence and self-reliance. For example, while an authoritarian perspective would want to make divorce more difficult, a liberal point of view would not support this. As some point out, though, it is also the case that authoritarian and liberal strands accommodate each other in their desire to roll back the welfare state (King, 1987).

Feminist criticisms of New Right thinking see it as backlash ideological support for a **patriarchal** view of family life based on **white middle-class** ideals, hiding behind supposed intellectual and academic arguments and using selective and suspect empirical evidence.

SUMMARY

New Right thinking on the family draws on both a social-authoritarian preoccupation with social order and family responsibility and a neo-liberal stress on freedom of choice above state regulation. The nuclear family is regarded as a key foundation for a stable society, civilizing and socializing men, women and children into socially beneficial moral values and self-reliant behaviour. A number of factors are said to be threatening to what New Right thinkers see as this socially useful unit, including feminism and the welfare state. While the social-authoritarian position advocates interventions to strengthen the family in the face of these threats, however, the neo-liberal perspective prioritizes the withdrawal of state intervention. Most feminists regard New Right ideas as fundamentally patriarchal.

FURTHER READING

Davies (1993) and Patricia Morgan (1996), and the websites of the Institute of Economic Affairs (IEA) (http://www.iea.org.uk/browse.jsp?type=book&pageID=34) and the Institute for the Study of Civil Society (http://www.civitas.org.uk/) all offer resources from New Right perspectives. Abbott and Wallace (1992) provide a review and critique.

Related concepts   *Family Change and Continuity; Functionalism; Problem Families; Public and Private*

Parenthood/Parents/ Parenting

DEFINITION

Parenthood concerns the processes of identification of individual adults (parents) who are considered to have particular connections with individual children, with associated expectations for their care (parenting) and social positioning. As a term, parenthood is gender neutral.

DISCUSSION

Concepts centred on the reproduction and care of infants and young people point to a cluster of terms around categories of people, institutionalized social forms, and activities in relation to children. *Parent* refers to a particular **status**, or category of person, of indeterminate gender, who is identified as standing in a special relationship with an individual child or related children. This term may also extend to expectations of performing a particular role as a parent. Paren*thood* refers to how this category or role is **institutionalized** as a social form. Parent*ing* generally refers to a set of practices and activities and thus draws attention to what a person does as a parent in relation to their child/ren. Reproduction and the care of children are features of all societies, at least at some minimal level (Montgomery, 2008), with individuals identified as parents in relationship to specific children. In most societies, there is an expectation that a child will have (at least) two parents, generally (although not universally) parents of different genders (Bornstein and Cheah, 2006). As well as being expected to care for children, parents may be important in providing children with a political, social and personal **identity**, including rights to **citizenship** in a certain nation state, and links to lines of kinship and **descent**.

Furthermore, since reproduction and the care of children are generally seen as a fundamental feature of 'family' lives, there are often close ties between ideas of parenthood and ideas of family (Ribbens, 1994). In those societies where the **nuclear family** form has been a influential idea, the presence and involvement of two parents may be seen as crucial to 'being a family', even if they do not live in the same household unit.

In contemporary policy and professional discussions, the terms 'parents' and 'parenting' are often used in preference to the gendered terms of 'mothers'/'mothering' and 'fathers'/'fathering'. While in some cultures both men and women are actively involved in childcare, the gendered roles and activities of parents also vary considerably across cultures and historical periods. The contemporary Western usage of the term 'parent' may be seen as promoting greater **gender** equality, and asserting that the gender of parents is not crucially significant for children's upbringing, rather than making assumptions about who are the key figures in children's lives. Nevertheless, use of the term 'parent' risks obscuring the way that daily practices of caring for children in such societies continue to be highly gendered (C. Lewis and Lamb, 2003). Furthermore, men and women are positioned differently with regard to the physical process of becoming a parent, since it is clear (at least to the woman herself) who is the birth mother (even if the child was conceived outside the womb), while historically it has not been so straightforward for a man to know if he is the father of a particular child.

There are thus political considerations underlying the use of different terms, as well as research implications. Different terms make some issues more or less visible and some questions more or less possible, such as 'Do men mother?' (Doucet, 2006). A further consideration, which has not received the same attention in policy and professional practice, is that the experience, relationship and activities of being a parent may differ significantly according to the gender of the child, as well as the gender of the parent, with different expectations of father–**son**, father–**daughter**, mother–son and mother–daughter relationships.

In European and New World societies there is a long history of understanding a link between parenthood and **reproduction** in terms of biological processes. Parenthood need not necessarily be understood as a biological 'given', however, since reproduction and the bearing and subsequent care of children are not necessarily straightforwardly connected, and understandings of their links vary across cultures and historical periods. English terminology allows room for a variety of parental relationships between individual adults and children, including **step-parents**, **foster parents** and **adoptive parents**, as well as individuals standing *in loco parentis*; that is, in the place of the parent and exercising parental responsibility and authority over children and young people below the age of legal adulthood (e.g. teachers). Furthermore, what constitutes the biological given in becoming a parent may entail complex legal adjudication, especially as new forms of **reproductive technology** and **surrogacy** are legitimated.

A variety of individuals and settings may be involved in the nurturance and care of children: **step-families** may see new adult household members acting as social parents to greater or lesser extents, while **childminders**, who care for children on a daily basis in childminder's own homes, may hold mixed views about whether they are acting as social parents to the children they are minding (Nelson, 1990). In the contemporary UK legislative context, however, **adoption** is seen as the termination of one set of parental relationships and their substitution by a new set, re-inscribing the view that a child can legally have only two parents. In other cultures, such as many African societies, a range of people may be involved in the upbringing of children, including older children parenting younger ones, or children being sent to other households to be fostered. In this way, a child may in effect have many (social) parents without this being seen to undermine their tie with their 'birth parent' (Montgomery, 2009). Furthermore, grandparents are centrally important for the parenting of younger children in many cultures, and increasingly so in some Western societies such as the USA (Bengston et al., 2002).

The term 'parent*ing*' arguably is a relatively recent feature of discussions about the care and upbringing of children, suggesting that adults engage in particular sets of practices as parents in relation to their children, that is, is an individual a 'parent' because of who they *are* or because of what they *do?* This contrasts with the idea that parent*hood* is the identification of individuals occupying the category of 'parent' – an **ascribed** status – regardless of activities with children. This shift in language is allied to a change in ideas about **children's needs** and a **moral** discourse of parenting **obligations**, such that children are understood to require particular forms of attention and care in order to reach their developmental potential, beyond basic physical survival needs. This moral discourse has been associated with a policy emphasis on **parenting skills**. Some argue that this shift towards parenting as a set of skills turns it from a relationship – with all the emotional content that potentially implies – into a set of tasks (Furedi, 2001; Ribbens McCarthy and Edwards, 2002). Furthermore, the new emphasis on special parenting skills and qualities has raised expectations and increased the scope for moral evaluation of parents, with some aspiring to 'heroic' levels of parenting (Bogenschneider, 2006: 11).

Various terms are used to describe what is thought to be required for good parenting in affluent Western societies, such as 'concerted culti- vation' (Lareau, 2003), and the practices of such parenting are likely to be time consuming and expensive of resources. Some writers suggest that this overlooks children's own **agency** and leads to a view of parental determinism as paramount (Furedi, 2001), which, in turn, marginalizes the significance of other social contexts and structural patterns, such as material or other **inequalities** in children's lives. It may also promote a particular view of parenting that is relevant to the lives of privileged children (Gillies, 2007).

In many Western societies, the state has promoted particular views of parenting practices, holding parents accountable for their children's behaviour and outcomes. This process, sometimes called the **responsi- bilization** of parents (in practice generally meaning mothers), includes a belief that changes in parenting will rectify many, if not most, soci- etal problems (Ribbens McCarthy, 2008). Within these political debates, parenting is posed as a crucial issue for wider social order and the state of the nation (Gillies, 2007). This emphasis on parenting as the locus for remedying social problems neglects structural issues of material resources and experiences of discrimination. At the same time, the increased emphasis on parental responsibilities, along with policies encouraging all parents to engage in paid **employment**, leads to questions about how to reconcile different priorities. While some governments have increased employment rights for parents, such as rights to **maternity** or **paternity leave**, or to ask for **flexible working hours**, or greater provision of subsidized **childcare**, such policies to support working parents may conflict with ideas about the impor- tance of intensive educational and psychological nurturance of their children by parents.

Furthermore, considerations of some parenting practices or styles as 'optimal' in relation to children's development are based on cultural assumptions embedded within **developmental psychology**. Such evalua- tions reflect an unacknowledged ethnocentrism and application of stereotypes (Phoenix and Husain, 2007). Across cultures, different ideas about parenting are linked to particular views of the value of children as economic and/or emotional assets within subsistence or affluent econo- mies. Varying views of what is important in human experiences of **autonomy** and **relatedness** are associated with different ideas of what is important in parent–child relationships, such that evaluations of parenting need to be understood in relation to specific cultural and political contexts (Kağitçibaşi, 2007). The impact of any particular aspect of parental behaviour (e.g. discipline methods) also varies with the meaning it holds for parents and children in different cultural contexts (O'Connor and Scott, 2007; Rogoff, 2003).

SUMMARY

Individuals with special responsibility for the care of children may be known as parents or, recognizing gender issues, as mothers and fathers. Distinctions may be drawn between parenthood as an institution, parent as a category of person, and parenting as a set of practices. Some also distinguish between parenthood as an institution and as everyday experience. Complex issues arise about how to describe and compare parenting practices, between genders and across cultures and historical periods. In recent years, parenting has been a key focus of policy attention in many Western societies, particularly the UK, regarded as the basis for social order and the state of the nation. What constitutes parenting has also become a major focus for adult moral identities, although evaluations of parenting risk imposing ethnocentric assumptions.

FURTHER READING

Rubin and Chung (2006) and Kağitçibaşi (2007) discuss parenting in varied cultural contexts. Changing parenting cultures in European and New World societies are discussed on the website of the Economic and Social Research Council seminar series 'Changing Parenting Cultures' (http://www.parentingculturestudies.org/seminar-series/index.html). Freeman and Richards (2006) and Richards (2007) discuss reproductive technologies, and Utting (2007) summarizes research evidence from the UK and USA on the consequences of parenting. Alwin (2007) provides an overview of parenting practices.

Related concepts   *Child Development; Division of Labour; Fatherhood; Motherhood*

parenthood/parents/parenting

Personal

DEFINITION

In contemporary English-speaking cultures, 'the personal' is used to refer to matters centred on individual experience, and sometimes intimate issues. As such it presupposes the concept of 'the person'.

DISCUSSION

The term 'personal' brings a variety of debates and topics into focus in the context of studying families. It draws attention to individual rather than collective experience.

Theories of 'the person' vary between disciplines. Anthropologists explore how the meaning of 'the person' varies across cultures; psychologists derive concepts on the basis of 'the person', such as **personality** and '(interior) personal experience'; while sociologists use it to consider how individual experiences occur in social, cultural and historical contexts. Other disciplines, such as economics or politics, theorize the person as a **rational economic actor** or as a **citizen**, drawn from analyses of economic systems and liberal democracies. Particular cultural understandings of personhood underpin the political systems of liberal democracies, in which the mature person is understood as **independent** and **autonomous**, capable of rationally reflecting on potential courses of action. This notion of personhood is also taken as the goal towards which child development must be oriented for the achievement of mature adult life.

Across the varying disciplinary perspectives, interactions among close family members, or in family-like relationships, are central for seeing how issues concerning the personal and the social occur in everyday experience. But it was in the later decades of the twentieth century that family researchers widened their focus beyond the **institutionalized** aspects of families to consider how personal lives are situated in the context of family lives, alongside cross-cutting social dimensions of **gender**, **class** and **race/ethnicity**. An important element here has been the increased attention paid to the life course perspective.

Anthropological work makes visible how understandings of 'the personal' may be embedded in taken-for-granted, but culturally specific,

key concepts in family studies

understandings. For example, the points at which life and **personhood** are deemed to have begun and ended (in terms of **birth** and **death**) are understood in varying ways in different cultures (Montgomery, 2008). These variations are associated with different experiences of survival, **life expectancy** and reproductive decision making. The beginnings of life are contested within European and New World cultures in terms of **abortion** debates. But in some countries with high infant mortality rates, babies may not be regarded as having personhood until they have survived the very hazardous early months and thus deemed to have shown the will to live (Scheper-Hughes, 1993).

The core idea of personhood is, culturally variable, with characteristics of age and gender understood as integral to personhood in some societies. Early anthropologists focused on 'the person' as a cultural category, rather than as an internal state of mind. This view of the person resonates with the concept of 'role'. In some societies the person is conceived of through one all-encompassing role (perhaps transmitted from an ancestor), rather than playing a series of roles. In this sense, the person is coterminous with their group membership and cannot be envisaged as separate from it. Whether human actions are regarded as caused by 'internal' motivations and moral conscience, by 'external' forces such as spirits, or by the moral stance of the groups (particularly families or kinship groups) to which the person belongs, is bound up with these cultural variations. Different perceptions of 'the person' also have consequences for expectations of personal and group goals, orientations to co-operation and emotional attachments. All of this offers very different understandings of the relationships between family members.

In contrast, a psychological approach focuses on **internal psychic experience**, a prevalent understanding of personhood in contemporary European and New World societies. From this perspective, people see themselves as having thoughts, emotions and experiences that are internal and unique, shaped by their personality and providing an 'authentic' sense of **self** that is known through their internal experience or **subjectivity**. This may be linked with differing understandings of families and close relationships. (Private) family life may be seen as a key place for being 'truly oneself', or younger family members may feel that only by leaving the family home can they become fully themselves. The meaning of a unified or authentic self has been debated within both post-structuralism and philosophy, while the concept of the self is central to theorizing about the nature of the person, experiences of **embodiment**, and **identity** in

personal

147

terms of a sense of self and a social category. Where an individual has more than one identity available to them, these might be in conflict with one another, for example between the identities of 'worker' and 'mother' for some women with children. Individuals may resist being associated with a particular identity, such as 'a deadbeat dad', or embrace others, such as 'a good mother'. Lack of a socially agreed identity may cause difficulties; for example, there may be no clear parenting identity for the partner of a lesbian mother.

The origin of subjectivity is understood differently within varying psychological theoretical frameworks, which may put emphasis on genetic and biological factors, or on social relationships and contextual experiences. While some **psychoanalytic** theories – notably **Freudian approaches** – understand the developing self primarily in terms of responses to internal psychological drives, others – notably **object relations theory** – emphasize how development occurs through interactions with others, especially parents in the case of children. Across these psychoanalytic approaches, however, the notion of the **subconscious** is seen as a powerful force for the construction of self and experience of reality.

The social nature of the self is a key theme for **psycho-social approaches**, which are underpinned by the idea that individual subjectivity is entwined with that of others and with social contexts. Thus, interior psychic life and external social realms cannot be understood apart from each other, so that what is experienced as an interior psychic life is argued to be profoundly merged with what are experienced as external social realms.

The social nature of subjectivity is extended through the concept of **intersubjectivity**, which points to the possibility of shared psychic space, and the social and psychological processes by which persons derive a sense of belonging and social integration. Another concept, that of **relationality**, points to varying notions of the individual as embedded within their close relationships. Each of the different theoretical perspectives carries different implications for how the relationship between individuality and connectedness is understood, and for how families and family relationships are theorized.

SUMMARY

The personal is a concept that evokes varying understandings of the person, the meanings of which may be embedded in different cultural systems and understandings of the links between the individual and their social groupings. Some argue for the value of this concept in distinguishing the individual from collective units, such as family. Linked concepts, such as self, subjectivity, intersubjectivity and relationality, also involve particular cultural understandings of the personal as entailing an interior psychic life even while its social nature is emphasized.

FURTHER READING

Carrithers (1999) reviews ideas of 'the person' across cultures, Smart (2007) advocates the concept of personal life. Lucey (2010) overviews psycho-social approaches to family relationships, and Mackenzie and Stoljar (2000) and Mason (2004) discuss relationality, while Crossley (2001) and Hollway (2006) discuss intersubjectivity from differing perspectives.

Related concepts   *Individualization; Public and Private; Rationalities*

Phenomenological Approaches

DEFINITION

Phenomenology is used here as an umbrella term covering a range of approaches to family studies that share a primary focus on people's own family meanings and face-to-face interactions in their families and close relationships.

DISCUSSION

Phenomenology is a philosophical approach taken up by both psychologists and sociologists, albeit with rather different emphases. Its primary orientation to human life is that it has to be understood through the meanings and perceptions by which people make sense of their daily lived experiences. Here, it encompasses a number of related approaches, including phenomenology itself as an elaborated philosophical approach, **social interactionism**, **ethnomethodology**, **interpretivism**, **social constructionism** and some **psycho-social** approaches, as well as some **narrative** methodologies that explore how people make sense of their biographies. As a philosophical framework, the emphasis on **meanings** is sometimes described as following a **hermeneutic** tradition.

These approaches within the social sciences are drawn upon to theorize the **micro** levels of family lives concerned with everyday lived experiences, in contrast with theories focused on **macro** levels of how institutions (including family) relate to each other in society as a whole – although it is important to recognize distinctions between varieties of micro theories, and the links between some micro and macro theories. Some forms of conflict theory and many areas of feminist work are thus also concerned with the daily interactions and understandings of family lives. Furthermore, much general social theorizing concerns the links between individual lives (the micro) and broad social patterns and structures (the macro).

The micro analysis of family lives includes a number of key themes, drawing attention to the routine and taken-for-granted aspects of family lives. The aim is to understand the **dailiness** of everyday lives (Apthekar, 1989) as a complex achievement between individuals, involving both talk and embodied practices, in the course of which meanings are shaped by individuals to create a particular view of reality. Meaning is built through interaction between others (as audience), between ourselves and others, and also with ourselves (internally). This approach emphasizes taking family members' (or social actors') points of view (their definition of **self** and their **definition of the situation**), to understand them on their own terms. The attention to everyday meanings comprises a number of elements, including **emotions**, **evaluations** (or moralities) and cognitions.

Phenomenological approaches also raise issues about how the social researcher her or himself participates in the process of constructing versions of reality in the encounters with family members that occur during the course of undertaking research. In this sense, the researcher is not regarded as an external observer who is collecting objective facts about family lives, but as a co-participant in an interaction through which meanings about family lives are constructed.

The phenomenological framework also draws attention to the routine and mundane ways in which individuals in their daily family interactions may (or may not) create microcosms of **social order** – even if such order is fragile and open to struggle and negotiation. Furthermore, through such family interactions people may experience a sense of security, as individuals jointly construct personal and social realities by which they make sense of the world and work out how to live their lives. People's experience of a firm feeling of who they are, their relationships and circumstances, is termed '**ontological security**'. Berger and Luckmann (1971) discuss primary socialization in family relationships as creating a sort of ontological illusion of solidity, constructing the individual's first experience of social reality, to which everything else is inevitably secondary. Similarly, **marriage** (or intimate couple) relationships may be understood as involving a joint construction of reality between the adults involved which, over time, may be experienced as taken for granted and solid. Such co-constructions may not only be idiosyncratic to the two people involved, but also build on wider shared expectations of what it means to be a husband and wife.

Phenomenological approaches have been criticized for neglecting wider social structures of power and inequalities that also shape individual meanings and interactional power dynamics within families (e.g. between men and women, or parents and children). There are indeed important issues about how to move from an analysis of individual family members' perspectives to an analysis of interactions and variable meanings, and how these relate to wider social patterns embedded in social structural and historical processes. Similar analytic difficulties concern how social scientists may move from a description of individual points of view that stay close to everyday terms and understandings (**first order constructs**), to an interpretive framework that looks across (or reconstructs) individual perspectives in terms of sociological concepts (**second order constructs**) that have a broader relevance.

One way of exploring sets of interconnected multiple realities is through the concept of '**family culture**'. This refers to a range of phenomena that may be viewed as unremarkable and 'normal' ways of doing things, but which may be idiosyncratic to particular families. Some aspects may be material – such as family photographs, household furnishings, choice of cars. Some may be more ephemeral – such as attitudes to work or money management, beliefs about childrearing, or what it means to be an independent person. There are thus tensions between understanding families as sets of individuals, and also seeing them as a site for a particular family reality of their own, that is greater than the sum of the individual parts. Yet, it is important to view family culture as dynamic, embracing tensions and differences of view (Davidoff et al., 1999).

Family phenomenology can go beyond academic analysis to be used as a basis for therapeutic approaches, particularly through the exploration of the multiple realities of different family members. An emphasis on meanings features as a basis for therapeutic interventions in terms of **meaning reconstruction** (Neimeyer and Anderson, 2002), and there are also links with some forms of systemic therapy.

SUMMARY

Phenomenological approaches prioritize an emphasis on the meanings and lived experiences of everyday lives. They offer detailed accounts of how family lives are managed through taken-for-granted routines in daily interactions. The emphasis on the actor's definition of the situation raises difficult issues about how to develop an interpretation that goes beyond individuals, to take account of multiple realities and understand links to wider social and historical processes.

FURTHER READING

David H.J. Morgan (1985) explains the main themes of phenomenological approaches in the context of family studies. The Stanford Encyclopedia of Philosophy webpage http://plato.stanford.edu/entries/merleau-ponty/ gives an introduction to the work of the philosopher Merleau-Ponty, whose ideas are central to phenomenological psychology in particular. Daly (2003) discusses how some family theory neglects such everyday family experiences, while White and Klein (2008) consider the contribution of social interactionism to family theories.

Related concepts   Conflict Theories; Family as Discourse; Negotiation; Socialization

key concepts in
family studies

152

Post-Coupledom: Separation/Divorce/ Widowhood

DEFINITION

The ending of ties between couples may take different forms, including separation, divorce and death. The ending of the couple relationship may or may not also signify the ending of a family.

DISCUSSION

Post-coupledom can only be understood in relation to the social arrangements by which alliances, personal ties and marriages are formed in the first place, which are often linked to the **gender order** of a society or culture. Most societies have customs about how coupledom or marriage may be ended, and what social arrangements should result, with religious ideas often being significant. Divorce is the annulment of a legally based marriage, but coupledom can also be ended by separation, abandonment and death.

The ending of a marriage or cohabiting couple relationship may take different forms, including couples maintaining co-residence but living separate lives (perhaps with sexual partners elsewhere), and couples living apart but maintaining regular contact, including sexual relationships. Much of the evidence on the ending of relationships is based on legal documentation, although some work has provided more personal accounts including from children's perspectives (Smart and Neale, 1998; Smart et al., 2001).

It was not until the second half of the twentieth century that **divorce** became a real option for ordinary people in most European and New World societies, although divorce legislation also varies in relation to the predominant religion of the country, and in many contemporary societies divorce is often harder for women to obtain than for men. Western societies thus saw a very steep increase in formal divorce in the later decades of the twentieth century, so that by the 1970s there was a greater probability of marriage ending in divorce than in death. Increases in **life expectancy** have meant that marriages that do not end in divorce or separation are likely to be significantly longer in duration than in previous times. The USA has generally had the highest rates of divorce, but there is some evidence of a plateau effect occurring across many affluent societies, or more recently a decline in the divorce rate (Paetsch et al., 2007).

The historical increase in divorce was also accompanied by shifts in the law towards mothers having custody of their children, in contrast with nineteenth-century practices of awarding custody to fathers. From the late twentieth century on, there have been shifts towards emphasizing fathers' continuing contact with their children, including shared residential arrangements and responsibilities. There have also been widespread changes in European and New World societies towards no-fault divorces based on the irretrievable breakdown of the marriage, meaning that it is the breakdown of the relationship that is at stake, rather than the breaking of a legal contract for which one party is blameworthy. Alongside these changes have been shifts in what is legally required with regard to divisions of property and income, and support for an ex-spouse.

There have been debates concerning the reasons for, and consequences of, these trends towards increases in separation and divorce in Western societies. Some argue that rising divorce rates are caused by the legal changes making divorce easier to obtain. By contrast, others suggest that divorce law changes have simply made it possible to formally regularize the ending of a couple relationship that might previously have continued in legal status only (e.g. desertion may have been more common historically). Other important issues that are identified include: a decline in religion and the **secularization** of society; women's increased financial independence through employment opportunities; reduced **social controls** whereby marriage is now seen as a matter of individual choice; rising expectations of fulfilment, **love** and intimacy through coupledom. While marriage and coupledom may bring benefits, including love, companionship, material and psychological support, sexual fulfilment, and a sense of **identity** and stability, it may also bring problems, including financial dependence, power struggles, conflict over roles and obligations, abuse and violence.

Divorce is socially patterned in relation to issues such as low income, differences in background between couples, and age when married. A woman's involvement in paid **employment** may be a consideration that makes both men and women more inclined to countenance the ending of a couple relationship (Paetsch et al., 2007). Across industrialized societies, higher **separation rates** are apparent among cohabiting rather than married couples, and couples who cohabit prior to marriage are also more likely to divorce than those who do not (Allan and Crow, 2001), but the reasons are complex. Rather than marriage *per se* keeping people together, it may be that those who cohabit start out with different attitudes – including religious beliefs – from those who marry. Cohabiting couples may have a greater sense of independence, for example by keeping their finances more separate than married couples. European and New World societies provide variable but limited rights for support or property-sharing after a cohabiting couple separate.

By contrast to the lack of attention to divorce or separations that do not involve children, research and policy have proliferated on the aftermath of divorce/separation where children are involved, generally from a **deficit model** which assumes that the ending of the couple family is undesirable for both adults and children. How children experience their parents' separation depends on the history of the relationships and who/what else is involved in the separation, but there is no evidence that parents undertake divorce lightly. The implications for children may be mediated by social, legal and cultural frameworks as well as the level of material, economic and social disruption involved. Children may express distress in the short term as a result of upheavals that may not have been explained to them, and some suggest that children cope better when parents enable them to have some control (Smart et al., 2001). Complex models have been developed to try to understand these various processes and their implications in the longer term. The implications for the adults involved are likely to include: economic and other material consequences; role changes; spousal conflict; and the loss of emotional support and **friendship** networks that have been structured around coupledom. These various processes are also likely to be different between men and women.

The ending of coupledom through the **death** of one of the partners has received attention primarily from psychologists, with varying theories, including stages of grief, **continuing bonds**, and the **dual process model** of restoration and loss orientations. Within theories of bereavement, the death of a spouse or partner is understood as a deeply significant process of **psycho-social transition** (Parkes, 1996). If emotional bonds with a deceased partner continue to be important for the widowed individual, for example, it may not be appropriate to describe **widowhood** as constituting a situation of *post*-coupledom. From a sociological perspective, uncertainty such as that associated with death and bereavement is distributed along lines of social inequalities (Marris, 1996). The death of a partner has been investigated with regard to the financial and health consequences and concomitant policy implications, as has the significance for children of the death of a parent (Ribbens McCarthy, 2006). These issues are often obscured by the contemporary association of death with ageing in affluent societies.

Whether the couple relationship is ended by separation, divorce or death, where children are involved this will generally lead to a situation in which they live primarily with one parent (usually the mother) or, less frequently, split their time between two parents. Lone parenthood can be a transitory phase, leading into cohabitation, and perhaps **remarriage** and/or **step-parenthood**, but then sometimes leading to divorce/separation again. The economic consequences of lone parenthood are generally disadvantageous for mothers as a result of gendered patterns in employment.

It is debateable whether the ending of a parenting couple relationship should be understood as the ending of a 'family'. This partly depends on how far the family is identified in terms of shared **residence**, and how far the couple relationship is seen as bound up with the parenting relationship. Some argue that the emphasis on children's continuing contact with both parents after divorce or separation means that **co-parenting** constitutes a continuation of the family, albeit in an altered form – known as the **durability model**, or 'post-familial family' (Beck-Gernsheim, 1998). This represents a shift away from earlier expectations of a 'clean break' after divorce or separation, which made it straightforward to then think of any new couple/step-parenting household as forming an alternative family – known as the **substitution model** (Thèry, 1989).

Post-coupledom also brings variable implications for relationships with wider kin networks. Some argue that rising rates of divorce mean that kin ties associated with **family of origin** are seen as more reliable than couple relationships (Duncan and Phillips, 2008). Kin ties that have been formed through the couple relationship itself (the **family of affinity**) may be ended along with the couple relationship, although not necessarily, especially if there are children involved. Furthermore, where marriage is seen as an alliance between kinship groups (as in many countries around the world), divorce will also have broader implications beyond the couple partnership itself.

SUMMARY

Post-coupledom is a complex idea, covering a wide variety of situations, from death or legal divorce to the informal ending of couple relationships that may not have involved expectations of durability and/or co-residence. Concerns about increases in divorce rates in European and New World societies have led to debates about 'family breakdown', and analyses of their causes and consequences, particularly with regard to the implications for children. Expectations of parental relationships after divorce or separation have shifted from a substitution model to a durability model.

FURTHER READING

Cheal (2002), Karraker and Grochowski (2006), and Allan and Crow (2001) offer overviews of debates and evidence around post-coupledom. Hetherington (2003) and Pryor and Trinder (2007) review the implications for children, and Duncan and Phillips (2008) look at changes in attitudes around divorce and separation.

Related concepts   *Attachment and Loss; Coupledom; Family Change and Continuity; Family Effects*

Power

power

DEFINITION

Power is defined in various ways in different theoretical perspectives. Generally, it is seen as the capacity of an individual to achieve desired outcomes against the wishes or interests of another. Alternatively, it is defined as a positive capacity to make things happen.

DISCUSSION

Power is a key concept in social science that raises questions about who is best positioned to identify when power is being exercised and whose interests are being served. Power in family relationships is complex, not least because it is not generally part of how people discuss their family lives. Rather, in contemporary European and New World societies, power is seen as a political language that is at odds with family ideals of love and togetherness. But analyses of power in family lives reveal the political dimensions of family relationships, often manifested through apparently mundane everyday details of family activities.

Power is analysed in different dimensions of social life: as a characteristic of individuals, as a feature of interactions between individuals, or as operating in systematic ways through society. These various macro and micro operations of power are interconnected. The exercise of personal power in family relationships is linked to wider structural processes of power, for example, through the operation of **patriarchy** (as traditional authority or physical violence), the institutionalized positioning of young people as dependent, and wider social norms about how resources are valued and distributed in society.

As an individual characteristic, power may refer to a perceived **locus of control**. Individuals may see themselves as having considerable capacity for self-direction (**autonomy**), or they may regard themselves as subject largely to forces beyond their control, or bound to act under the direction of others (**heteronomy**). These perceptions may be linked to active or passive styles of coping. The **outcomes** for children living in difficult circumstances, for example, are found to vary according to their parents' coping style (e.g. Seiffge-Krenke, 2000). Nevertheless, such differences in orientation to power may also be linked to structural patterns, such as **poverty** or other problematic life events, and the value placed on autonomy or heteronomy may also vary across cultures (Kağitçibaşi, 2007).

At macro and micro levels, power may be analysed as a manifestation of conflict, or as a form of energy or capacity that allows outcomes to be achieved. At **macro** levels, conflict theories see power as working systematically to the benefit of some groups or classes of people over others, whereas functionalist theories see power as working to the benefit of all through the achievement of societal goals. Similarly, at the **micro** level of family relationships, conflict theories see power as enabling certain individuals to assert their needs and interests over and against those of other family members, whereas functionalist approaches see power as operating to the smooth functioning of the family as a whole.

Where power is understood as the capacity to achieve one's goals despite opposition, this comes close to the related concepts of **control** and coercion. Within this view, operations of power may be identified in terms of either who is successful in asserting their wishes in situations of conflict, or on who seems to be benefitting most from the outcomes or effects of actions. Some ideas of power depend on intentionality, while other perspectives may include unintended consequences, particularly in families – where individuals may be expected to pay attention to the consequences of their actions for those they care about. In longer-term family relationships, however, subtler forms of power, such as social influence, or expectations built up over time, may operate.

One way of approaching power within family relationships has been to examine **decision making** by asking spouses who makes family decisions. There are methodological difficulties with this approach, such as which spouse to ask, and which decisions are regarded as key. There are also conceptual issues concerning whether or not decision making is the most significant route through which power is manifested. Perhaps power is most effective when it is least noticeable, operating as part of the unquestioned routines of daily lives. Furthermore, open discussion and negotiation may be more apparent than actual in practice. An alternative approach is to identify whose interests are best served by family arrangements.

The distribution of **resources** in families is important to identifying power. On the one hand, resources can be deployed to reinforce or assert power, while on the other hand, inequalities of resources are an outcome of the operations of power. Power is key for thinking about **inequalities** within families. But it is also important that power helps to explain continuing attachments alongside negative experiences, even including violence and abuse. The notion of '**false consciousness**' has been used to suggest that family members fail to see where their true interests lie, and thus accept the oppressive operations of power. The language of '**sharing**', for example, may serve to mystify inequalities of resources, and feminist work has been crucial in opening up the question of how money is distributed in households and families (Pahl, J., 2005).

Identifying how resources feature in relationships of power is complex, however, because much depends on the meanings given to them. It is possible, for example, for both the spending and withholding of **money** to be seen as an absence of proper care, since 'money can't buy you love', and may be seen as no substitute for spending **time** with someone, and yet the lack of basic provision by a non-resident employed parent can be seen as uncaring (Ribbens McCarthy et al., 2003). Further, spending time with someone not only may be seen as part of a loving relationship, but may also be seen as meeting one individual's interests more than another's. Are wives spending afternoons making tea and looking after children at their husbands' cricket matches an example of 'false consciousness' or of loving togetherness? Everyday resources in households, such as providing cooked **food**, can also carry power through their symbolic importance (as with a Christmas or Thanksgiving family dinner), as well as imposing obligations on the receivers. When a wife cooks regular meals for her husband and children, is she acting through an idea of the 'good housewife and mother' that has been imposed on her, and/or is she also creating an obligation on other family members to come home for dinner at the expected time and respect the importance of the family meal?

To explain how power operates while maintaining commitment from the subordinate partner, Bell and Newby (1976) described the marital relationship in terms of a '**deferential dialectic**'. From this perspective, the **traditional authority** given to men as heads of household means that men's power is seen as unquestionable and immutable. In European and New World societies, it occurs, for example, through expectations that male partners will be taller and older than female partners. At the same time, Bell and Newby argue that the more powerful individual mitigates the harsher connotations of power through providing **gifts** and symbolic acts of care.

A more benign view of power sees it as the capacity to achieve common goals, in which case power does not entail anyone losing out. Some social psychological theories view power as a necessary part of group dynamics, enabling people to achieve joint goals, and sometimes also acknowledging mediation by wider structural inequalities.

Where individuals are **dependent** on others, as in families, they are vulnerable to the exercise of others' power, but this may operate either in abusive or in nurturant ways. Where one spouse is emotionally dependent on another, for example, the more emotionally independent spouse may have relational power (O'Connor, 1991). Young children and people with high dependency needs are vulnerable to abuse, or are the object of care and nurturance. A more equal power relationship occurs with **interdependence**, where individuals look to each other for the achievement of desired outcomes and the meeting of their needs.

Some feminist writers avoid dichotomizing power and **love** (Meyer, 1991), raising the possibility of conceptualizing power as a form of care. The classic notion of power as a struggle of interests between individuals depends on a Western notion of the individual as separate, to whom interests are attached. But if individuals are understood in relational terms, with interests that are bound up with those of others, power needs to be conceptualized in more complex ways. For example, mothers may describe the exercise of power over their children as fulfilling what they see as the **children's needs** for discipline or order (Ribbens, 1994). Much depends on the meanings attributed to actions and on how people's interests and needs are understood. Indeed, family members' particular interests and needs, especially children's, are framed by expert theories of knowledge, such as child development, which constitute power and a key form of **governance** in themselves (Rose, N., 1999).

SUMMARY

Power may be seen as destructive or productive. While some focus on power as involving a direct clash of interests, others draw attention to the importance of people's perceptions of their own interests and what counts as authority, expertise and so on. Wider social norms as well as structural inequalities and access to resources are important factors in family power. Feminist analyses of power in family lives have been crucial in making inequalities and abuse in households visible. Power may also be understood in relational terms, as a form of care.

FURTHER READING

Allan and Crow (2001) are unusual in offering a brief but explicit overview of power as a pervasive part of family relationships. J. Pahl (2005) offers a recent discussion of money in households, while Kirchler et al. (2001) provide a social psychological perspective on resources and love in close relationships. On families and food, see DeVault (1991) for a groundbreaking study, and Jackson (2009) for recent empirical work.

power

Related concepts   *Care; Division of Labour; Domestic Violence and Abuse; Social Divisions*

DEFINITION

'Problem families' is one of a range of terms used for those families said to be on the margins of mainstream society in terms of their behaviour and values.

DISCUSSION

Versions of the idea of 'problem families' have reoccurred throughout the history of industrial society (Welshman, 2007). As well as 'problem families', other terms that have been used include dysfunctional families, a cycle of deprivation, the underclass, anti-social families and socially excluded families. Drawing on theories about appropriate parenting and family lives, problem families are judged to be, variously, structurally deficient or internally chaotic, socially excluded or withdrawn from the dominant social and moral order, causing problems for wider society through parental inability to control children and transmitting a subculture of **poverty** and inadequacy across generations within particular families.

A recurring feature of these debates is that expert and institutionalized discourses, such as **developmental psychology**, are drawn on by professionals to judge these families as presenting difficulties both for themselves and for wider society because of parents' inadequate **childrearing** practices and deviant or disorganized domestic life. Whether or not the values and behaviour of families defined as problematic are founded in culture or structure is subject to debate (discussed further below), but some commentators argue that such a definition involves value judgements about **working-class** and minority **ethnic** family life, rather than scientific precision.

Dysfunctional families are judged to be failing to instil acceptable family values and behaviour, and economic and work values. Family systems and therapeutic approaches make reference to dysfunctional, disorganized or chaotic families, in which **neglect**, **conflict**, misbehaviour and **abuse** occur continually and are accommodated and regarded as normal by family members. Many of these approaches fail to make a sociological link to the state of wider society. An influential example of a concern with dysfunctional families that does make this link is Coleman's (1988) discussion of the structural features of contemporary family life that weaken its **social capital** function. Most notably, Coleman argues that parents in certain types of family – **lone parent**, dual-earner or welfare-dependent families – are unable adequately to socialize and monitor their children or to make community-based links with families who are functioning in a socially acceptable manner. This is then said to have repercussions for wider society in the form of young people underachieving educationally, holding 'free-rider' attitudes, flouting acceptable behavioural norms and engaging in delinquent behaviour.

The **cycle of deprivation**, and other associated terms such as cycle of disadvantage, **cycle of poverty** and cycle of dependency, also focuses on failure of the intergenerational transmission of the work ethic and stable family relationships. It posits the development of a self-perpetuating **sub-culture** of deviant attitudes and behaviour among some families that plays a causal role in the perpetuation of disadvantage. Poverty, irresponsible parenting and out-of-control large families are said to reproduce themselves across the generations in particular families, resulting in social problems such as 'maladjustment', educational failure, child abuse, **delinquency** and **mental ill-health**. While empirical evidence does not support this view, the idea of a transmitted cycle of deprivation or disadvantage continues to have a purchase in both professional and political thinking.

Another term, the **underclass** family, captures a sense of families who are **socially excluded**, or have withdrawn, from mainstream society. In the context of conceptualizations of social class and structure that are founded on skill and occupational rankings, dependence on state **welfare benefits** rather than the labour market is seen as a major indicator of the underclass (and, in some versions, as causal). There are different explanations for the existence of this residual category that prioritize cultural or structural factors. The cultural explanation focuses on the **moral** mindset and activities of the underclass, arguing that welfare dependency has created the break-up of the nuclear family household and socialization into a counter-culture that devalues employment and encourages dependency and/or delinquency and criminality, with lone mother households seen as prime cases.

In contrast, the structural underclass explanation emphasizes structured **inequalities** that disadvantage particular groups in society. The economy has failed to provide sufficient secure **employment** and, consequently, has destabilized the male **breadwinner** role and encouraged criminality. In particular, labour market restructuring away from manufacturing and towards the service sector in developed countries has led to poor employment opportunities for men who lack training and skills. In US discussions of the underclass, there has been a strong racial element to both cultural and structural arguments, which has led to debates about whether **race** or class is the primary factor in the production of an underclass.

More recently in the British context, the term **anti-social families** has become familiar both politically and popularly, again linked to ideas about social exclusion. There is a particular focus on the perceived inability of parents to socialize and control children adequately such that young people cause social disorder in the community and for wider society. Such families' adjudged failure to absorb, or their active rejection of, the norms and behaviour of the majority are then dealt with either by **education** (such as **parenting skills** advice) or by sanction, which defines their behaviour as criminal (such as compulsory parenting skills classes, local child curfews and Anti-social Behaviour Orders, commonly referred to as ASBOs) (Edwards, R. and Gillies, 2004). In stark contrast to this version of what constitutes familial anti-social behaviour, some feminists have argued that it is the nuclear family itself that is 'anti-social', in institutionalizing women's oppression and labelling all other forms of family life as inferior.

The supervision of families considered to be problematic has been and is a feature of most welfare systems (Rodgers, 1996). A solution to problem families who resist the kinds of intervention or sanction outlined above for anti-social families, or who fail to benefit from them and change their behaviour, is for children and young people to be removed and taken into state care (sometimes referred to as **'looked after' children**). In some countries and points in history, including the Netherlands (Van Wel, 1992, cited in Rodgers, 1996) and the UK (Garrett, 2007), whole families considered to be in need of intervention may be placed in residential care, with the aim of resocializing them into acceptable mainstream patterns of behaviour.

Conceptually, ideas about dysfunctional families, a cycle of deprivation, the underclass and anti-social families, locate the threat that the problem families who comprise them are seen to pose as somehow 'outside' of society. This placing of problem families as not really a part of 'normal' society, allows society then to be perceived as internally cohesive and free from significant challenge (Morris, 1994). Notions of 'problem families' thus have an appeal to professional groups in bolstering a casework approach to dealing with these families, working closely with family members to encourage and monitor changing behaviour (Welshman, 1999).

'Problem family' labels, however, have been argued to have little validity as conceptual tools of sociological analysis, lacking in both theoretical and empirical precision and often confounding cause and effect. Critics point out that, overwhelmingly, it is poor families who do not conform to standards grounded in **middle-class** privilege who are given the various labels that denote definition as a problem family and subjected to regulation through state intervention (Gillies, 2007). Simple linear models of **causality** of, say, delinquency and criminality, ignore the complex interaction over time of social deprivation, low income, unemployment and so on, with family practices.

SUMMARY

Key axes of debate about problem families concern whether the purported deviant behaviour and values of such families are founded in culture or structure. Others question the values and motivations behind definitions of problem families, however, arguing that such labels have little conceptual or empirical purchase. A number of terms are used variously for problem families, including dysfunctional families, judged to be structurally deficient or internally chaotic; underclass families, deemed to be socially excluded or withdrawn from the dominant social and moral order; and anti-social families, regarded as causing problems for wider society through parental inability to control children. The idea of a cycle of deprivation poses a sub-culture of poverty transmitted across generations within particular families. Problem families, and especially the parents in such families, are viewed as in need of education or sanction.

FURTHER READING

Welshman (2007) provides a historical overview. Gillies (2007) discusses 'marginalized mothers' in the UK who are the focus of public concern and intervention.

Related concepts   Child Development; Conflict Theories; Family Policies; Social Divisions

problem families

DEFINITION

In relation to families, public and private are often used to refer to a distinction between worlds of work and home, or between the state and domestic family life.

DISCUSSION

Social scientists vary as to whether, and how far, they see the terms public and private as mutually dependent, and how to define them. Their meanings are complex, not least because they may be invoked in different contexts of debate. Public and private, for example, may be used to distinguish between public (State) and private (non-State) ownership of companies, or the public may refer to the activities of the state while the private refers to activities of economic or other formal organizations outside of the state. In relation to families, the distinction is different, with reference to what might be broadly described as the worlds of work and of home, although the terms may also be used to distinguish between both work and political life on the one hand (public) and domestic family life on the other (private).

It is important to note that the private needs to be distinguished from **privacy**, which is contrasted with public. Public in this context refers to being visible and known to others, and may involve legal notions of the right of the individual not to be exposed to the public gaze and intrusion.

Concepts of public and private have been important for analyses of gender, including suggestions that all societies involve gender **inequalities** based on women's subordination in a **domestic** domain, contrasted with male power in the public and political domain (Rosaldo, 1974). This analysis, however, may impose inappropriate Western-based political distinctions. Rather, notions of public and private may be better understood through the variable **gender orders** of particular cultures (Overing, 2003).

Distinctions of public and private may be more relevant to some societies than others, since it was the emergence of large-scale **industrialization** that led to the characterization of '**work**' (as paid waged labour) as being located in non-domestic sites. A strong set of ideas about the nature of the home as a respite from work, and a particularly appropriate site for the experience of a particular form of childhood, accompanied this differentiation. This private domestic world was idealized as expressing particular values and as providing a refuge from the harsh economic realities of the amoral world outside. It was women – 'the angel in the home' – who were seen to be the moral custodians and also the physical **embodiments** of these ideals (Davidoff, 1995). Home was private in the sense of being removed from public gaze. It was also a haven from state intrusion, but in this sense, it was male authority as the **head of household** in the home that was safeguarded from public intervention.

While this construction of the private sphere may have only ever been available to a minority of the population in developed societies, the ideals and values it represents continue to exert a strong hold over people's imaginations. In this respect, family scholars have analysed the distinction between public and private as representing something more complex than a division between the physical locations of workplace and home. They have drawn distinctions between contrasting principles of social organization (Cheal, 1991); different value systems (Ferree, 1985); different modes of organizational consciousness (Smith, 1987); or different **ways of being** in the world (Ribbens and Edwards, 1998). Ribbens McCarthy and Edwards (2002) thus suggest that the terms refer to a range of interlocking tensions that, in European and New World societies, are focused around understandings of childhood. These tensions involve differing ideas of the **personhood**, of orientations towards present and future, of formal and informal relationships, and different orientations to **time** and **emotions**. In this sense, public ways of being may at times be relevant to domestic sites (e.g. where non-family members are being paid for domestic work) while private ways of being may be relevant to non-domestic sites (e.g. where people develop close **friendships** with work colleagues). Nevertheless, the way that some social locations are seen as appropriate for children while others are considered inappropriate (e.g. taking children into the office) mean that public and private may be experienced as different 'worlds' (Bell and Ribbens, 1994).

The variable understandings of public and private mean that they may be used in contradictory ways, or may 'slip' between one usage and another in debates. In relation to their use in family studies, feminist scholars have explored their meanings in relation to gendered experiences of home and family lives, but with differing **evaluations** of the terms as a hindrance or a help.

On the one hand, the meanings of public and private are said historically to work to the disadvantage of women who became marginalized from paid employment and political power, and oppressed by the ideology that promulgated a particular role for women within the private sphere (Benhabib, 1998). From this perspective the distinction between public and private is part of an oppressive ideology that distorts the actual lived experiences of the majority of women. Furthermore, experiences of public and private, in this sense, are likely to be significantly shaped by issues of **class** and **ethnicity** as well as **gender** (Fraser, 1998; Hill Collins, 1997).

On the other hand, because domestic family lives have often been treated by social scientists as lying outside of society – part of a **natural** order that is separate from societal contexts of political and economic power – the terms public and private are useful in revealing the socially constructed and significant activities of women and children in the domestic sphere. Indeed, feminist writers have argued that social science attention from the nineteenth-century 'founding fathers' onwards, was largely preoccupied with the public sphere, reproducing the notion that women's and children's lives in the private sphere are somehow 'outside' of society (Yeatman, 1986).

The terms offer an alternative theoretical framework from the predominant sociological notion of **macro** and **micro** levels of social analysis, in which family is inevitably situated at the interface between the two, but largely consisting of small-scale interactions between individuals. In this framework, family lives are generally theorized as shaped by the macro social forces of politics and the economy. Using public and private as an alternative way of understanding the relationship between families and economic and political life, however, facilitates an analysis of the interdependence of these different activities and arenas.

SUMMARY

The concepts of public and private are complex and may be used in variable ways in different contexts and disciplines. In family studies, public is often used to refer to the world of work, and private to family life in the domestic sphere. Various writers argue that these terms also need to be understood as value orientations or 'ways of being' (particularly focused around experiences of childcare) rather than demarcated physical locations and specific social sites in any simple sense. Some writers argue that these distinctions are unhelpful and may be ideologically loaded, while others suggest that they can be useful in clarifying the socially and historically constructed nature of family experiences.

FURTHER READING

Weintraub (1997) and Ribbens McCarthy and Edwards (2002) provide, respectively, political and feminist overviews of the use of the concepts of public and private.

Related concepts   *Childhood; Division of Labour; Feminisms; Home*

Rationalities

DEFINITION

The notion of 'rationalities' in family life provides a theoretical approach to how family members make sense of choices and decide what is the right thing to do. In the rationalities framework there are two main approaches: economic rationality (*homo economicus*) and moral rationalities (*homo sociologicus*).

DISCUSSION

The use of 'rationalities' to analyse family life assumes that people have choices in their lives, and then seeks to understand how people decide on their choices, such as whether to stay single or marry, whether and when to have children, how to divide responsibilities and resources between men and women. There are two main explanations for how the choices are made in the rationalities framework: rational choice theory and the concept of moral rationalities. Each poses quite a different view of human motivations.

Rational choice theory applies classical, neo-liberal, economic ideas to family behaviour, and is thus closely allied to post-industrial Enlightenment thinking in European and New World societies. It poses people as separate, individual agents who have consistent, ranked preferences ('tastes'). Faced with a range of options, they rationally calculate the costs and benefits for themselves of different choices, with decisions determined by what they believe will give them the maximum feasible benefit ('utility'). This process is seen as separate from the 'external' social situation that produces and shapes these options and preferences. The instrumental individual portrayed is often termed *homo economicus*. This 'pursuit of self-interest' approach is often seen as the economic version of **genetic drive** arguments.

Becker has built on this framework to develop what is termed '**family economics**', where these ideas are applied to aspects of family life. He has argued that **marriage** is governed by economic laws of supply and demand, where each spouse possesses their own level of qualifications, skills and experience (**human capital**) – men particularly as **breadwinners** in the labour market, women as carers and **homemakers**. They then contract a partnership with each other to 'trade' their complementary specialisms to maximize productivity and efficiency. People decide to marry when the advantages they expect from marriage outweigh those that they expect to receive either from staying single or from searching for another marriageable partner (Becker, 1976), and similarly with decisions to **divorce**. The rise in women's **employment**, and the development of childcare provision outside of the household, may modify the equation of costs and benefits, but not the principle. Similarly, others have argued that the rise in **childbearing** outside of marriage, in cohabitation or as a **lone mother**, is the consequence of rational choice in a context of economic insecurity – it does not make economic sense to marry low-waged or unemployed men, particularly when mothers have higher levels of education and job experience and more employment opportunity (Moffitt, 2000).

In contrast, the concept of **moral rationalities** prioritizes the social and the relational over economic and individual interest. In this perspective, economic rationality cannot proceed without a socially produced normative understanding, which means that moral rationality is primary and rational economic choice is secondary in family behaviour. People still act rationally, but **intersubjectively**, in accord with assessments about what is the right and proper thing for them to do in the particular social and cultural context in which they live. Economic considerations may still be important, but these are embedded in, and logically secondary to, moral and normative choices. This situated moral actor is *homo sociologicus* rather than *economicus.*

For example, based on their study of higher-income couples' choices about employment, Jordan et al. (1994) argue that economic rationality is used in a secondary way to support and legitimate what are essentially moral commitments to a gendered division of labour. Duncan and Edwards (1999) have gone further to develop the more socially embedded concept of 'gendered moral rationalities' in relation to mothers' uptake of paid **work**. They argue that the decisions that mothers make about paid employment and mothering are not based solely on economic cost and benefit calculations, but primarily on moral values about what constitutes a 'good' mother. These decisions and the values underpinning them are negotiated in the context of variable social networks, social groups and cultural settings, so that people have different understandings of the proper or right course of action.

Overall, rational choice theory's assumptions that family members act according to the economic consequences of their actions in the light of fixed preferences and self-interest, have been criticized for failing to capture the moral reasoning that people use in making decisions about family life in social context. In response, Becker (1996) has incorporated notions of personal and **social capital** into his rational choice 'family economics' model – to debatable effect. His assumptions also appear limited to the USA in the mid-twentieth century (Therborn, 2004). Despite this, others argue it is often a rational economic choice framework that is adopted explicitly or implicitly in contemporary family policy initiatives to motivate people in particular ways. In this view, rational economic choice theory and its implementation in policy becomes a 'rationality mistake' (Barlow et al., 2002).

SUMMARY

Rationalities concern explanations of how family members understand choices and make decisions about the best way to act. Different models pose different views of human motivation. Rational choice theory presumes *homo economicus* – an instrumental individual who calculates the economic cost and benefit consequences of choices in order to gain the maximum feasible benefit for themselves. Moral rationalities, and specifically the concept of gendered moral rationalities, addresses *homo sociologicus* – a socially embedded actor who negotiates what is the right and proper thing to do in the context of variable social networks and cultural settings.

FURTHER READING

Introductory economics and philosophy texts discuss reason and rationality in general; Casper and Bianchi (2002) introduce economic rationality theories of family lives and some of their continuing uses, while White and Klein (2008) offer a fuller discussion. Carling et al. (2002) critique family-related behaviour as governed by economic rationality; Brynin and Ermisch (2009) compare economic and sociological approaches to the analysis of families and relationships.

Related concepts   *Division of Labour; Household; Negotiation; Role Theory*

Role Theory

DEFINITION

Role theory attempts to explain the way that people in particular social positions are expected to behave, or the way in which they develop particular patterns of behaviour when they occupy such positions. In relation to family, these include roles associated with kinship, generation and gender, such as those of grandfather, mother, daughter, aunt, cousin.

DISCUSSION

Role theory is often referred to as dramaturgical because it draws on the metaphor of the theatre. It attempts to provide a pivotal link between individual behaviours and economic and cultural patterns and structures, with flows in both directions. People's individual experiences of their position/s in family life are shaped by collective conventions; in turn, social expectations are shaped by people's actions in their family roles. Expectations in regard to the typical **emotions** and behaviour associated with a particular family role can come from the 'actor' occupying the role themselves, family members and other members of society, such as neighbours, or of social institutions, such as healthcare workers and judges. Some family roles are **ascribed** from birth (such as when the roles of father or daughter are regarded as fixed by biology) while others are **achieved** through developing or taking on relationships (e.g. as wife or **step-father**). A role approach can be used in an everyday and implicit way to talk about family relationships and associated behaviour, such as 'in her role as a mother …', or it can be used more explicitly in scholarly attempts to understand and explain family life.

A central tenet of role theory is that a person's sense of **identity** and their behaviour are shaped by their social position, but within that broad umbrella there is a range of different strands. Looking at sociologically informed role theory, a functionalist approach argues that roles give people their place in society, that they are prescribed and learned and that often they are rooted in biology. Echoing some of this approach, **structuralist** role theory focuses more on the way in which family and other social roles follow relatively fixed 'scripts' that are 'written' by what is needed for the smooth functioning of society, and inculcated through repeated interactions. In families, young **sons** and **daughters**, for example, are socialized during childhood into their **gendered** roles they will adopt as adults. **Symbolic interactionism**, on the other hand, regards roles as giving guidance and meaning to social life in a much more fluid way (notably stemming from Goffman, 1959). Within this approach, people negotiate and develop their roles, both in their family and more widely, and refine the emotions and activities associated with those roles through interaction with others, rather than 'taking on' pre-existing prescriptions. Cognitive role theory, which is associated more with social psychology, also focuses on the ways in which individuals negotiate role expectations and behaviour, but in particular where there is disagreement rather than consensus about the role.

The **conjugal roles** of husband and wife have received much attention from all role theory perspectives, with particular classic texts from the mid-twentieth century helping to shape sociological ideas and understanding of family life. Taking a functionalist approach, Talcott Parsons (Parsons and Bales, 1955) drew a distinction between what he regarded as the 'natural' **instrumental roles** performed by the male head of household as **breadwinning husband** and father, and the **expressive roles** performed by the woman as **caring wife** and mother. In functionalist thinking these distinct roles are regarded as 'complementary' to each other, fitting together for maximum effectiveness. In some contrast, Berger and Kellner's (1964) interpretive study of **marriage** looked at what it meant to take on and act out the roles of **husband** and wife. They argued that the reality of marriage is an ongoing construction that is constantly negotiated and affirmed between the spouses. In another classic, more structural, text, Bott (1957) identified two main types of conjugal role. Segregated roles refers to distinct divisions of labour between husband and wife, usually along conventional gender lines. In contrast, joint roles refer to decision making and domestic tasks that husband and wife share between them. While researchers have taken variable views on whether marital roles have become less segregated in European and New World societies in recent decades, the continued implicit assumption of particular parenting roles being associated with particular genders is evident in the term '**role reversal**', where mothers take on primary breadwinning and fathers primary caring roles.

A lot of attention has also been paid to role strain, role conflict and role overload, especially in relation to expectations of contemporary fathering and mothering. The terms are often used (interchangeably) to describe tensions between the demands of social norms and activities or chosen behaviour within and between roles, although they have some-what different nuances. 'Overload' points towards having too many roles to fulfil, for instance, while 'conflict' points more to contradictions between different roles, although both can happen at the same time. For example, contemporary fathers are often said to be pulled between a good *breadwinner* father role, working hard to earn enough money to support their children, and a good *involved* father role, present and active in their children's daily upbringing. Similarly, contemporary mothers are often said to find it stressful to meet all the different expec-tations, from both themselves and others, associated with a mothering role, a role as wife or partner and a paid worker role, perhaps also along-side the role of daughter to elderly parents. Such issues often underpin calls for **work–family balance** policies. Far less attention has been paid to the roles occupied by children in families, although the way in which young people can feel torn between the expectations of family and their peers could also be described as role conflict.

Criticisms of role theory, especially in its more structuralist form, highlight the dangers of oversimplifying the complexities of actual behaviour in families, variously ignoring different material and structural circumstances, as well as shifting historical, social and normative con-texts, all of which can shape the substance and emphasis of family life and activities. Role theory developed in European and New World societies can be **culturally imperialistic**, imposing ideas about the existence of particular types of family roles on contexts in which they do not occur in the same way at all.

Some feminists have been critical of the role framework as supporting **patriarchy** and shifting attention away from **inequalities**, power and resistance in families (Rapp et al., 1979), and omitting to take account of sexual politics. Tensions, for example, are explained only as a product of multiple roles that are failing to mesh, especially for women. This implies that if either the multiplicity of roles disappeared (women went back to the kitchen) or a bit more skilful juggling took place (women got themselves better organized), harmony would ensue. Another strand, however, questions the adequacy of role theory as an explanation of individual identity and behaviour. Family relationships, such as being a mother, are not on a par with being, say, a solicitor, secretary or student. Role theory drains family relationships of their significance as complex core identities invested with **love**, tears, effort and ambivalence. Nonetheless, it can highlight the ways in which individuals may feel constrained to attempt to play particular roles in ways that fail to mesh with their sense of personal identity and their emotions.

SUMMARY

Role theory draws on the metaphor of theatre to make links between individual behaviours and economic and cultural patterns and structures. There is a range of different strands of role theory. Functionalism sees family and other roles as prescribed and learned, and necessary for the smooth running of society as a whole. Structuralist role theory focuses on roles within families, and elsewhere, as inculcated by society. Symbolic interactionism sees family and other roles as giving meaning to social life and as negotiated through interactions with others. Role strain, conflict and overload have received attention in combining family roles with employment. Critics of role theory regard it as oversimplifying family life and relationships.

FURTHER READING

Biddle (1986) provides overviews of role theory in its various versions, and Cheal (2002) discusses role theory in relation to family life in general terms.

Related concepts *Coupledom; Division of Labour; Functionalism; Phenomenological Approaches*

DEFINITION

Full siblings are children who share both biological parents, while half-siblings share one biological parent. Step-siblings are not biologically related, but each has a biological parent who has formed a new partner relationship together.

DISCUSSION

Relationships with sisters and brothers form one of the longest-lasting family bonds that people may experience. Ties with siblings form part of many people's lives, from their early years into older adulthood. Young children may spend just as much, if not more, time with siblings, as time with their parents. A further distinctive feature of sibling relationships is their seriality: that is, being one among a series of more than one.

The **diversity** of family structures in most European and New World societies means that the question of who is a sibling is complex. Children may have full, half-, step- or foster sisters and brothers living in the same or a different parental household to them, or who are no longer dependent and live outside these households, and who constitute some form of biological and/or social **tie**. This complexity has led some researchers to develop typologies and terminologies of forms of sibling relationships, encompassing features such as common genes, common history, family values and cultures, and common legal status, or to distinguish between 'core', 'kin' or 'social' siblings. An anthropological focus on kinship networks in cultures other than Western post-industrialized societies also underlines the variable definition of who is considered as a sibling (Cicirelli, 1994).

The language of siblingship – **sister** and **brother** – is also a symbolic means of expressing social or political relationships and connections more broadly. Reference to friends being 'like a sister or brother to me' is made to express the feeling that the **friendship** is more than just an ordinary social relationship. It attempts to convey a sense of close emotional attachment, loyalty, **trust**, everyday **reciprocity** and other idealized sibling-tie-like qualities within the friendship relationship. The quality of sibling relationships is also part of collective language and political understandings. The socialist and trade union practice of referring to co-members as 'brothers' and, more recently, 'sisters', the feminist notion of women as 'sisters', and some black, Asian or other minority **ethnic** use of 'brother' and 'sister' to refer to co-ethnics, for example, signal a particular sort of relationship – a political sense of the idealized subjective quality of the sibling bond as part of a particular social or political group 'family', such as standing up for each other and sticking together even in difficult times.

Child **outcomes** are an enduring concern of work on siblings, especially in the psychological and social functionalist fields. The focus is on sibling group 'constellation' or 'configuration' – number of children, birth order, age gap, gender composition and so on. These variables are then correlated with development and outcomes for children, relating to intelligence, personality type, educational achievement and career/occupational success, eating disorders, incest, gender identity and sexuality (Carr Steelman et al., 2002).

Parents are usually posed as key in relationships between siblings, with a focus on their own characteristics and how they socialize their children. From a functionalist perspective, the greater the number of children they have, the less parents are said to be able to invest **time** and attention in them, with detrimental consequences for children's socialization and outcomes (Coleman, 1988). From an **evolutionary psychological** perspective, the genetic link between parent and child is understood to lead parents to feel love and commitment towards their biological offspring and to reject non-biological children, with a similar relationship between biological and non-biological siblings, and even biological siblings in rivalry for parental attention (e.g. Daly and Wilson, 1998).

In **psychoanalytic theory**, the relationship between parents and their child is presumed to establish the emotional and psychic foundations of all other relationships, with siblings viewed as marginal and/or 'transitional' relationships and as provoking 'primal hatred' in their conflict for psychic attachment to the parent (e.g. Bank and Kahn, 1982). Recently, however, there have been challenges to the psychoanalytical preoccupation with parent–child relationships. These challenges claim that 'lateral' relationships between siblings are relatively autonomous and just as, or even more, important than 'vertical' parent–child relationships in psychic and social learning, and the construction and workings of internal worlds (Mitchell, 2003). Family systems approaches also include siblings as integral to the processes that are needed to achieve **homoeostasis** in the system; here **conflict** in relationships between sisters and brothers may be viewed as evidence of a **dysfunction** in the family system as a whole.

While mainstream research on sibling relationships is largely interested in the socialization of children and in child development, there is a strand of work on middle and later **adulthood**. As well as looking at the strength of relationships between sisters and brothers over the life course, such work is also concerned with who provides care and help to elderly parents. In this respect, research often draws out **gender** differences, which it links to a stronger culture of caring among women. Adult **sexuality** has also been linked to sibling gender and birth order (see review in Edwards, R. and Weller, 2010).

A relational sociological perspective on sibling relationships has focused on the intricate and variable dynamics of emotional and practical care and power at play in child and adult sibling relationships, grounded in their own understandings (e.g. Mauthner, 2002). Relational perspectives, drawing on **social constructionism** and **psycho-dynamics**, have also shown how relationships between sisters and brothers are redolent with understandings about themselves as people and their place in the social world, and so are linked to wider divisions in society as a whole (Gillies and Lucey, 2006). At the same time as sibling **identity** and relationships are fluid, shifting over time and according to **context,** they are also shaped by social differences of gender, social **class** and **race/ ethnicity**, as well as **age** status.

SUMMARY

Sibling relationships comprise a complex interplay of biological, social, emotional and cultural elements, not merely a simple association between biology, law and **residence**. Different theoretical approaches underpin different emphases in the study of sibling relationships. Developmental and functionalist perspectives focus on sibling characteristics and their relationships to child outcomes, posing parents' actions as key. Recent psychoanalytic ideas, however, see relationships with sisters and brothers as foundational, while relational sociological perspectives emphasize diversity in sibling ties, and suggest that deeply embedded social divisions are produced and reproduced in these family bonds.

R. Edwards et al. (2006) provide critical overviews of perspectives on children's sibling relationships. Contributions to Caspi (2010) discuss a range of cultural and environmental aspects of sibling relationships.

Related concepts   *Functionalism; Household; Kinship; Social Divisions*

Social Divisions

DEFINITION

'Social divisions' refers to regular patterns of division in society that are associated with membership of particular social groupings, generally in terms of advantages and disadvantages, inequalities and differences. Systematic social divisions – such as generation, gender, sexuality, race/ethnicity and social class – are both shaped by, and shape, family experiences.

DISCUSSION

Social divisions are important for individual life experiences and **life chances** in the context where social characteristics provide the basis for differential treatment, unequal access to **resources** and judgemental evaluations. Social divisions are associated with **inequalities** and a hierarchical order between categories or groups of people, theorized through the concept of '**stratification**'. Such divisions emerge through both institutional processes and everyday routine social interactions (Anthias, 2005). The **boundaries** that are found between categories and groups of people generally depend, at least partly, on what are seen as individual biological characteristics, but are embedded in social processes. They may also be experienced as both 'external' to individuals, and imposed as a result of **social structure**, or 'internal', and implicated in people's **identities** and self-perceptions.

Social divisions are crucial in various aspects of everyday family lives and experiences. These include systematic differences both between

social divisions

179

family members and between the families of particular groups of people. Social divisions that are especially important in relation to families include: generation, gender, sexuality, race/ethnicity and class.

Generation can form a social division in several ways. **Birth cohort** generation refers to people who were born in a particular year or at approximately the same time and are therefore all of a similar age. Studies of the effects of family on children's development and outcomes often use surveys that track members of a particular cohort over time. People who belong to a particular cohort not only share a similar age, they also share the experience of growing up during a particular historical period and thus constitute an historical generation.

The term 'family generation' is more concerned with differences between family members in terms of positioning in family lines of **descent** or lineage, stretching backwards and forwards in time. Within families, generation cross-cut with age is associated with **dependency**, power or **authority**, as well as flows of **obligation** and responsibility up and down generations.

Generational issues are important for family processes over time. All kinds of material and symbolic resources, artefacts and traits may be regarded as being **inherited** or 'passed on' in families. Besides material and economic resources, these include: the family name; **family traditions** and **family culture** (which can intersect with religious or ethnic heritage); and family **resemblances** of character or appearance.

Despite suggestions that **gender** no longer plays a significant part in contemporary European and New World societies, it continues to be a key social division through which family lives are patterned in all cultures, although some suggest that not every culture is associated with gender inequality or subordination (Nzegwu, 2006). Gendered family lives are most obvious in relation to heterosexual parenting roles. Children are also identified as male or female from the moment of birth (or in the womb), with importance for their family relationships and upbringing. The social consequences of gender within a society is known as the **gender order**.

The significance of gender as a social structure, rather than a reflection of 'natural' differences, has been a feature of academic debates since second wave feminism demonstrated how gender is the product of social expectations and interactions. A distinction was drawn between **sex** – understood as fixed biological characteristics; and gender – understood as a role and identity produced by socialization and the wider social order. This sex/gender distinction, however, treated **bodies** as somehow existing outside of the social order. More recent discussions have explored how bodies are gendered and 'performed' through social discourses and actions (Butler, 2004).

Gender categories are closely linked with expectations about sexuality. Indeed, without the binary categories of gender, heterosexuality is meaningless. Compulsory **heterosexuality** describes the situation where heterosexuality is institutionalized as 'normal' – in both evaluative and statistical senses. In the UK, for example, **marriage** has been reserved as an exclusively heterosexual institution, despite legislation that recognizes **civil partnerships** between **same-sex couples**.

The term 'sexuality' encompasses sexual desires, identities and relationships. As with other social divisions, heterosexuality may be viewed as biological, and thus a universal 'fact' underpinning how **labour** is divided between the sexes in family life and society more widely – drawing on associated ideas of **masculinity** and **femininity**. In this view, marriage and family life are regarded as important in the production and regulation of heterosexuality, based on assumptions about the male sex drive and the reactive character of female sexuality. Another biologically based view argues that women's sexuality is controlled by men through **patriarchy** in order to ensure the legitimacy of their offspring. While its extent and forms may vary, patriarchy has arguably been a predominant social form across global history (Therborn, 2004).

Other perspectives consider sexuality as a key aspect of family socialization and/or **psychic processes**. Children are said to 'learn' normative heterosexuality in the crucible of family. At the same time, anything linking children and sexuality is condemned, since childhood is seen as a time of (sexual) innocence in affluent societies. Nevertheless, societies vary in whether and how far heterosexuality is imposed. Some argue that the sanctioned association between heterosexuality and family life is breaking down, liberating sexuality from traditional family values.

Ideas about fixed biological differences are also important for race and ethnicity as social divisions. The terms '**race**' and '**ethnicity**' are used in a variety of ways, and sometimes as though they are interchangeable. Indeed, both terms interweave issues of kinship, **citizenship**, **religion**, **history**, language, culture and identity.

'Race' is associated with a history of divisions between hierarchically ranked races, seen as a product of distinct **ancestries**. Early studies of race combined some observable physical differences, such as skin colour, hair texture, facial features and skull shape, with what lies below the body surface, such as blood, bones and brain size, as well as being associated with sensibilities such as courage and aesthetic appreciation. Bars on **intermarriage** are predicated on such ideas. Although modern **genetics** has undermined notions of biological fixedness by providing evidence that there is more genetic variation within than between so-called racial groups, biological notions of race still persist – both in political and popular ideas that oppress people (e.g. fascism) and mobilization to resist such ideas (e.g. black power). Whiteness often remains invisible in racial terms, but is often the norm from which the difference of all 'others' is measured. In studies of **parenting** styles or the prevalence of particular family forms, for example, the family lives and experiences of racial minorities may be either unacknowledged or pathologized.

'Ethnicity' links into a range of non-biological communal identifications. A degree of cultural distinctiveness is seen as the mark of an ethnic grouping, both by insiders and by outsiders: members of the group believe that they share a common **descent**, **heritage** or tradition, and others accept this. There is debate about how far people can negotiate their own ethnic identity and whether it is a deep, primary identification or a symbolic instrumental resource. Rigid ideas about ethnic cultural practices (such as particular **food** and clothing), on the one hand, can result in stereotypes held about, say, 'the Asian family', or, on the other hand, can mean that some family or parenting practices are criticized by co-ethnics as inauthentic. As with race, the term 'ethnicity' can be used to refer only to minority groups who are different physically or culturally from the assumed norm, rather than also encompassing dominant ethnicity.

Class (sometimes called **socio-economic grouping**) is also a key social division that may be more visible to those who are further down the hierarchy, with problematic consequences for their lives. Although academic attention to social class has fluctuated over time, it remains central to social theory and research, including family studies. **Mortality rates** and parenting practices, for example, are each linked to social class differences.

Class may be used to indicate broad social inequalities. The main understanding of social class, however, is derived from the occupational structure of industrialized societies. In mid-twentieth-century social research, the class position of the family unit as a whole was derived from the occupation of the 'head of household', generally seen as the **male breadwinner**. Studies of **intergenerational mobility** examine how far individuals, over their life course, move from the occupational class position of their families of origin. This occupational perspective on class is problematic in relation to families as a collection of individuals who are co-resident or closely related. An alternative is to theorize class as cutting across both work and family, as a feature of taken-for-granted cultural differences that individuals absorb from childhood through experiences, relationships and environment (which Bourdieu (1990) theorized as '**habitus**').

Overall, social divisions result in differences within and between families. Although they are identified through separate concepts, such as generation, gender, sexuality, race/ethnicity and class, as part of everyday lives, social divisions are experienced as cross-cutting or articulating with each other (sometimes referred to as **intersectionality**). The social division that seems most salient at any one time depends on the particular context. Social divisions experienced in and through families are also linked to wider social networks, meaning that people often interact with other families who share similar social characteristics. Likewise, people tend to partner with similar others, resulting in patterns of **homogamy** that reproduce shared family cultures, with important consequences for social structure more broadly (Brynin et al., 2009). Some argue that the primary experience of divisions and hierarchies within families underpins social hierarchies and inequalities in society at large.

SUMMARY

Social divisions cross the biological, the psychic and the social in ways that reflect and shape wider social structures, while also becoming part of internalized identities and experiences of the world. Social divisions can be understood: as based in biology, or as produced in and through social structures and institutions; as part of everyday family and social practices; through cultural discourses; and within individual subjectivities.

FURTHER READING

For general overviews, Payne (2006) addresses social divisions and Pilcher and Whelehan (2004) discuss gender. Gillies (2007) discusses class and mothering in the UK, and see Lareau (2003) for the USA. Ochieng and Hylton (2010) and McAdoo (2006) look at black family lives in the UK and the USA, respectively. Alanen (2001) discusses generation in the lives of children, while Finch (1989) addresses generational responsibilities in families. Carabine (2004) and Scott and Jackson (2000) provide introductions to sexualities and personal lives.

Related concepts   *Biology; Family Effects; Feminisms; Power*

DEFINITION

Socialization refers to the processes by which children, and also adults, learn all aspects of the behaviours and customs of the social groups to which they belong or are joining, enabling them to become functioning human beings in the contexts in which they live.

DISCUSSION

The process by which people learn the culture – behaviour and customs – of their societies and settings is known as socialization. **Primary sociali-zation** generally occurs in families or other care relationships when children are infants. It involves the internalization of norms and expec-tations and the acquisition of the behaviours necessary to function as a member of society. Socialization can also refer to learning the culture of a new group that an individual has joined, such as starting a new job. This is sometimes referred to as **secondary socialization**, a process that continues throughout life.

The significance of social contact for young children in learning to participate in social life is illustrated graphically by accounts of 'feral' children. These instances provide evidence of the effects on children of being without human contact for long periods of time, especially at a young age, and demonstrate the importance of socialization for the most basic features of being recognizably 'human', such as language, upright posture, social interaction and moral awareness (Candland, 1993).

Socialization is an important sociological concept because it acts as an interface between the individual and their membership of a particular society or social context. In this regard, family links small-scale **(micro)** levels of interaction with broader **(macro)** patterns of society. Some argue that particular family forms are inadequate for satisfactory social-ization; for example, lone mothers and **absent fathers** are said to fail to socialize young men into acceptable adult male roles. The concept of socialization itself does not necessarily entail such evaluations, however, since such young men are still being socialized, albeit into behaviours that others find unsatisfactory. Nevertheless, some sociological theories do implicitly evaluate socialization in varying ways.

From the point of view of functionalism, as an overarching 'grand' theory of **social order**, family socialization is said to ensure that children, and later adults, not only know how to behave, but also **internalize** the norms and values of society, so that these then constitute their own internal worlds. Socialization thus functions to produce social order by reproducing society within the individual's psyche. Indeed, **personality** may be seen as produced through socialization. Within this form of macro analysis, the needs of the **social system** as a whole determine family formations and processes, with the family acting as the agent of society. This approach sees parents as agents of **cultural transmission**, and children as passive recipients of socialization, with little room for a sense of **agency**. Furthermore, socialization within families is seen as shaped by the demands of wider social systems, with no conception of economic life being shaped by family practices of socialization, for example.

Theories concerned with conflict and **inequality** in social life tend to use the term **reproduction** in preference to socialization, but similarly to functionalist views, conflict theories also see socialization as shaping the passive individual to 'fit in' with social life. In this framework, however, the macro social system does not operate to the benefit of all, but instead reproduces inequalities to the advantage of the ruling groups. By internalizing the norms and values of society, individuals are said to develop a **false consciousness** that works against their own best interests. For example, both in their family lives and other contexts, boys and girls are said to internalize their gender roles, even though these serve to reproduce inequalities between men and women.

A rather different account of socialization is provided by broadly phenomenological approaches. From a **symbolic interactionist** perspective, socialization produces the capacity for thought and the development of meaning. Cooley's concept of the 'looking glass self' captures the idea that we only know ourselves through our interactions with others, who reflect our characteristics back to us. The writings of George Herbert Mead built on this concept, suggesting that children first develop a sense of themselves as an object in the eyes of others through taking on the role of the **'significant other'**; for example, by playing the part of a parent caring for a baby. As children interact with larger groups, they develop an understanding of a 'generalized other', learning to see themselves within the larger culture. **Ethnomethodological** theories are more concerned with everyday interactions between children and those around them, offering a dynamic notion of socialization, in which individuals actively reason, invent and respond in unique ways. Thus socialization is studied in terms of children's interpretive competencies in family interactions, and elsewhere. Such theories resonate with more recent interactional accounts of child development. At the same time, routine ways of behaving and thinking become so deeply internalized that they become completely **taken-for-granted** unless the assumptions on which they are based are challenged, for example by encountering radically different cultures.

Phenomenologists Berger and Luckmann (1971) describe socialization as a creative process by which the individual 'takes over' the world in which (significant) others live, such that a shared internalized social world results. The **primary social world** of family life comes to be seen as inevitable, having a greater solidity than will ever be experienced with any subsequent socialization experiences.

In recent years, socialization has perhaps received less attention. One reason for this may be the development of the 'new' childhood studies, which view children as active social agents, who are 'beings' in the present, rather than passive objects to be shaped through socialization for their 'becomings' in the future. Another factor may be postmodern theories, which stress the plurality of lifestyles and identities with which individuals may experiment, rendering obsolete accounts of children being socialized into the values that fit them into society.

The example of feral children (discussed earlier) points to how extensively human-ness depends on nurture. Indeed, the concept of socialization depends to some extent on the distinction between nature and nurture, with socialization stressing nurture, while the more psychological concept of child development was founded in ideas of biological change in children. Since the distinction between nature and nurture has been increasingly questioned, the concept of socialization becomes less useful. Genes, organisms and environments may be implicated in each other, rather than studied as if they are separate entities.

Nevertheless, the concept of socialization continues to be used by contemporary theorists. Giddens (1990, 1991), for example, argues for the importance for children of learning **trust** within families, as a basis for a sense of **ontological security** in the world, while Bourdieu (1990) developed the concept of **'habitus'** to refer to individuals' learned and internalized mental structures as a result of socialization experiences shaped by **class** inequalities and produced in local material contexts. From some perspectives, then, socialization may arguably be ever more important as children (and adults) learn to internalize – but also, perhaps, to resist or subvert – the demands of the complex social worlds in which they find themselves.

SUMMARY

The key sociological concept of socialization has been theorized as a central feature of family lives. Functionalist and conflict theories risk presenting a view of individuals as over-socialized, shaped by external forces that are mediated through family (and other) experiences. Phenomenological approaches provide more scope for seeing individuals as actively appropriating their social experiences and creating their own internal worlds, but these theoretical perspectives risk neglecting wider social structures that help to shape family lives. Although examples of feral children point to the importance of social contact for becoming recognizably 'human', more recent theorizing questions longstanding debates based on a dualism of nature and nurture. Recent theories increasingly point to the complexity of the processes by which children internalize, but also resist or reframe, the expectations of wider social groups and structures.

FURTHER READING

David H.J. Morgan (1975) and Ribbens (1994) overview accounts of socialization, while Ritzer (1996) considers socialization embedded within varying theoretical perspectives. Karraker and Grochowski (2006) discuss parenting and socialization in the contemporary US context; the collection edited by Denzin (2009) addresses childhood socialization across a range of contexts. The website FeralChildren.com (http://www.feralchildren.com/en/index.php) offers a variety of materials (including academically robust references) concerning feral children.

Related concepts   *Child Development; Conflict Theories; Functionalism; Phenomenological Approaches*

Transnational Families

DEFINITION

'Transnational families' refers to sustained ties of family members and kinship networks across the borders of multiple nation states. The term recognizes that migration is not necessarily unidirectional, with the permanent resettlement of families, or parts of families, in a country of destination, but more often involves fluid relationships between family members in two or more countries.

DISCUSSION

Transnational families involve the creation and maintenance of a feeling of 'family' connections, shared welfare and a sense of a **belonging** across two or more national boundaries, through the long- or short-term **migration** and settlement of some family members. Transnationalism raises challenges for the understanding of family forms as being organized around shared household **residence** and participation in **reproduction** and **consumption**. In transnational kinship groups, for example, one parent, both parents, or adult children may be producing income abroad, while other family members carry out reproduction and care in the country of origin. Partnering and **marriage** across nation-state borders can create, or reinforce and extend, transnational kinship ties (e.g. Ballard, 1994). Family networks, **identities** and allegiances, therefore, become stretched and reconfigured, with commitment and reciprocal **obligations** being practised across national boundaries. Statistics that are collected within national boundaries may completely overlook family **ties** and activities that cross such spatial categories.

In the context of advances in, and increased availability of, communication technology, such as email and mobile telephones, and the reduced costs of transportation, such as air travel, many migrants in a 'receiving' society are able regularly to keep in touch with and visit family members in the 'sending' country of origin, and vice versa. An established strand of work in the field focuses on family provisioning, care and **rituals** that sustain family life across **time** and distance. Bryceson and Vuorela (2002) conceptualize the creation and maintenance of kinship for transnational families as involving 'frontiering' and 'relativising'. 'Frontiering' refers to the practices involved in the creation of familial space and network ties across national boundaries, while 'relativising' captures the ways in which relational ties between family members are established, maintained or curtailed. Within these broad forms of creating and maintaining transnational families, there can be different practices for different **ethnic** groups. Indeed, several studies compare and contrast the experiences of migrants from one sending country with those from another country of origin within a single receiving country (e.g. Goulbourne et al., 2009).

Mass migration and international **labour markets** mean that some national and ethnic groups are more likely than others to practise transnational family life, and the circumstances under which they do so vary considerably. For example, labour market migration within Europe is more likely to be from east to west than vice versa, and the conditions and resources for poor migrants working in the manual and domestic sectors of the labour market are quite different from those who work in more professional elite sectors of the economy. In other words, social **class** shapes how transnationalism is experienced. Most of the work on transnational families with a labour market focus has concentrated on the international market in domestic workers rather than on the elite sectors. In particular, attention has been given to **global care chains**, looking at the **commodification** of the work of social reproduction in the domestic sphere, such as care and home maintenance in affluent countries. Most attention has been paid to women domestic workers from poorer nations taking up caring and domestic work as women in affluent and developed economies increase their participation in paid employment, although male migrant workers are also a feature of this sector of the economy.

The global care chain not only involves migrant workers carrying out care for other families in another nation state, but also caring for and about their own transnational family of origin. Research shows how migrant women can play a key economic role in supporting the families they leave behind, sending back substantial remittances that maintain family solidarity and **reciprocity** as well as ensuring material survival. Transnational mothers who leave their children behind or return them to the family country of origin to be cared for by (usually female) relatives, can feel pulled between, on the one hand, their work commitments in immigrant countries and economic support of their children and other family members, and, on the other hand, images of a 'good' mother as involving physically present caring (Erel, 2002).

Other transnational family care practices involve men working abroad to support their families, which can mean practising transnational fathering while wives stay in the country of origin to bring up children; and grandparents joining parents and grandchildren in immigrant countries to take up family care and domestic responsibilities while parents are in employment. Studies have also paid attention to the issues facing children in transnational families that are involved in global care chains. These studies have shown children experiencing not only gains in **material** terms but also pain as a result of **separation** from parents; they have also pointed to the difficulties of family reunification after a parent returns home or their child joins them in the migrant country (e.g. Parreñas, 2005).

While it is important to bear ethnic differences in mind in making overarching statements about transnational families, aspects of maintaining family relationships across **nation states** can reflect the **gendered** nature of family life generally. As has been found for families generally, women in transnational families are often pivotal in maintaining kin ties. Despite geographical distance and prolonged separation, ways in which they do this include sending presents, organizing family visits and celebrations, and instituting new family customs in the transnational context (e.g. Zontini, 2004).

The issue of **diasporic** identities is also highlighted in work on transnational families, even where one part of the family has been settled in another nation state for generations. This work addresses the ways in which kinship networks across geographical **boundaries** help shape a sense of belonging, home and values. Family members may have another actual or imaginary home away from the one in which they lead their day-to-day lives. The evidence suggests that transnational family links provide people with a sense of fluid and multiple ethnic and national identities and allegiances, on which they may draw in different ways, according to time, location and audience.

SUMMARY

Transnational family life is an increasingly common practice in a globalized world with mass migration and international labour markets, alongside new technologies of communication. Resources and circumstances vary between and within different ethnic groups, and these can result in variable transnational family practices around provisioning, care and ritual, and fluid senses of belonging. While both men and women are involved in supporting transnational family life, women tend to be crucial in maintaining kin ties across multiple nation-state boundaries. Children can experience gains and losses as part of transnational family life.

FURTHER READING

Goulbourne et al. (2009) explore a variety of aspects of transnational family practices. Globalized care chains and migrant workers across a range of countries are addressed by Hochschild (2000) and Yeates (2009).

Related concepts   Care; Division of Labour; Family Forms; Kinship

key concepts in family studies

index of sub-concepts

As explained in the Introduction, this Index specifically offers a way of tracing sub-concepts that are not main entries in their own right, but are nevertheless important in the study of families. This index shows where each sub-concept is most significantly discussed in each of the relevant main entries, and it is bolded at those points in the text. *See also* indicates other relevant sub-concepts.

Abortion: Personal, 147

Absent father: Socialization, 184; *see also Non-resident father*

Absent parent: Family Policies, 186; *see also Non-resident*

Abuse: Problem Families, 162; *see also Child neglect, Elder abuse, Marital rape, Sexual abuse*

Accessibility: Fatherhood, 97

Achieved: Biology, 13; Families of Choice, 57; Fatherhood, 97; Intimacy, 124; Role Theory, 173

Adolescence: Family Life Cycle and Life Course, 81; *see also Developmental psychology, Youth*

Adoption: Demography, 44; Families of Choice, 57; Household, 115; Parenthood, 143; *see also Social parenting*

Adoptive parents: Parenthood, 142

Adulthood: Child Development, 23; Childhood, 26; Conflict Theories, 35; Family Life Cycle and Life Course, 81; Fatherhood, 95; Home, 112; Siblings, 178

Adult-worker model: Division of Labour, 48; Family Change and Continuity, 64; *see also Breadwinner*

Affectional communities: Families of Choice, 57; *see also Community care*

Affinities: Kinship, 129; *see also Connectedness, Relationality, Ties*

Age(s): Child Development, 22; Family Life Cycle and Life Course, 81; Family Practices, 89; Household, 117; Individualization, 122; Motherhood, 134; Siblings, 178; *see also Old age*
>   **Age of marriage:** Family Change and Continuity, 64
>   **Age status:** Care, 19; Family Life Cycle and Life Course, 81

Ageing population: Demography, 44

Agency: Families of Choice, 56; Family Effects, 67; Functionalism, 105; Individualization, 121; Parenthood, 144; Socialization, 185; *see also Autonomy, Decision making*

Agrarian societies: Family Change and Continuity, 63; *see also Pre-industrial*

Alliances: Coupledom, 38; Kinship, 127

Ancestries/Ancestors: Attachment and Loss, 11; Social Divisions, 181; *see also Lineage*

Anti-social families: Problem Families, 164

Archival sources: Comparative Approaches, 30

Arranged marriages: Coupledom, 38

Ascribed: Biology, 13; Families of Choice, 57; Fatherhood, 97; Intimacy, 124; Negotiation, 136; Parenthood, 143; Role Theory, 173

Asymmetrical: Grandparents, 107

Authoritative parenting: Child Development, 23

Authority: Intimacy, 124; Kinship, 128; Negotiation, 135; New Right, 139; Social Divisions, 180; *see also Traditional authority*

Autonomy/ous: Care: 20; Demography, 45; Family Systems, 93; Grandparents, 109; Home, 112; Household, 116; Individualization, 119; Parenthood, 144; Personal, 146; Power, 158; *see also Agency, Heteronomy, Independence, Self*

Bean pole families: Grandparents, 106

Belonging: Home, 111; Transnational Families, 188; *see also Affinities, Ties*

Bereavement: Attachment and Loss, 11; *see also Death, Grief, Widowhood*

Biography/ies: Family Life Cycle and Life Course, 81; Family Practices, 89; *see also Life history*

Biological father: Fatherhood, 96; *see also Social father*

Biological parents: Family Law, 77; *see also Social parenting*

Birth: Coupledom, 38; Demography, 42; Family Life Cycle and Life Course, 81; Kinship, 127; Personal, 147; *see also Childbearing, Childbirth, Fertility*
> **Birth cohort:** Social Divisions, 180; *see also Cohort*
> **Births outside marriage:** Family Law, 77; New Right, 139; *see also Legitimacy, Never-married motherhood*
> **Birth registration:** Demography, 43

Blended families: *See Step-families*

Blood ties: Demography, 44; Family Law, 77; Family Practices, 88; Household, 115; *see also Connectedness*

Body/ies: Biology, 13; Family as Discourse, 60; Family Practices, 89; Social Divisions, 180; *see also Embodiment, Genetics*

Boundary/ies: Conflict Theories, 34; Coupledom, 40; Demography, 43; Family as Discourse, 60; Family Forms, 73; Family Systems, 93; Household, 116; Social Divisions, 179

Bourgeois family form: Conflict Theories, 35; *see also Middle class*

Breadwinner(s): Conflict Theories, 35; Division of Labour, 47; Fatherhood, 97; Feminisms, 99; New Right, 138; Problem Families, 164; Rationalities, 170, Role Theory, 173; Social Divisions, 182; *see also Adult-worker model, Male breadwinner (family), Work*

Brothers: Biology, 15; Siblings, 176

Capitalism/Capitalist societies: Conflict Theories, 35; Feminisms, 100; **Caring/caring for/caring about:** Care, 18; Role theory, 173

Causality: Family Effects, 69; Problem Families, 165

Causal laws: Comparative Approaches, 31

Census returns: Demography, 43

Child abuse: Domestic Violence and Abuse, 55

Childbearing: Family Change and Continuity, 64; Rationalities, 170; *see also Birth, Fertility*

Childbirth: Feminisms, 101

Childcare: Division of Labour, 48; Family Policies, 84; Home, 114; Motherhood, 131; Parenthood, 144

Child labour: Division of Labour, 47

Childminders: Parenthood, 143

Child neglect: Domestic Violence and Abuse, 55; *see also Abuse*

Children's 'needs': Child Development, 21; Parenthood, 143; Power, 161; *see also Moral*

Childrearing: Feminisms, 101; New Right, 139; Problem Families, 162

Citizen/ship: Care, 19; Child Development, 23; Childhood, 28; Family Policies, 85; Parenthood, 141; Personal, 146; Social Divisions, 181

Civic participation: Childhood, 26

Civil partnerships: Coupledom, 41; Families of Choice, 56; Social Divisions, 181

Class: Care, 19; Comparative Approaches, 30; Conflict Theories, 35; Coupledom, 40; Family Life Cycle and Life Course, 81; Family Practices, 89; Family Systems, 94; Feminisms, 101; Individualization, 119; Intimacy, 125; Motherhood, 132; Personal, 146; Public and Private, 168; Siblings, 178; Social Divisions, 182; Socialization, 186; Transnational Families, 189; *see also Diversity, Equality, Inequality, Middle class, Working class*

Clinical case studies: Family Effects, 67

Cohabitation: Comparative Approaches, 31; Coupledom, 40

Cohort: Family Life Cycle and Life Course, 83; *see also Birth cohort*
     Cohort studies: Family Effects, 67

Commodification: Transnational Families, 189

Common law: Family Law, 76

Community care: Care, 18; *see also Affectional communities*

Community mothering: Motherhood, 131; *see also Fictve kin*

Community of need: Individualization, 120

Companionate marriage: Coupledom, 40; *see also Marriage*

Compulsory education: Motherhood, 133; *see also Education, Schooling*

Compulsory schooling: Child Development, 21

Concerted cultivation: *See Intensive mothering*

Conflict: Problem Families, 162; Siblings, 178; *see also Abuse, Control, Exploitation*

Conjugal roles: Role Theory, 173

Connectedness: Family Systems, 93; *see also Affinities, Belonging, Continuing bonds, Relationality, Ties*

Connubium: Coupledom, 40

Consumerism/consumption: Introduction, 7; Coupledom, 40; Functionalism, 105; Individualization, 121; Transnational Families, 188; *see also Commodification, Weddings*

Contexts: Comparative Approaches, 30; Domestic Violence and Abuse, 55; *see also Ecological model, Social contexts*

Continuing bonds: Attachment and Loss, 11; Post-Coupledom, 155; *see also Bereavement, Dual process model, Grief, Widowhood*

Contraception: Coupledom, 41; Individualization, 119; *see also Abortion, Fertility*

Control: Care, 18; Power, 158; *see also Discipline*

Convergence theory: Comparative Approaches, 31

Conversation analysis: Family as Discourse, 59

Co-parenting: Post-Coupledom, 156

Co-resident/ce: Coupledom, 41; Demography, 43; *see also Absent fathers*

Couples: Family Forms, 71

Couple households: Demography, 44; *see also Living-apart-together (LATs), Non-resident, Residence*

Critical discourse analysis: Family as Discourse, 59

Cross-sectional: Family Effects, 67; *see also Surveys*

Culture: Comparative Approaches, 30; *see also Family culture*
    Cultural imperialism/Culturally imperialist: Child Development, 25; Comparative Approaches, 31; Role Theory, 175
    Cultural relativism/t: Comparative Approaches, 32; Domestic Violence and Abuse, 55
    Cultural transmission: Functionalism, 104; Socialization, 185

Cycle of deprivation: Problem Families, 163; *see also Dependency/ dependent, Welfare benefits*

Cycle of poverty: Family Life Cycle and Life Course, 80; Problem Families, 163; *see also Inequality/ies*

Cyclical change: Family Change and Continuity, 63

Dailiness: Family Practices, 89; Phenomenological Approaches, 150; *see also Everyday experience, Taken-for-granted*

Daughter(s): Families of Choice, 57; Parenthood, 142; Role Theory, 173; *see also Son*

Death: Attachment and Loss, 11; Demography, 42; Family Life Cycle and Life Course, 81; Kinship, 127; Personal, 147; Post-Coupledom, 155; *see also Ancestries, Bereavement, Continuing bonds, Dual process model, Generation/al, Widowhood*

Decision making: Power, 159; *see also Agency*

Deferential dialectic: Power, 160; *see also Gifts, Traditional authority*

Deficit model: Post-Coupledom, 155; *see also Evaluation(s)*

Definition of the situation: Phenomenological Approaches, 150; *see also Taken-for-granted*

Delinquency: Problem Families, 163; *see also Adolescence, Youth*

Democratization: Childhood, 27; Feminisms, 102; Individualization, 119

Demographic transition: Demography, 45; Family Change and Continuity, 65

Dependency/dependent: Childhood, 27; Domestic Violence and Abuse, 54; Power, 160; Social Divisions, 180; *see also Autonomy, Independence, Vulnerability*

Descent: Kinship, 127; Parenthood, 141; Social Divisions, 180, 182; *see also Ancestries, Heritage, Lineage*

Deservingness: Care, 18; *see also Obligation(s)*

Detraditionalization: Families of Choice, 56; Individualization, 119; *see also Industrialization, Secularization*

Developmental cycle: Family Life Cycle and Life Course, 80

Developmental psychology: Child Development, 22; Parenthood, 144; Problem Families, 162; *see also Adolescence, Children's 'needs'*

Developmental progression: Child Development, 22

Diasporic: Transnational Families, 190

Difference feminism: Division of Labour, 49; *see also Inequality*

Discursive psychology: Family as Discourse, 59

Discipline: Domestic Violence and Abuse, 54; *see also Authoritative parenting, Authority, Control*

Discourses: Negotiation, 137; *see also Critical discourse analysis*

Displaying families: Family practice, 90; *see also Rituals*

Diversity: Child Development, 25; Demography, 45; Family Change and Continuity, 64; Intimacy, 123; Siblings, 176; *see also Ethnic/ity*

Divorce: Comparative Approaches, 31; Coupledom, 41; Demography, 43; Family Change and Continuity, 64; Family Forms, 73; Family Law, 77; Grandparents, 108; Home, 111; New Right, 139; Post-Coupledom, 153; Rationalities, 170

Domestic/domestic ideology/ideal: Motherhood, 133; Public and Private, 166; *see also Domestic space/sphere, Housewife*
    Domestic labour (debate): Biology, 13; Conflict Theories, 36; *see also Exchange theory, Surplus labour value, Women's work*
    Domestic space/sphere: Functionalism 104; Home, 111

Dowry: Coupledom, 38; *see also Alliances*

Dual process model: Post-Coupledom,155; *see also Bereavement, Grief, Widowhood*

Durability model: Post-Coupledom, 156; *see also Step-families*

Dysfunction/al: Family Life Cycle and Life Course, 80; Family Practices, 88; Family Systems, 94; Problem Families, 162; Siblings, 178; *see also Deficit model*

Ecological model: Child Development, 24; Family Systems, 93; *see also Contexts, Macro*

Economic choice/determinism: Division of Labour, 77; Functionalism, 105; *see also Industrialization, Macro*

Economic development: Family Change and Continuity, 62; *see also Industrialization, Macro*

Economic rationality: Intimacy, 125; *see also Moral rationality*

Economic transactions: Conflict Theories, 36; *see also Resource(s)*

Education: Family Change and Continuity, 62; Family Life Cycle and Life Course, 82; Family Policies, 85; Problem Families, 164; *see also Compulsory education, Schooling*

Elder abuse: Domestic Violence and Abuse, 53; *see also Ageing population*

Elective affinities: Individualization, 120; *see also Connectedness, Democratization, Relationality*

Elective kin: Families of Choice, 57; *see also Fictive kin, Quasi kin*

Embodiment: Personal, 147; Public and Private, 167; *see also Body/ies*

Emotions/al: Introduction, 7; Care, 19; Family Practices, 90; Home, 112; Intimacy, 123; Negotiation, 137; Phenomenological Approaches, 150; Public and Private, 167; Role Theory, 172; *see also Conflict, Love*
    Emotional labour: Division of Labour, 49; *see also Expressive role*

Employment: Coupledom, 39; Family Policies, 84; Parenthood, 144; Problem Families, 164; Rationalities, 170; *see also Breadwinner(s), Work*

Endogamy: Coupledom, 38; Kinship, 127; *see also Alliances, Exogamy*

Equality: Childhood, 28; Division of Labour, 50; Individualization, 119; Intimacy, 124; *see also Class, Gender, Inequality*

Ethical reasoning: Care, 19; *see also Evaluation(s), Moral*

Ethnic/ity: Domestic Violence and Abuse, 54; Family Life Cycle and Life Course, 81; Family Practices, 89; Family Systems, 94; Feminisms, 101; Home, 113; Individualization, 122; Intimacy, 125; Motherhood, 132;

Personal, 146; Problem Families, 162; Public and Private, 168; Siblings, 177; Social Divisions, 181; Transnational Families, 188; *see also Diversity, Race*

Ethnomethodology: Phenomenological Approaches, 150; Socialization, 185; *see also Taken-for-granted*

Eugenics: Biology, 13; *see also Genetics, Heritage, Race*

Evaluation(s): Family as Discourse, 60; Family Practices, 88; Phenomenological Approaches, 150; Public and Private, 167; *see also Cultural imperialism, Cultural relativism, Moral evaluations*

Everyday experience: Motherhood, 131; *see also Dailiness, Definition of the situation, Taken-for-granted*

Everyday interactions: Negotiation, 136; *see also Micro*

Evolutionary psychology: Biology, 13; *see also Genetics*

Exchange theory: Division of Labour, 47; *see also Resources*

Exogamy: Coupledom, 38; Kinship, 127; *see also Alliances, Endogamy*

Exploitation: Conflict Theories, 35; *see also Surplus labour value*

Expressive role: Division of Labour, 47; Functionalism, 104; Role Theory, 173; *see also Emotional labour*

Extended family: Family Forms, 72; Household, 117; *see also Joint family, Multigenerational households*

External environment: Family Systems, 92; *see also Contexts; Ecological model, Social contexts*

Fairness: Care, 20; *see also Justice*

False consciousness: Conflict Theories, 35; Power, 159; Socialization, 185; *see also Domestic ideology/ideal, Family ideology*

Familialization: Childhood, 28

Family business: Division of Labour, 50

Family culture: Phenomenological Approaches, 151; Social Divisions, 180; *see also Culture*

Family discourse: Family as Discourse, 58

Family economics: Rationalities, 170

Family formation: Family Life Cycle and Life Course, 80; *see also Childbearing, Fertility*

Family ideology: Conflict Theories, 35; Family as Discourse, 59; *see also False consciousness*

Family of affinity: Coupledom, 38; Post-Coupledom; *see also Affinities*

Family of origin: Coupledom, 38; Post-Coupledom, 156

Family therapy: Family Systems, 92

Family ties: Conflict Theories, 35; *see also Ties*

Family time: Family Life Cycle and Life Course, 82

Family traditions: Social Divisions, 180

Family wage: Division of Labour, 47; Fatherhood, 96; Motherhood, 133; New Right, 139; *see also Breadwinner(s), Resource(s)*

Feedback mechanisms: Family Systems, 92; *see also Ecological model*

Femininity: Social Divisions, 181; *see also Roles, Sexuality*

Fertility: Demography, 42; *see also Childbearing, Family formation*

Fictive kin: Biology, 15; Kinship, 129; *see also Elective affinities, Quasi kin*

Financial: Coupledom, 41; *see also Economic transactions, Money, Resources*
    Financial support: Fatherhood, 96; Grandparents, 107; *see also Breadwinner(s), Resource(s)*

First order constructs: Phenomenological Approaches, 151; *see also Second order constructs*

Flexible working hours: Parenthood, 144

Food: Introduction, 7; Coupledom, 38; Family Practices, 89; Home, 113; Household, 115; Kinship, 129; Power, 160; Social Divisions, 182; *see also Consumerism/consumption, Resource(s), Rituals*

Forced marriages: Coupledom, 38; *see also Control*

Foster carer/parents: Care, 18; Parenthood, 142; *see also Social parenting*

Foucauldian approaches: Family as Discourse, 59; *see also Critical discourse analysis*

Freudian approaches: Personal, 148; *see also Psycho-social, Psychoanalytic*

Friends/ship: Coupledom, 40; Families of Choice, 56; Intimacy, 125; Kinship, 130; Post-Coupledom, 155; Public and Private, 167; Siblings, 176; *see also Connectedness, Isolation, Relationality*

Function(s): Comparative Approaches, 31; *see also Role(s)*

Gender/gendered: Care, 17; Demography, 45; Domestic Violence and Abuse, 52; Family Change and Continuity, 65; Family Life Cycle and Life Course, 81; Family Practices, 89; Family Systems, 94; Home, 112; Household, 117; Individualization, 119; Intimacy, 125; Negotiation, 137; Parenthood, 142; Personal, 146; Public and Private, 168; Role Theory, 173; Siblings, 178; Social Divisions, 180; Transnational Families,

190; *see also Domestic ideology; Breadwinner(s); Employment; Equality; Inequality/ies*

  Gender order(s): Coupledom, 37; Post-Coupledom, 153; Public and Private, 166; Social Divisions, 180; *see also Social structure*

  Gender roles: Feminisms, 99; *see also Gender, Gender order(s)*

Genealogy: Biology, 15; *see also Ancestries/Ancestors,Heritage*

Generation/al: Childhood, 28; Coupledom, 38; Family Life Cycle and Life Course, 83; Home, 112; Household, 117; Individualization, 119; Intimacy, 125; Negotiation, 137; Social Divisions, 180; *see also Age, Ancestries/Ancestors*

Genetic(s): Social Divisions, 182; *see also Bodies, Maternal instinct*

  Genetic drive: Rationalities, 170

  Genetic inheritance: Biology, 13; Family Effects, 67

Gifts: Power, 160; *see also Deferential dialectic, Rituals*

Global: Comparative Approaches, 31; *see also Cultural imperialism, Global care chains*

  Global care chains: Care, 19; Transnational Families, 189; *see also Global*

Governance: Child Development, 25; Power, 161; *see also Discourse; Moral evaluations, Welfare state regimes*

Grandchildren: Grandparents, 109; *see also Generation/al*

Grief: Attachment and Loss, 10; *see also Bereavement, Continuing bonds; Death; Dual process model, Widowhood*

Habitus: Social Divisions, 183; Socialization, 186; *see also Internalize/ation, Taken-for-granted*

Head of household: Household, 116; Public and Private, 167; *see also Breadwinner(s), Household reference person, Traditional authority*

Health: Family Policies, 85; *see also Mental ill-health*

Hegemonic: Family as Discourse, 60; *see also Domestic ideology, Family ideology, Governance*

Heritage: Social Divisions, 182; *see also Culture, Genetic(s)*

Hermeneutic: Phenomenological Approaches, 150; *see also Meaning(s)*

Heteronomy: Power, 158; *see also Autonomy, Control*

Heteronormativity: Coupledom, 41; Families of Choice, 57; Family Change and Continuity, 65; Family Systems, 93; *see also Heterosexuality, Sexuality*

Heterosexual/ity: Feminisms, 101; Individualization, 119; Intimacy, 123; New Right, 139; Social Divisions, 181; *see also Heteronormativity*

Historical arc: Family Change and Continuity, 63

Historical time: Family Life Cycle and Life Course, 83; Kinship, 130; *see also Time*

History: Family Practices, 89; Social Divisions, 181; *see also Cohort, Generation/al*

Homemakers: Division of Labour, 47; Home, 112; Rationalities, 170; *see also Expressive role, Housewife*

Homoeostasis: Family Systems, 93; Siblings, 178

Homogamy: Coupledom, 40; Social Divisions, 183

Homosexual: Intimacy, 123; *see also Heteronormativity, Same-sex couples*

Household reference person: Household, 116; *see also Head of household*

Household size: Demography, 44; Family Change and Continuity, 64; *see also Multigenerational households*

Household technologies: Division of Labour, 49; *see also Resource(s), Time use studies*

Housekeeping: Coupledom, 41; *see also Housewife, Work*

Housewife: Division of Labour, 48; Motherhood, 133; *see also Domestic ideology, Wife*

Housework: Division of Labour, 48; Household, 115; *see also Work*

Housing: Family Policies, 85; *see also Resources*

Human capital: Rationalities, 170; *see also Resources*

Hunter-gatherer societies: Biology, 13; *see also Agrarian societies, Pre-industrial*

Husband(s): Division of Labour, 47; Domestic Violence and Abuse, 53; Home, 112; Negotiation, 137; Role Theory, 174; *see also Breadwinner(s), Role(s)*

Identity(ies): Child Development, 24; Childhood, 28; Fatherhood, 95; Feminisms, 101; Home, 111; Individualization, 120; Intimacy, 123; Kinship, 128; Motherhood, 132; Parenthood, 141; Personal, 147; Post-Coupledom, 154; Role Theory, 173; Siblings, 178; Social Divisions, 179; Transitional Families, 188; *see also Personhood, (the) Self*

Income: Family Policies, 85; *see also Equality, Inequality/ies, Money, Resource(s)*

Independence/t: Child Development, 23; Coupledom, 39; Personal, 146; *see also Autonomy, Dependency, Heteronomy, Interdependence, Vulnerability*

(the) Individual(s): Child Development, 23; *see also Biography/ies, Time*

Individual biographies: Family Life Cycle and Life Course, 81

Individual time: Family Life Cycle and Life Course, 82

Individualism: Family Change and Continuity, 65; Individualization, 120; Intimacy, 124; New Right, 139

Individuality: Individualization, 121; Motherhood, 134

Industrial (/ized, Societies): Division of Labour, 46; Family Change and Continuity, 63; *see also Agrarian societies*

> **Industrialization:** Comparative Approaches, 31; Coupledom, 39; Family Change and Continuity, 63; Family Forms, 72; Home, 111; Motherhood, 133; Public and Private, 166; *see also Economic determinism*

Inequality/ies: Care, 19; Conflict Theories, 34; Domestic Violence and Abuse, 52; Home, 112; Negotiation, 137; Parenthood, 144; Power, 159; Problem Families, 163; Public and Private, 166; Role Theory, 175; Social Divisions, 179; Socialization, 185; *see also Class, Equality, Exploitation, Resource(s)*

Inherit/ed/ance: Biology, 13; Conflict Theories, 36; Coupledom, 39; Family Law, 76; Social Divisions, 180; *see also Genetic inheritance*

Institution: Conflict Theories, 36; Motherhood, 131; *see also Social structure*

> **Institutionalized/ation:** Childhood, 26; Parenthood, 141; Personal, 146

Instrumental role(s): Functionalism, 104; Role Theory, 173; *see also Role(s)*

Intensive mothering: Motherhood, 134; *see also Responsibilization*

Interactional sociolinguistics: Family as Discourse, 59

Interdependence/t: Care, 20; Division of Labour, 47; Family Systems, 91; Individualization, 121; Power, 160; *see also Autonomy, Connectedness, Dependency, Independence/t, Vulnerability*

Intergenerational mobility: Social Divisions, 182; *see also Class, Habitus*

Intermarriage: Social Divisions, 182; *see also Endogamy, Homogamy*

Internal psychic experience: Personal, 147

Internal psychic life: Child development, 23

index of sub-concepts

Internalize/ation: Functionalism, 104; Socialization, 185; *see also Psycho-social*

Interpretivism: Phenomenological Approaches, 150; *see also Social constructionism/t*

Intersectionality: Feminisms, 101; Motherhood, 132; Social Divisions, 183; *see also Class, Diversity, Ethnic/ity, Gender*

Intersubjectivity: Motherhood, 134; Personal, 148; *see also Connectedness, Love, Psycho-social, Relationality, Subjectivity*

Isolation: Motherhood, 133

Joint family: Family Forms, 72; *see also Extended family*

Justice: Care, 19; *see also Fairness*

Kin: Comparative Approaches, 32; *see also Fictive kin, Quasi kin*
    Kin-keeping: Kinship, 129

Labour: Household, 117; Intimacy, 125; Social Divisions, 181; *see also Breadwinner(s), Emotional labour, Employment, Exploitation, Housewife, Surplus labour value, Work*
    Labour market: Transnational Families, 189; *see also Economic determinism*

Language: Family as Discourse, 59

Late or high modernity: Family Change and Continuity, 63; *see also Postmodernity*

LATs: Family Forms, 71; *see Living-apart-together*

Legitimacy/ation: Family Law, 77; Fatherhood, 96; *see also Births outside marriage, Marriage, Patriarchy*

Leisure: Coupledom, 40; Family Practices, 89; *see also Time*

Liable relatives: Family Law, 78; *see also Obligation(s), Responsibility/ies*

Life chances: Family Effects, 67; Social Divisions, 179

Life expectancy: Personal, 147; Post-Coupledom, 154

Life history/ies: Family Effects, 67; Family Life Cycle and Life Course, 81; Family Practices, 90; *see also Biography/ies, Trajectory*

Life span: Demography, 44; Family Life Cycle and Life Course, 81; Motherhood, 134

Lineage: Grandparents, 108; Household, 117; *see also Ancestries/ Ancestors, Heritage, Matrilineal, Patrilineal*

Linked lives: Family Life Cycle and Life Course, 82

Liquid love: Individualization, 119; Intimacy, 123; *see also Emotions/al, Love*

Living-apart-together (LATs): Coupledom, 41; Household, 117; *see also Non-resident*

Locality: Coupledom, 40; *see also Ecological model, Localized networks, Social contexts, Space*

Localized networks: Motherhood, 133; *see also Community mothering, Isolation*

Locus of control: Power, 158; *see also Control*

Lone father: Fatherhood, 98; *see also Lone parent*

index of sub-concepts

Lone mother(s)/hood: Comparative Approaches, 30; Family Change and Continuity, 64; Family Policies, 86; Motherhood, 132; Rationalities, 170; *see also Lone parent, Never-married motherhood, Single mother(s)*
    Lone mother households: Family Change and Continuity, 64

Lone parent (families): Family Forms, 73; Problem Families, 163

Longitudinal studies: Family Effects, 67; *see also Qualitative longitudinal research*

Looked after children: Problem Families, 164

Love: Attachment and Loss, 9; Care, 17; Coupledom, 41; Domestic Violence and Abuse, 53; Families of Choice, 56; Intimacy, 123; Post-Coupledom, 154; Power, 161; Role Theory, 175; *see also Liquid love, Romantic love*

Macro: Child Development, 24; Family Change and Continuity, 62; Family Life Cycle and Life Course, 82; Phenomenological Approaches, 150; Power, 158; Public and Private, 168; Socialization, 184; *see also Economic choice determinism, Institution*
> **Macro social level:** Functionalism, 104
> **Macro social order:** Conflict Theories, 34; *see also Institution, Social structure*
> **Macro system:** Child Development, 24

Male breadwinner (family): Feminisms, 99; Social Divisions, 182; *see also Breadwinner(s)*

Marital breakdown: Family Policies, 84; *see also Divorce*

Marital conversation: Negotiation, 136; *see also Social constructionism*

Marital rape: Domestic Violence and Abuse, 53

Marriage: Comparative Approaches, 31; Coupledom, 37; Demography, 42; Division of Labour, 47; Family Law, 77; Family Life Cycle and Life Course, 80; Family Practices, 88; Fatherhood, 96; Feminisms, 100; Household, 115; Kinship, 127; Negotiation, 135; New Right, 138; Phenomenological Approaches, 151; Rationalities, 170; Role Theory, 174; Social Divisions, 181, Transnational Families, 188; *see also Civil partnership, Heteronormativity, Heterosexuality, Husband, Wife*
> **Marriage rates:** Family Change and Continuity, 64

Masculinity: Social Divisions, 181; *see also Femininity, Heteronormativity, Heterosexuality*

Mass media: Family Change and Continuity, 62

Material/ity: Family as Discourse, 61; Transnational Families, 189; *see also Resource(s)*

Maternal instinct: Biology, 13; *see also Genetics*

Maternal thinking: Care, 19; Feminisms, 102; Motherhood, 131

Matriarchal: Kinship, 127; *see also Authority*

Matrifocal: Grandparents, 108; Household, 117; Kinship, 127

Matrilineal: Kinship, 127; *see also Lineage, Patrilineal*

Meaning(s): Comparative Approaches, 32; Family Practices, 89; Home, 112; Phenomenological Approaches, 150; *see also Hermeneutic*
 Meaning reconstruction: Phenomenological Approaches, 152; *see also Definition of the situation, Interpretivism*

Measure: Comparative Approaches, 32; *see also Quantitative*

Mental ill-health: Problem Families, 163; *see also Health*

Meta-system: Family Systems, 92; *see also Ecological model, Macro*

Micro: Family Change and Continuity, 62; Family Life Cycle and Life Course, 82; Phenomenological Approaches, 150; Power, 158; Public and Private, 168; Socialization, 184; *see also Social interactionism*
 Micro interactions: Conflict Theories, 34; Functionalism, 104; *see also Dailiness, Everyday experience*

Middle class: Child Development, 25; Fatherhood, 98; Motherhood, 133; Problem Families, 165; *see also Bourgeois family form, Capitalism, Class, Inequality/ies, White middle class, Working class*

Migration: Demography, 42; Family Forms, 72; Motherhood, 132; Transnational Families, 188

Models: Family Effects, 69; *see also Ecological model*

Modernity: Childhood, 26; Family Change and Continuity, 63; Individualization, 119; *see also Industrialization, Postmodernity*

Money: Introduction, 7; Intimacy, 125; Power, 159; *see also Resource(s)*

Monogamy/ous: Coupledom, 38; Family Forms, 72; New Right, 138; *see also Marriage, Polygamy*

Moral: Family Practices, 88; Fatherhood, 97; Individualization, 121; Intimacy, 124; Parenthood, 143; Problem Families, 163; *see also Children's 'needs', Evaluation(s)*
    Moral decay: New Right, 139
    Moral evaluations: Motherhood, 133
    Moral rationalities: Rationalities, 170; *see also Gender*
    Moral values: New Right, 139

Mortality: Demography, 42; *see also Death, Life span*
    Mortality rates: Social Divisions, 182

Multidimensional developmental pathways: Family Life Cycle and Life Course, 82; *see also Trajectory*

Multigenerational households: Family Change and Continuity, 64; *see also Extended family, Household size*

Narrative: Phenomenological Approaches, 150; *see also Biography/ies, Life history/ies, Meaning(s)*

Nation states: Comparative Approaches, 31; Demography, 42; Transitional families, 190; *see also Citizenship, Welfare state regimes*

Natural: Domestic Violence and Abuse, 54; Family Practices, 88; Public and Private, 168

Nature: Biology, 14; Kinship, 128

Nature versus nurture: Biology, 14; *see also Nurture*

Neglect: Problem Families, 162; *see also Abuse, Child neglect*

Neo-liberalism: New Right, 138

Never-married motherhood: Motherhood, 132; *see also Lone mother(s)/hood*

Non-resident: Biology, 13; *see also Co-resident/ce, Living-apart-together (LATs)*
> **Non-resident father:** Family Forms, 74; *see also Absent father*

Nuclear: Demography, 45
> **Nuclear family/ies:** Conflict theories, 35; Family Change and Continuity, 63; Family Forms, 72; Family Life Cycle and Life Course, 80; Family Policies, 85; Family Systems, 93; Functionalism, 104; Household, 117; Kinship, 127; New Right, 138; Parenthood, 141; *see also Traditional family*
> **Nuclear family household:** Conflict Theories, 35

Nurture: Care, 17; *see also Nature*

Object relations theory: Attachment and Loss, 9; Child Development, 23; Personal, 148; *see also Psycho-social, Psychoanalytic*

Obligation(s): Coupledom, 39; Family Law, 76; Family Policies, 85; Feminisms, 102; Grandparents, 107; Intimacy, 124; Negotiation, 136; Parenthood, 143; Social Divisions, 180; Transnational Families, 188; *see also Responsibility/ies*

Old age: Family Life Cycle and Life Course, 81; *see also Elder abuse*

Ontological security: Phenomenological Approaches, 151; Socialization, 186; *see also Trust*

Outcomes: Child Development, 23; Family Effects, 68; Power, 158; Siblings, 177; *see also Causal laws*

Parental leave: Family Policies, 86

Parenting: Child Development, 23; Family Law, 77; Post-coupledom, 156

Parenting skills: Parenthood, 143; Problem Families, 164

Parenting styles: Family Effects, 67; Social Divisions, 182; *see also Cultural relativism/t, Evaluation(s)*

Paternal engagement: Fatherhood, 97

Paternity leave: Parenthood, 144

Patriarchal: Domestic Violence and Abuse, 52; Kinship, 127; New Right, 140; *see also Deferential dialectic*

Patriarchy: Conflict Theories, 36; Fatherhood, 95; Feminisms, 100; Power, 158; Role Theory, 175; Social Divisions, 181; *see also Head of household, Traditional authority*

Patrifocal: Grandparents, 108; Kinship, 127

Patrilineal: Fatherhood, 95; Kinship, 127; *see also Ancestries/Ancestors; Lineage, Matrilineal*

Personal-kind terms: Kinship, 129

Personal life: Family Practices, 90

Personality: Personal, 146; Socialization, 185; *see also (the) Self*

Personhood: Child Development, 23; Kinship, 128; Personal, 147; *see also Status*

Plastic sexuality: Individualization, 119; Intimacy, 123; *see also Sexuality*

Polyamory: Coupledom, 41

Polygamy: Coupledom, 38; *see also Monogamy/ous*

Populations: Demography, 42
    Population studies: Demography, 45

Post-structuralist: Family as Discourse, 59

Postmodernity: Family Change and Continuity, 63; Family Life Cycle and Life Course, 83; *see also Modernity*

Poverty: Family Life Cycle, 80; Feminisms, 100; Household, 117; Power, 158; Problem Families, 162; *see also Inequality/ies, Resource(s)*

Pre-industrial: Division of Labour, 46; *see also Agrarian societies, Hunter-gatherer societies, Industrialization*

Predict: Family Effects, 69; *see also Causal laws*

Primary carers: Fatherhood, 97

Primary social world: Socialization, 186; *see also Social constructionist/m*

Primary socialization: Socialization, 184

Privacy: Grandparents, 109; Home, 112; Public and Private, 166

Property: Family Law, 76; Household, 117; Kinship, 128; *see also Class, Inequality/ies, Resource(s)*

Protection: Care, 18; *see also Maternal thinking, Nurture*

Psychic capacity: Motherhood, 132

Psychic processes: Social Divisions, 181; *see also Internal psychic life, Intersubjectivity, Psycho-social*

Psycho-dynamics: Siblings, 178; *see also Psycho-social*

index of sub-concepts

Psycho-social (approaches): Introduction, 7; Personal, 148; Pheno-menological Approaches, 150; *see also Internalize/ation, Intersubjectivity*

Psycho-social transition: Attachment and Loss, 11; Post-Coupledom, 155

Psychoanalytic: Personal, 148; *see also Freudian approaches*

Psychoanalytic psychology: Child Development, 22; *see also Object relations theory*

Psychoanalytic theory: Siblings, 177

Public law: Family Law, 76; *see also Common law*

Public sphere: Motherhood, 133; *see also Domestic space/sphere*

Pure relationship(s): Coupledom, 40; Intimacy, 124; *see also Democra-tization, Equalities, Love*

Qualitative: Comparative Approaches, 30; Family Effects, 67; *see also Biography/ies, Life history/ies, Meanings*
    Qualitative longitudinal research: Family Life Cycle and Life Course, 81

Quantitative: Comparative Approaches, 30; Family Change and Continuity, 64; Family Effects, 67; *see also Measure, Statistical association*

Quasi kin: Kinship, 129; *see also Elective affinities, Fictive kin*

Race: Care, 19; Comparative Approaches, 30; Problem Families, 164; Social Divisions, 181; *see also Diversity, Ethnic/ity, Inequality/ies*
    Race/ethnicity: Personal, 146; Siblings 178; *see also Ethnic/ity*

Rates: Demography, 43

Rational choice theory: Rationalities, 169; *see also Decision making*

Rational economic actor: Personal, 146; *see also Moral rationalities*

Rational economic choice: Division of Labour, 47; Domestic Violence and Abuse, 53

Reciprocity: Care, 18; Coupledom, 38; Family Law, 78; Intimacy, 124; Siblings, 176; Transnational Families, 189; *see also Asymmetrical, Obligation(s)*

Reconstituted families: *see Step-families*

Relatedness: Kinship, 129; Parenthood, 144; *see also Affinities, Connectedness, Kin*

Relationality: Personal, 148; *see also Intersubjectivity*

Relatives: Kinship, 129; *see also Extended family*

Religion: Family Change and Continuity, 62; Family Law, 75; Individualization, 119; Social Divisions, 181; *see also Secularization*

Remarriage: Post-Coupledom, 156; *see also Step-families*

Reproduction: Conflict Theories, 35; Coupledom, 37; Individualization, 119; Intimacy, 123; Kinship, 127; Parenthood, 142; Socialization, 185; Transnational Families, 188; *see also Childbirth*

Reproductive technology/ies: Biology, 16; Fatherhood, 96; Feminisms, 101; Kinship, 130; Motherhood, 131; New Right, 139; Parenthood, 143; *see also Surrogacy*

Resemblances: Biology, 15; Social Divisions, 180; *see also Genetic(s)*

Residence: Family Forms, 71; Household, 115; Post-Coupledom, 156; Siblings, 178; Transnational Families, 188; *see also Co-resident/ce and Non-resident*

Resilience: Family Effects, 69; *see also Risks*

Resource(s): Conflict Theories 36; Domestic Violence and Abuse, 53; Fatherhood, 96; Home, 112; Household, 117; Kinship, 127; Power, 159; Social Divisions, 179; *see also Money, Poverty, Property*
    Resource theory: Division of Labour, 47; *see also Decision making*

Responsibility/ies: Care, 18; Family Law, 75; Family Practices, 88; Fatherhood, 97; Home, 113; Negotiation, 136; New Right, 140; *see also Obligation(s)*

Responsibilization: Parenthood, 144

Retrospective: Family Effects, 67; *see also Life history/ies*

Right(s): Coupledom, 39; Family Law, 76; Grandparents, 110; *see also Justice*

Risk: Domestic Violence and Abuse, 54; Intimacy, 124; *see also Resilience*
    Risk factor: Family Effects, 68; *see also Outcomes*

Rituals: Coupledom, 38; Grandparents, 109; Kinship, 129; Transnational Families, 188; *see also Food, Gifts, Weddings*

Role(s): Care, 18; Intimacy, 123 *see also Gender/gendered, Status*
    Role allocation: Functionalism, 104
    Role reversal: Role Theory, 174; *see also Gender/gendered*

Romantic love: Coupledom, 39; Intimacy, 124; *see also Liquid love, Love*

Roots: Biology 15; *see also Ancestries/Ancestors, Genealogy*

Ruling class: Conflict Theories, 35; *see also Class, Middle class, Working class, Surplus labour value*

Same-sex couples: Coupledom 41; Family Forms, 71; Social Divisions, 181; *see also Heteronormativity*

Same-sex marriage: Coupledom, 38; Families of Choice, 56; *see also Civil partnerships; Marriage*

Schooling: Childhood , 26; Divisions of Labour, 47; Home, 113; *see also Education*

Secondary socialization: Socialization, 184; *see also Primary socialization*

Second order constructs: Phenomenological Approaches, 151; *see also First order constructs*

Second wave feminism: Division of Labour, 48

Secularization: Post-Coupledom, 154; *see also Industrialization, Religion*

Selection effects: Family Effects, 69; *see also Statistical association*

(the) Self : Introduction, 7; Child Development, 24; Family Practices, 88; Individualization, 120; Intimacy, 124; Personal, 147; Phenomenological Approaches, 150; *see also Autonomy/ous , Identity(ies), Personhood*

Self-disclosure: Intimacy, 123; *see also Trust*

Separation: Attachment and Loss, 9; Transnational Families, 189

Separation rates: Post-Coupledom, 155

Sex: Social Divisions, 180; *see also Fertility, Gender/gendered, Nature*
    Sexual abuse: Domestic Violence and Abuse, 52; *see also Child abuse*
    Sexual fulfilment: Coupledom, 40
    Sexual union: Coupledom, 41
    Sexuality: Feminisms, 100; Motherhood, 132; Siblings, 178; *see also Heteronormativity, Heterosexuality*

Shell institutions: Individualization, 119; *see also Institution*

Significant other: Socialization, 185; *see also Primary socialization*

Single mother(s): Family Forms, 73; New Right, 139; *see also Lone mother(s)/hood, Lone parent (families), Never-married mother/hood*

Sisters: Biology, 15

Social authoritarianism: New Right, 138; *see also Tradition*

Social capital: Problem Families, 163; Rationalities, 171; *see also Resources*

Social constructionism/t: Child Development, 24; Family as Discourse, 59; Phenomenological Approaches, 150; Siblings, 178; *see also Interpretivism*

Social contexts: Domestic Violence and Abuse, 55; *see also Contexts; Ecological Model*

Social controls: Post-Coupledom, 154; *see also Control*

Social father: Fatherhood, 96; *see also Step-families*

Social interactionism: Phenomenological Approaches, 150; *see also Social constructionism, Micro*

Social order: Functionalism, 105; Phenomenological Approaches, 151; Socialization, 185; *see also Control, Responsibilization*

Social parenting: Family Law, 77; *see also Adoptive parents, Step-families, Social father*

Social structure: Social Divisions, 179; *see also Institutions, Macro*

Social system: Socialization, 185

Socially excluded: Problem Families, 163; *see also Poverty*

Socio-biology: Biology, 13

Solo living: Demography, 44; Household, 115

Son(s): Domestic Violence and Abuse, 54; Motherhood, 132; Parenthood, 142; Role Theory, 173; *see also Daughter(s)*

Spaces: Childhood, 27; *see also Locality*

Stabilization of adult personalities: Functionalism, 104; *see also Social order*

State intervention: Family Policies, 84; *see also Evaluation(s), Governance, Welfare State regimes*

Statistical association: Family Effects, 68; *see also Causal laws, Quantitative*

Statistical data banks: Comparative Approaches, 32; *see also Quantitative*

Status: Family Law, 75; Negotiation, 136; Parenthood, 141; *see also Role(s)*

Step-cluster(s): Family Forms, 73; *see also Step-families*

Step-families: Family Forms, 73; Family Law, 77; Parenthood, 143; *see also Social parenting*

Step-father(s): Fatherhood, 97, Role Theory, 173; *see also Social father*

Step-grandparenting: Grandparents, 108

Step-mothers: Motherhood, 132

Step-parenthood: Post-Coupledom, 156

Step-parents: Parenthood, 142

Stratification: Social Divisions, 179

Structuralist: Role Theory, 173; *see also Macro*

Subconscious: Personal, 148; *see also Freudian approaches, Internal psychic life, Psychoanalytic*

Subjectivity: Introduction, 7; Personal, 147; *see also Internal psychic life, Intersubjectivity, Psycho-social, Self*

Substitution model: Post-Coupledom, 156; *see also Durability model*

Surplus labour value: Conflict Theories, 35; *see also Exploitation*

Surrogacy: Parenthood, 143; *see also Childbirth, Reproductive technology/ies*

index of sub-concepts

Surveys: Demography, 43; Household, 115; *see also Quantitative*

Symbolic interactionism/t: Family as Discourse, 59; Role Theory, 173; Socialization, 185; *see also Micro, Social constructionism*

Symmetrical family/ies: Coupledom, 40; Division of Labour, 48; *see also Equality, Sharing*

Taken-for-granted: Socialization, 186; *see also Dailiness, Everyday experience*

Technologies: Family as Discourse, 60

Teenage mothers: Motherhood, 132; *see Adolescence, Never-married motherhood*

Ties: Demography, 44; Transnational Families, 188; *see also Affinities, Connectedness, Family ties, Relationality*

Time: Introduction, 7; Family Life Cycle and Life Course, 79; Family Systems, 93; Home, 112; Negotiation, 136; Power, 159; Public and Private, 167; Siblings, 177; Transnational Families, 188; *see also Family time, Historical time, Individual time, Social time, Leisure*
    Time period: Demography, 45; *see also History*
    Time use studies: Division of Labour, 49

Tradition: Family Change and Continuity, 63; Intimacy, 124; *see also Family culture, Family traditions, Rituals*
    Traditional authority: Power, 160; *see also Authority*
    Traditional family: Family Forms, 72; *see also Nuclear Family/ies*

Trajectory: Demography, 44; Family Life Cycle and Life Course, 82; *see also Life span, Multidimensional developmental pathways*

Transnationalism: Feminisms, 101; *see also Diasporic, Nation States*

Trust: Siblings, 176; Socialization, 186

Turning point: Family Life Cycle and Life Course, 82

Underclass: Problem Families, 163; *see also Class, Inequality/ies*

Violence: Feminisms, 99; Home, 112; *see also Control, Marital rape*

Vulnerability: Care, 20; Domestic Violence and Abuse, 54; *see also Dependency/dependent, Interdependence/t*

Wages for housework: Division of Labour, 48; Feminisms, 100; *see also Money, Resource(s), Work*

Ways of being: Public and Private, 167

Weddings: Kinship, 129; *see also Consumerism/consumption, Rituals*

Welfare benefits: Family Law, 76; Problem Families, 163; *see also Justice, Underclass*

Welfare state: Comparative Approaches, 30; Home, 113; Individualization 121; New Right, 139

Welfare state regimes: Family Policies, 85

Widowhood: Family Forms 73; Post-Coupledom, 156; *see also Death, Grief*

Wife/ves: Division of Labour, 47; Negotiation, 137; *see also Husband(s), Marriage*

   Wife-battering: Domestic Violence and Abuse, 54; *see also Violence*

Women's work: Feminisms, 100

Work: Introduction, 7; Care, 18; Family Life Cycle and Life Course, 82; Motherhood, 133; Public and Private, 166; Rationalities, 171; *see also Employment*

Work–family balance: Role Theory, 174

Work–life balance: Family Policies, 87

index of sub-concepts

Working class: Conflict Theories, 35; Coupledom, 39; Domestic Violence and Abuse, 55; Fatherhood, 98; Home, 113; Household, 116; Motherhood, 132; Problem Families, 162; *see also Class, Exploitation, Surplus labour value*

Youth: Family Life Cycle and Life Course, 81; *see also Adolescence*

references

Abbasi-Shivazi, M.J. and McDonald, P. (2008) 'Family change in Iran: religion, revolution, and the State', in R. Jayakody, A. Thornton and W.G Axinn (eds), *International Family Change: Ideational Perspectives*. New York: Lawrence Erlbaum Associates.

Abbott, P. and Wallace, C. (1992) *The Family and the New Right*. London: Pluto Press.

Abbott, P. and Wallace, C. (1997) *An Introduction to Sociology: Feminist Perspectives* (2nd edn). London: Routledge.

Agathonos-Georgopoulou, H. (2006) 'Cross-cultural perspectives in child abuse and neglect', *Child Abuse Review*, 1 (2): 80–8.

Alanen, L. (2001) 'Explorations in generational analysis', in L. Alanen and B. Mayall (eds), *Conceptualising Child–Adult Relations*. London: Routledge.

Alanen, L. and Bardy, M. (1991) Childhood as Social Phenomenon: National Report for Finland. *Eurosocial Report*. Vienna: European Centre for Social Welfare.

Aldous, J. (1995) 'New views of grandparents in intergenerational context', *Journal of Family Issues*, 15 (1): 104–22.

Allan, G. (1996) *Kinship and Friendship in Modern Britain*. Oxford: Oxford University Press.

Allan, G. (2005) 'Boundaries of friendship', in L. McKie and S. Cunningham-Burley (eds), *Families in Society: Boundaries and Relationships*. Bristol: Policy Press.

Allan, G. and Crow, G. (2001) *Families, Households and Society*. Basingstoke, Hants: Palgrave.

Allen, K.R. (2000) 'A conscious and inclusive Family Studies', *Journal of Marriage and Family*, 62 (1): 4–17.

Allen, K.R. (2009) 'Reclaiming feminist theory, methods, and praxis for family studies', in S.A. Lloyd, A.L. Few and K.R. Allen (eds), *Handbook of Feminist Family Studies*. Los Angeles: Sage, pp. 3–17.

Alwin, D.F. (2007) 'Parenting practices', in J. Scott, J. Treas and M. Richards (eds), *The Blackwell Companion to the Sociology of Families*. Malden, MA: Blackwell, pp. 142–57.

Amato, P. (2004) 'Divorce in social and historical context: changing scientific perspectives on children and marital dissolution,' in M. Coleman and L.H. Ganong (eds), *Handbook of Contemporary Families: Considering the Past, Contemplating the Future*. Thousand Oaks, CA: Sage, pp. 265–81.

Anderson, M. (1971) *Family Structure in Nineteenth Century Lancashire*. Cambridge: Cambridge University Press.

Anthias, F. (2005) 'Social stratification and social inequality: models of intersectionality and identity', in F. Devine, M. Savage, J. Scott and R. Crompton (eds), *Rethinking Class: Culture, Identities and Lifestyle*. Basingstoke, Hants: Palgrave Macmillan, pp. 24–45.

Apthekar, B. (1989) *Tapestries of Life: Women's Work, Women's Consciousness and the Meaning of Daily Experience*. Amherst, MA: University of Massachusetts Press.

Archard, D. (1993) *Children, Rights and Childhood*. London: Routledge.

Backett, K. (1982) *Mothers and Fathers: A Study of the Development and Negotiation of Parental Behaviour*. London: Macmillan.

Bailey-Harris, R. (ed.) (2000) *New Families for a New Society?* Family Law: Essays for a New Millennium. Bristol: Jordan Publishing.

Ballard, R. (1994) *Desh Pardesh: The South Asian Presence in Britain*. London: Hurst.

Bank, S. and Kahn, M. (1982) *The Sibling Bond*. New York: Basic Books.

Barlow, A., Duncan, S. and James, G. (2002) 'New Labour, the rationality mistake and family policy in Britain', in A. Carling, S. Duncan and R. Edwards (eds), *Analysing Families: Morality and Rationality in Policy and Practice*. London: Routledge.

Barlow, A., Duncan, S., James, G. and Park, A. (2005) *Cohabitation, Marriage and the Law: Social Change and Legal Reform in the 21st Century*. Oxford: Hart.

Barlow, A., Burgoyne, C., Clery, E. and Smithson J. (2008) 'Cohabitation and the law: myths, money and the media', in A. Park, J. Curtice, K. Thomson, M. Phillips, M. Johnson and E. Clery (eds), *British Social Attitudes: the 24th Report*. London: Sage, pp. 29–52.

Barlow, J., Shaw, R. and Stewart-Brown, S. (2004) *Parenting Programmes and Minority Ethnic Families*. London: National Children's Bureau/Joseph Rowntree Foundation.

Barrett, M. and MacIntosh, M. (1982) *The Anti-Social Family*. London: Verso.

Bauman, Z. (2001) *The Individualized Society*. Cambridge: Polity Press.

Bauman, Z. (2003) *Liquid Love: On the Frailty of Human Bonds*. Cambridge: Polity Press.

Baumle, A.K. (ed.) (2006) *Demography in Transition: Emerging Trends in Population Studies*. Newcastle: Cambridge Scholars Press.

Baumrind, D. (1989) 'Rearing competent children', in W. Damon (ed.), *Child Development Today and Tomorrow*. San Francisco: Jossey-Bass.

Beck, U. (1992) *Risk Society: Towards a New Modernity*. London: Sage.

Beck, U. (1997) 'Democratisation of the family', *Childhood*, 4 (2): 151–68.

Beck, U. and Beck-Gernsheim, E. (1995) *The Normal Chaos of Love*. Cambridge: Polity Press.

Beck, U. and Beck-Gernsheim, E. (2002) *Individualisation*. London: Sage.

Becker, G. (1976) *The Economic Approach to Human Behaviour*. Chicago: University of Chicago Press.

Becker, G. (1996) *Accounting for Tastes*. Cambridge, MA: Harvard University Press.

Beck-Gernsheim, E. (1998) 'On the way to a post-familial family: from a community of need to elective affinities', *Theory, Culture and Society*, 15 (3–4): 53–70.

Bell, C. and Newby, H. (1976) 'Husbands and wives: the dynamics of the deferential dialectic', in D. Barker and S. Allen (eds), *Dependence and Exploitation in Work and Marriage*. London: Longman.

Bell, L. and Ribbens, J. (1994) 'Isolated housewives and complex maternal worlds: the significance of social contacts between women with young children in industrialised societies', *Sociological Review*, 42 (2): 227–62.

Belsky, J. (2007) 'Childcare matters', in J. Oates (ed.), *Attachment Relationships: Quality of Care for Young Children*. Milton Keynes: The Open University.

Belsky, J. and Pluess, M. (2010) 'The nature (and nurture?) of plasticity in early human development', *Perspectives in Psychological Science*, 4: 345–51.

Benavente, J. and Gains, S. (2008) Families of Choice. http://www.ext.colostate.edu/pubs/COLUMNCC/cc050111.html, Colorado State University (accessed 31 March 2010).

Bengston, V., Biblarz, T. and Roberts, R. (2002) *How Families Still Matter: A Longitudinal Analysis of Youth in Two Generations.* Cambridge: Cambridge University Press.

Benhabib, S. (1998) 'Models of public space: Hannah Arendt, the liberal tradition, and Jurgen Habermas', in J.B. Landes (ed.), *Feminism: the Public and the Private.* Oxford: Oxford University Press.

Benjamin, O. (1998) 'Therapeutic discourse, power and change: emotion and negotiation in marital conversations', *Sociology*, 32: 771–93.

Berger, P.L. and Kellner, H. (1964) 'Marriage and the construction of reality', *Diogenes*, 1–23.

Berger, P.L. and Luckmann, T. (1971) *The Social Construction of Reality: A Treatise in the Sociology of Knowledge.* Harmondsworth: Penguin.

Bernardes, J. (1985) '"Family ideology": identification and exploration', *Sociological Review*, 33: 275–97.

Bernardes, J. (1986) 'Multidimensional developmental pathways: a proposal to facilitate the conceptualisation of "Family Diversity"', *Sociological Review*, 34 (3): 590–610.

Bersani, L. (1995) *Homos.* Cambridge, MA: Harvard University Press.

Bianchi, S.M., Casper, L.M. and Berkow King, R. (eds) (2005) *Work, Family, Health and Well-being.* London: Routledge.

Biddle, B.J. (1986) 'Recent development in role theory', *Annual Review of Sociology*, 12: 67–92.

Blood, R. and Wolfe, D. (1960) *Husbands and Wives.* Glencoe: Free Press.

Bogenschneider, K. (2006) *Family Policy Matters: How Policymaking Affects Families and What Professionals Can Do.* Mahwah, NJ: Lawrence Erlbaum.

Booth, A. and Crouter, A.C. (eds) (2005) *The New Population Problem: Why Families in Developed Countries Are Shrinking and What It Means.* Mahwah, NJ: Lawrence Erlbaum Associates.

Bornstein, M.H. and Cheah, C.S.L. (2006) 'The place of "culture and parenting" in the ecological contextual perspective on developmental science', in K. Rubin and O.B. Chung (eds), *Parenting Beliefs, Behaviors, and Parent-Child Relations: A Cross-Cultural Perspective.* New York: Psychology Press.

Boss, P.G., Doherty, W.J. and LaRossa, R. (eds) (2009) *Sourcebook of Family Theories and Methods: A Contextual Approach.* New York: Springer.

Bott, E. (1957) *Family and Social Networks.* London: Tavistock.

Bourdieu, P. (1990) *The Logic of Practice.* Cambridge: Polity Press.

Bourdieu, P. (1996) 'On the family as a realized category', *Theory, Culture and Society*, 13 (3): 19–26.

Boyden, J. (1997) 'Childhood and the policy makers: a comparative perspective on the globalisation of childhood', in A. James and A. Prout (eds), *Constructing and Reconstructing Childhood: Contemporary Issues in the Sociological Study of Childhood.* Lewes: Falmer.

Boyden, J. (2003) 'Children under fire: challenging assumptions about children's resilience', http://www.colorado.edu/journals/cye/13_1/Vol13_1Articles/CYE_CurrentIssue_Article_ChildrenUnderFire_Boyden.htm (accessed 24 March 2009).

Brannen, J., Heptinstall, E. and Bhopal, K. (2000) *Connecting Children: Care and Family Life in Later Childhood*. London: Routledge Falmer.

Brannen, J. and Nilsen, A. (2005) 'Individualisation, choice and structure: a discussion of current trends in sociological analysis', *The Sociological Review*, 53 (3): 412–28.

Bronfenbrenner, U. (1979) *The Ecology of Human Development*. Cambridge, MA: Harvard University Press.

Brooker, L. and Woodhead, M. (eds) (2008) *Developing Positive Identities: Diversity and Young Children*. Early Childhood in Focus. Milton Keynes: Open University with the Bernard van Leer Foundation.

Broome, D.M., Knafl, K.A., Feetham, S. and Pridham, K. (eds) (1998) *Children and Families in Health and Illness*. London: Sage.

Bryceson, D. and Vuorela, U. (eds) (2002) *The Transnational Family: New European Frontiers and Global Networks*. Oxford: Berg.

Brynin, M. and Ermisch, J. (2009) 'Introduction: the social significance of relationships', in M. Brynin and J. Ermisch (eds), *Changing Relationships*. New York: Routledge, pp. 3–28.

Brynin, M., Longhi, S., Pérez, M. (2009) 'The social significance of homogamy', in M. Brynin and J. Ermisch (eds), *Changing Relationships*. New York: Routledge, pp. 73–90.

Budig, M. (2007) 'Feminism and the family', in J. Scott, J. Treas and M. Richards (eds), *The Blackwell Companion to the Sociology of Families*. Oxford: Blackwell Publishing.

Burman, E. (1994) *Deconstructing Developmental Psychology*. London: Routledge.

Butler, J. (2004) *Undoing Gender*. New York: Routledge.

Byng-Hall, J. (1985) 'Family scripts: a useful bridge between theory and practice', *Journal of Family Therapy*, 7 (3): 301–6.

Bynner, J. (2001) 'Childhood risks and protective factors in social exclusion', *Children and Society*, 15 (5): 285–301.

Caballero, C. and Edwards, R. (2008) *Parenting Mixed Heritage Children: Negotiating Difference and Belonging*. York: Joseph Rowntree Foundation.

Candland, D.K. (1993) *Feral Children and Clever Animals: Reflections on Human Nature*. New York: Oxford University Press.

Carabine, J. (ed.) (2004) *Sexualities*. Bristol: Policy Press.

Carling, A. (1992) *Social Division*. London: Verso.

Carling, A., Duncan, S. and Edwards, R. (eds) (2002) *Analysing Families: Morality and Rationality in Policy and Practice*. London: Routledge.

Carr Steelman, L., Powell, B., Werum, R. and Carter, S. (2002) 'Reconsidering the effects of sibling configuration: recent advances and challenges', *Annual Review of Sociology*, 28: 243–69.

Carrithers, M. (1999) 'Person', in A. Barnard and J. Spencer (eds), *Encyclopedia of Social and Cultural Anthropology*. London: Routledge.

Carsten, J. (2004) *After Kinship: New Departures in Anthropology*. Cambridge: Cambridge University Press.

Casper, L.M. and Bianchi, S.M. (2002) *Continuity and Change in the American Family*. Thousand Oaks, CA: Sage.

Caspi, J. (ed.) (2010) *Sibling Relationships in Practice: Cultural and Environmental Influences*. New York: Springer Publishing.

Celsius (2010) 'Centre for Longitudinal Study Information and User Support', London School of Hygiene and Tropical Medecine, http://www.celsius.lshtm.ac.uk (accessed 13 February 2010).

Chamberlain, M. (1999) 'A lateral perspective on Caribbean families', in E. Silva and C. Smart (eds), *The New Family?* London: Sage.

Chandler Sabourin, T. (2003) *The Contemporary American Family*. Thousand Oaks, CA: Sage.

Charles, N., Davies, C.A. and Harris, C. (2008) *Families in Transition: Social Change, Family Formation and Kin Relationships*. Bristol: Policy Press.

Chase, S.E. and Rogers, M.F. (2001) *Mothers and Children: Feminist Analyses and Personal Narratives*. Chapel Hill, NC: Rutgers University Press.

Cheal, D. (1991) *Family and the State of Theory*. New York: Harvester Wheatsheaf.

Cheal, D. (2002) *Sociology of Family Life*. Basingstoke, Hants: Palgrave Macmillan.

Chodorow, N. (1979) *The Reproduction of Mothering: Psychoanalysis and the Sociology of Gender*. Berkeley, CA: University of California Press. Second edition (1999).

Cicirelli, V. (1994) 'Sibling relationships in cross-cultural perspective', *Journal of Marriage and the Family*, 56: 7–20.

Cieraad, I. (ed.) (1999) *Introduction: Anthropology at Home*. Syracuse, NY: Syracuse University Press.

Clarke, A.M. and Clarke, A.D.B. (1976) *Early Experience: Myth and Evidence*. Chicago: Open Books.

Clarke, A.M. and Clarke, A.D.B. (2000) *Early Experience and the Life Path*. London: Jessica Kingsley.

Clarke, J. and Fink, J. (2008) 'Unsettled attachments: national identity, citizenship and welfare', in W. van Oorschot, M. Opielka and B. Pfau-Effinger (eds), *Culture and Welfare State: Values and Social Policy in Comparative Perspective*. Cheltenham: Edward Elgar, pp. 225–46.

Coleman, J.S. (1988) 'Social capital in the creation of human capital', *American Journal of Sociology*, 94 (Suppl): pp. 95–120.

Coleman, M. and Ganong, L.H. (eds) (2004) *Handbook of Contemporary Families: Considering the Past, Contemplating the Future*. Thousand Oaks, CA: Sage.

Coll, C.G. and Magnuson, K. (2000) 'Cultural differences as sources of developmental vulnerabilities and resources' in J.P. Shonkoff and S.J. Meisels (eds), *Handbook of Early Childhood Intervention* (2nd edn). Cambridge: Cambridge University Press, pp. 94–114.

Collier, R. and Sheldon, S. (eds) (2006) *Fathers' Rights Activism and Law Reform in Comparative Perspective*. Oxford: Hart Publishing.

Collier, R. and Sheldon, S. (2008) *Fragmenting Fatherhood: A Socio-Legal Study*. Oxford: Hart Publishing.

Collins, R. and Coltrane, S. (2001) *Sociology of Marriage and the Family: Gender, Love and Property*. Florence, KY: Wadsworth Publishing Co.

Cooper, C., Selwood, A., Blanchard, M., Walker, Z., Blizard, R. and Livingston, G. (2009) 'Abuse of people with dementia by family carers: representative cross sectional survey', *British Medical Journal*, 338: 1–3.

Crompton, R., Lewis, S. and Lyonette, C. (eds) (2010) *Women, Men, Work, and Family in Europe*. Basingstoke, Hants: Palgrave Macmillan.

Crossley, N. (2001) *Intersubjectivity*. London: Sage.

Crow, G. (2002) *Social Solidarities: Theories, Identities and Social Change*. Buckingham: Open University Press.

Crozier, G. and Reay, D. (2005) *Activating Participation: Parents and Teachers Working Towards Partnership*. Stoke-on-Trent: Trentham.

Cunningham-Burley, S. and Jamieson, L. (eds) (2003) *Families and the State: Changing Relationships*. Basingstoke, Hants: Palgrave Macmillan.

Daly, K. (2003) 'Family theory versus the theories families live by', *Journal of Marriage and Family*, 65: 771–84.

Daly, M. and Wilson, M. (1998) *Truth About Cinderella: A Darwinian View of Parental Love*. London: Weidenfeld and Nicolson.

Davidoff, L. (1995) *Worlds Between: Historical Perspectives on Gender and Class*. Cambridge: Polity Press.

Davidoff, L. and Hall, C. (2002) *Family Fortunes: Men and Women of the English Middle Class 1780–1850*. London: Routledge.

Davidoff, L., Doolittle, M., Fink, J. and Holden, K. (1999) *The Family Story: Blood, Contract and Intimacy, 1830–1960*. London: Longman.

Davies, J. (ed.) (1993) *The Family: Is it Just Another Lifestyle Choice?* London: IEA Health and Welfare Unit.

Dawson, A. and Rapport, N. (1998) *Migrants of Identity*. Oxford: Berg.

De Cruz, P. (2010) *Family Law, Sex and Society: A Comparative Study of Family Law*. Abingdon, London: Routledge.

Delphy, C. and Leonard, D. (1992) *Familiar Exploitation: A New Analysis of Marriage in Contemporary Western Societies*. Cambridge: Polity Press.

Dempsey, K. (1997/1999) *Inequalities in Marriage: Australia and Beyond*. Melbourne: Oxford University Press.

Dench, G. (1997) *Rewriting the Sexual Contract*. London: Institute of Community Studies.

Dench, G. and Ogg, J. (2002) *Grandparenting in Britain: A Baseline Study*. London: Institute of Community Studies.

Denzin, N. (ed.) (2009) *Childhood Socialization*. NJ: Transaction Publishers.

Dermott, E. (2008) *Intimate Fatherhood: A Sociological Analysis*. London: Routledge.

DeVault, M.L. (1991/1994) *Feeding the Family: The Social Organisation of Caring as Gendered Work*. Chicago: University of Chicago Press.

Dilworth-Anderson, P., Burton, L.M. and Boulin Johnson, L. (1993) 'Reframing theories for understanding race, ethnicity and families', in P.G. Boss, W.J. Doherty, R. LaRossa, W.R. Schumm and S.K. Steinmetz (eds), *Sourcebook of Family Theories and Methods*. New York: Plenum Press, pp. 627–49.

Dinnerstein, D. (1987) *The Rocking of the Cradle and the Ruling of the World* (2nd edn). London: The Women's Press.

Doucet, A. (2006) *Do Men Mother? Fathering, Care and Domestic Responsibility.* Toronto: University of Toronto Press.

du Bois-Raymond, M., Sünker, H. and Krüger, H.H. (eds) (2001) *Childhood in Europe: Approaches, Trends, Findings.* New York: Peter Lang Publishing.

Duncan, S. and Edwards, R. (1999) *Lone Mothers, Paid Work and Gendered Moral Rationalities.* London: Macmillan.

Duncan, S. and Phillips, M. (2008) 'New families? Tradition and change in modern relationships', in A. Park, J. Curtice, K. Thomson, M. Phillips, M. Johnson and E. Clery (eds), *British Social Attitudes: the 24th Report.* London: Sage, pp. 1–28.

Duncan, S., Edwards, R. and Alexander, C. (eds) (2010) *Teenage Parenthood: What's the Problem?* London: Tufnell Press.

Dunne, G. (1997) *Lesbian Lifestyles: Women's Work and the Politics of Sexuality.* London: Macmillan.

Dutton, D.G. (2007) 'Female intimate partner violence and developmental trajectories of abusive females', *International Journal of Men's Health*, 6 (1): 54–70.

Edgar, D. (2007) 'Globalization and western bias in family sociology', in J. Scott, J. Treas and M. Richards (eds), *The Blackwell Companion to the Sociology of Families.* Malden, MA: Blackwell.

Edwards, J. (2000) *Born and Bred.* Oxford: Oxford University Press.

Edwards, R. (2002) 'Introduction: conceptualising relationships between home and school in children's lives', in R. Edwards (ed.), *Children, Home and School: Resistance, Autonomy or Connection?* London: Routlege Falmer.

Edwards, R. (2008) 'Introduction', in R. Edwards (ed.), *Researching Families and Communities: Social and Generational Change.* London: Routledge and Kegan Paul, pp. 1–10.

Edwards, R. and Alldred, P. (2000) 'A typology of parental involvement in education centring on children and young people: negotiating familialisation, institutionalisation and indivualisation', *British Journal of Sociology of Education*, 21 (3): 435–55.

Edwards, R. and Gillies, V. (2004) 'Support in parenting: values and consensus concerning who to turn to', *Journal of Social Policy*, 33 (4): 627–47.

Edwards, R. and Weller, S. (eds) (2010) *A Sideways Look at Gender and Sibling Relationships.* New York: Springer Publishing.

Edwards, R., Ribbens McCarthy, J. and Gillies, V. (1999) 'Biological parents and social families: legal discourses and everyday understandings of the position of step-parents', *International Journal of Law, Policy and the Family*, 13: 78–105.

Edwards, R., Bäck-Wiklund, M., Bak, M. and Ribbens McCarthy, J. (2002) Stepfathering: comparing policy and everyday experiences in Britain and Sweden. *Sociological Research Online*, 7 (1) (http://www.socresonline.org.uk/7/1/edwards.html).

Edwards, R., Hadfield, L., Lucey, H. and Mauthner, M. (2006) *Sibling Identity and Relationships.* London: Routledge.

Eekelaar, J. and Nhlapo, T. (eds) (1998) *The Changing Family: International Perspectives on the Family and Family Law.* Oxford: Hart.

Elder, G.H. (1999) *Children of the Great Depression: Social Change in Life Experience, 25th Anniversary Edition.* Boulder, CO: Westview Press.

references

Elder, G.H., Park R.D. and Modell, J. (eds) (1994) *Children in Time and Place: Developmental and Historical Insights*. Cambridge: Cambridge University Press.

Elder, G.H., Johnson, M.K. and Crosnoe, R. (2003) 'The emergence and development of life course theory', in J.T. Mortimer and M.J. Shanahan (eds), *Handbook of the Life Course*. New York: Kluwer Academic/Plenum Publishers.

Elshtain, J.B. (1981) *Public Man, Private Woman*. Princeton NJ: Princeton University Press.

Engels, F. (1884) *The Origin of the Family, Private Property and the State*. http://www.marxists.org/archive/marx/works/1884/origin-family/index.htm (accessed 24 July 2010).

Erel, U. (ed.) (2002) 'Reconceptualising motherhood: Experiences of migrant women from Turkey living in Germany', in D. Bryceson and U. Vuorela (eds), *The Transnational Family: New European Frontiers and Global Networks*. Oxford: Berg.

Esping-Anderson, G. (1990) *The Three Worlds of Welfare Capitalism*. London: Polity Press.

Etzioni, A. and Bloom, J. (2004) *We Are What We Celebrate: Understanding Holidays and Rituals*. New York: New York University Press.

Farmer, A. and Tiefenthaler, J. (1997) 'An economic analysis of domestic violence', *Review of Social Economy*, 55 (3): 337–58.

Farrington, K. and Chertok, E. (2009) 'Social conflict theories of the family', in P.G. Boss, W.J. Doherty, R. LaRossa, W.R. Schumm and S.K. Steinmetz (eds), *Sourcebook of Family Theories and Methods: A Contextual Approach*. New York: Springer, pp. 357–81.

Featherstone, B. (2009) *Contemporary Fathering: Theory, Policy and Practice*. Bristol: Policy Press.

Ferguson, N., Douglas, G., Lowe, N., Murch, M.A. and Robinson, M. (2004) *Grandparenting in Divorced Families*. Bristol: Policy Press.

Ferree, M.M. (1985) 'Between two worlds: German feminist approaches to working class women and work', *Signs*, 10 (2): 517–36.

Fevre, R. (2000) *The Demoralisation of Western Culture*. London: Continuum.

Finch, J. (1989) *Family Obligations and Social Change*. Cambridge: Polity Press.

Finch, J. (2007) 'Displaying families', *Sociology*, 4 (1): 65–81.

Finch, J. and Mason, J. (1993) *Negotiating Family Responsibilities*. London: Routledge.

Fink, J. (2004) 'Questions of care', in J. Fink (ed.), *Care: Personal Lives and Social Policy*. Bristol: Open University/Policy Press.

Firestone, S. (1979) *The Dialectic of Sex: The Case for Feminist Revolution*. London: Women's Press.

Flax, J. (1984) 'Theorising motherhood', *Women's Review of Books*, 1(9).

Fortes, M. (1958) 'Introduction', in J. Goody (ed.), *The Developmental Cycle in Domestic Groups*. New York: Cambridge University Press.

Fortin, J. (2009) 'Children's right to know their origins – too far, too fast?', *Child and Family Law Quarterly*, 21: 336–355.

Fox, R. (1967) *Kinship and Marriage: An Anthropological Perspective*. London: Pelican.

Fraser, N. (1998) 'Sex, lies and the public sphere: reflections on the confirmation of Clarence Thomas', in J.B. Landes (ed.), *Feminism: the Public and the Private*. Oxford: Oxford University Press.

key concepts in family studies

Freeman, T. and Richards, M. (2006) 'DNA testing and kinship: paternity, genealogy and the search for the "truth" of genetic origins', in F. Ebtehaj, B. Lindley and M. Richards (eds), *Kinship Matters*. Oxford: Hart Publishing.

Friedan, B. (1963) *The Feminine Mystique*. London:Victor Gollancz.

Furedi, F. (2001) *Paranoid Parenting: Abandon Your Anxieties and Be a Good Parent*. London: Allen Lane.

Furstenberg, F.F. (1988) 'Good dads – bad dads: two faces of fatherhood', in A.J. Cherlin (ed.), *Making Men Into Fathers: Men, Masculinities and the Social Politics of Fatherhood*. Cambridge: Cambridge University Press.

Gabb, J. (2008) *Researching Intimacy and Sexuality in Families*. Basingstoke, Hants: Palgrave Macmillan.

Garland-Thomson, R. (2006) 'Integrating disability, transforming feminist theory' in L.J. Davis (ed.), *The Disability Studies Reader*. London: Routledge, pp: 257–74.

Garmezy, N. (1994) 'Reflections and commentary on risk, resilience and development', in R.J. Haggerty, L.R. Sherrod, N. Garmezy and M. Rutter (eds), *Stress, Risk and Resilience in Children and Adolescents: Processes, Mechanisms and Interventions*. Cambridge: Cambridge University Press.

Garrett, P.M. (2007) '"Sinbin" solutions: the "pioneer" projects for "problem families" and the forgetfulness of social policy research', *Critical Social Policy*, 27 (2): 203–30.

Gergen, K.J. (2009) *An Invitation to Social Construction*. Thousand Oaks, CA: Sage.

Giddens, A. (1990) *The Consequences of Modernity*. Cambridge: Polity Press.

Giddens, A. (1991) *Modernity and Self Identity: Self and Society in the Late Modern Age*. Cambridge: Polity Press.

Giddens, A. (1992) *The Transformation of Intimacy: Sexuality, Love and Eroticism in Modern Societies*. Cambridge: Polity Press.

Giddens, A. (1998) *The Third Way: The Renewal of Social Democracy*. Cambridge: Polity Press.

Giddens, A. (1999) *Runaway World: How Globalisation is Reshaping Our Lives*. London: Profile.

Gillies, V. (2003) *Family and Intimate Relationships: A Review of the Sociological Literature*. London: London South Bank University, Families and Social Capital Research Group.

Gillies, V. (2007) *Marginalised Mothers: Exploring Working-Class Experiences of Parenting*. London: Routledge.

Gillies, V. (2008) 'Perspectives on parenting responsibility: contextualising values and practices', *Journal of Law and Society*, 35: 95–112.

Gillies, V. and Lucey, H. (2006) '"It's a connection you can't get away from": Brothers, sisters and social capital', *Journal of Youth Studies*, 9 (4): 479–93.

Gilligan, C. (1982) *In a Different Voice: Psychological Theory and Women's Development*. Cambridge, MA: Harvard University Press.

Gillis, J. (1997) *A World of Their Own Making: the History of Myth and Ritual in Family Life*. Oxford: Oxford Paperbacks.

Gittins, D. (1989) *The Family in Question: Changing Households and Familiar Ideologies*. Basingstoke: Macmillan.

Glendon, M.A. (1997) *The Transformation of Family Law: State, Family and Law in the United States and Western Europe*. Chicago: University of Chicago Press.

Glenn, E.N. (1985) 'Racial ethnic women's labor: the intersections of race, gender and class oppression', *Review of Radical Political Economics*, 17 (3): 86–108.

Goffman, E. (1959) *The Presentation of Self in Everyday Life*. New York: Anchor Books.

Goldberg, S. (2000) *Attachment and Development*. New York: Oxford University Press.

Goldthorpe, J.E. (1987) *Family Life in Western Societies: A Historical Sociology of Family Relationships in Britain and North America*. Cambridge: Cambridge University Press.

Golombok, S. (2000) *Parenting: What Really Counts?* London: Routledge.

Gopaul-McNicol, S.-A. (1999) 'Ethnocultural perspectives on childrearing practices in the Caribbean', *International Social Work*, 42 (1): 79–86.

Goulbourne, H., Reynolds, T., Solomos, J. and Zontini, E. (2009) *Transnational Families: Ethnicities, Identities and Social Capital*. Abingdon. London: Routledge.

Gray, A. (2006) The time economy of parenting. *Sociological Research Online*, 11 (3) http://www.socresonline.org.uk.libezproxy.open.ac.uk/11/3/gray.html (accessed 22 June 2009).

Greenstein, T.N. (2006) *Methods of Family Research*. Thousand Oaks, CA: Sage.

Gubrium, J.F. and Holstein, J.A. (1990) *What Is Family?* Mountain View, CA: Mayfield Publishing.

Gubrium, J.F. and Holstein, J.A. (2000) *Constructing the Life Course*. Dix Hills, NY: General Hall.

Gubrium, J.F. and Holstein, J.A. (2009) 'Phenomenology, ethnomethodology, and family discourse', in P.G. Boss, W.J. Doherty, R. LaRossa, W.R. Schumm and S.K. Steinmetz (eds), *Sourcebook of Family Theories and Methods: A Contextual Approach*. New York: Springer, pp. 651–72.

Gustafson, D.L. (2005) *Unbecoming Mothers: The Social Production of Maternal Absence*. Bingham, NY: Haworth Clinic Practice Press.

Hackstaff, K.B. (2009) '"Turning points" for aging genealogists: claiming identities and histories in time', *Qualitative Sociology Review* 5(1), www.qualitativesociologyreview. org.

Hantrais, L. (2004) *Family Policy Matters: Responding to Family Change in Europe*. Bristol: Policy Press.

Hareven, T. (1993) *The Home and Family in Historical Perspective*, in A. Mack, *Home: A Place in the World*. New York: New York University Press.

Hartmann, H. (1979) 'The unhappy marriage of Marxism and feminism: towards a more progressive union', *Capital and Class*, 8: 1–33.

Haskey, J. (1994) 'Stepfamilies and stepchildren in Great Britain', *Population Trends* 76: 17–28.

Hays, S. (1996) *The Cultural Contradictions of Motherhood*. New Haven, CT: Yale University Press.

Hearn, J. and Pringle, K. (eds) (2003) 'Thematic network on the social problem and societal problematization of men and masculinities (MEN)', Luxembourg Office for Official Publication of the European Communities.

Heaton, C., McCallum, L. and Jogi, R. (2009) *Forced Marriage: A Special Bulletin*. Bristol: Jordan Publishing.

Held, V. (2006) *The Ethics of Care: Personal, Political and Global*. Oxford: Oxford University Press.

Hendricks, H. (1994) *Child Welfare: England 1872–1989*. London: Routledge.

Hendry, J. (1999) 'Rethinking marriage and kinship', Unpublished lecture given as part of the *MA in Family Research*, Oxford Brookes University, Oxford.

Hendry, J. (2008) *An Introduction to Social Anthropology: Sharing Our Worlds*. Basingstoke, Hants: Palgrave Macmillan.

Hetherington, E.M. (2003) 'Social support and the adjustment of children in divorced and remarried families', *Childhood: A Global Journal of Child Research*, 10 (2): 217–53.

Hill Collins, P. (1990/2008) *Black Feminist Thought: Knowledge, Consciousness and the Politics of Empowerment*. London: HarperCollins/Routledge.

Hill Collins, P. (1997) *The More Things Change, the More They Stay the Same: African American Women and the New Politics of Containment*. British Sociological Association Annual Conference, 7–10 April, University of York, York.

Himmelweit, S. (ed.) (2000) *Inside the Household: From Labour to Care*. Basingstoke, Hants: Macmillan.

Hochschild, A.R. (2000) 'Global care chains and emotional surplus value', in W. Hutton and A. Giddens (eds), *On the Edge: Living with Global Capitalism*. London: Jonathan Cape.

Hochschild, A. (2003) *The Commercialisation of Intimate Life: Notes From Home and Work*. Berkeley, CA: University of California Press.

Hollinger, M.A. (2007) 'Ethical reflections for a globalized family curriculum: a developmental paradigm', in B. Sherif Trask and R.R. Hamon (eds), *Cultural Diversity and Families: Expanding Perspectives*. Thousand Oaks, CA: Sage, pp. 244–78.

Hollway, W. (2006) *The Capacity to Care*. London: Routledge.

hooks, B. (1991) *Yearning: Race, Gender and Cultural Politics*. London: Turnaround.

Hooper, C.A. (1992) *Mothers Surviving Child Sexual Abuse*. London: Routledge.

Horne, A. and Ohlsen, M.M. (2002) *Family Counselling and Therapy*. Florence, KY: Wadsworth.

Howe, D., Schofield, G., Brandon, M. and Hinings, D. (1999) *Attachment Theory, Child Maltreatment and Family Support: A Practice and Assessment Model*. London: Routledge.

Humphries, J. (1995) 'Women's labour force participation and the transition to the male breadwinner family, 1790–1865', *Economic History Review*, XLVIII: 89–117.

Jackson, P. (ed.) (2009) *Changing Families, Changing Food*. Basingstoke, Hants: Palgrave Macmillan.

Jacobsen, J. (2007) *The Economics of Gender*. Malden, MA: Blackwell Publishing.

James, A. and James, A.L. (2008) *Key Concepts in Childhood Studies*. London: Sage.

James, A., Jenks, C. and Prout, A. (eds) (1998) *Theorizing Childhood*. Cambridge: Polity Press.

Jamieson, L. (1998) *Intimacy: Personal Relationships in Modern Societies*. Cambridge: Polity.

Janeway, E. (1971) *Man's World, Women's Place*. New York: Bell.

Jayakody, R., Thornton, A. and Axinn, W. (eds) (2008) *International Family Change: Ideational Perspectives*. New York: Lawrence Erlbaum.

Johnson, M.P. (1992) 'Patriarchal terrorism and common couple violence: two forms of violence against women', *Journal of Marriage and the Family*, 57: 283–94.

Johnson, P. (2005) *Love, Heterosexuality and Society*. London: Routledge.

Jordan, B., Redley, M. and James, S. (1994) *Putting the Family First*. London: UCL Press.

Kağitçibaşi, Ç. (2005) 'Autonomy and relatedness in cultural context: implications for self and family', *Journal of Cross-Cultural Psychology*, 36 (4): 403–22.

Kağitçibaşi, Ç. (2007) *Family, Self and Human Development Across Cultures: Theory and Applications*. Mahwah, NJ: Lawrence Erlbaum.

Kamerman, S. and Moss, P. (eds) (2009) *The Politics of Parental Leave Policies: Children, Parenting, Gender and the Labour Market*. Bristol: Policy Press.

Karraker, M.W. and Grochowski, J.R. (2006) *Families with Futures: A Survey of Family Studies for the 21st Century*. Mahwah, NJ: Lawrence Erlbaum.

Katz, S.M. (2007) 'New directions for family law in the United States', *InDret* http://ssrm.com/abstract=1371031 (accessed 17 February 2010).

Kiernan, K. (2007) 'Changing European families: trends and issues', in J. Scott, J. Treas and M. Richards (eds), *The Blackwell Companion to the Sociology of Families*. Malden, MA: Blackwell.

Kingsbury, N. and Scanzoni, J. (2009) 'Structural-functionalism' in P.G. Boss, W.J. Doherty, R. LaRossa, W.R. Schumm and S.K. Steinmetz (eds), *Sourcebook of Family Theories and Methods: A Contextual Approach*. New York: Springer.

Kirchler, E., Rodler, C., Hoezl, E. and Meier, K. (2001) *Conflict and Decision-Making in Close Relationships: Love, Money and Daily Routines*. Hove: Psychology Press/ Taylor and Francis.

Kjørholt, A.T. and Lidén, H. (2004) 'Children and youth as citizens: symbolic participants or political actors?' in H. Brembeck, B. Johansson and J. Kampmann (eds), *Beyond the Competent Child: Exploring Contemporary Childhoods in the Nordic Welfare Societies*. Roskilde: Roskilde University Press.

Klass, D., Silverman, P.R. and Nickman, S.L. (eds) (1996) *Continuing Bonds: New Understandings of Grief*. London: Taylor and Francis.

Laham, S.M., Gonsalkorale, K. and von Hippel, W. (2005) 'Darwinian grandparenting: preferential investment in more certain kin', *Personality and Social Psychology Bulletin*, 31 (1): 63–72.

Laing, R.D. (1971) *The Politics of the Family and Other Essays*. London: Tavistock.

Lamb, M.E. (2007) 'Child-parent attachment' in J. Oates (ed.), *Attachment Relationships: Quality of Care for Young Children*. Milton Keynes: The Open University.

Lamb, M.E. (2010) *The Role of the Father in Child Development*. Chichester: John Wiley and Sons.

Lamb, M.E., Pleck, J.H., Charnov, E.L. and Levine, J.A. (1987) 'A biosocial perspective on paternal behavior and involvement', in J.B. Lancaster, J. Altmann, A.S. Rossi and

L. Sherrod (eds), *Parenting Across the Lifespan: Biosocial Dimensions.* New York: Aldine, pp. 111–142.

Land, H. (ed.) (1995) *Families and the Law*, in J. Muncie, M. Wetherell, R. Dallos and A. Cochrane (eds) *Understanding the Family.* London: Sage.

Lareau, A. (2003) *Unequal Childhoods: Class, Race and Family Life.* Berkeley, CA: University of California Press.

Lee, G.R. and Haas, L. (2004) 'Comparative methods in family research ', in P.G. Boss, W.J. Doherty, R. LaRossa, W.R. Schumm and S.K. Steinmetz (eds), *Sourcebook of Family Theories and Methods: A Contextual Approach.* New York: Springer, pp. 117–134.

Lee, N. (2001) *Childhood and Society: Growing Up in an Age of Uncertainty.* Buckingham: Open University Press.

Leslie, L.A. and A.L. Southard (2009) 'Thirty years of feminist family therapy: moving into the mainstream', in S.A. Lloyd, A.L. Few and K.R. Allen (eds), *Handbook of Feminist Family Studies.* Los Angeles: Sage, pp. 328–39.

Levi-Strauss, C. (1969) *The Elementary Structures of Kinship.* Boston, MA: Beacon Press.

Levner, L. (1998) 'A "dysfunctional" triangle or love in all the right places: social context in the therapy of a family living with AIDS', in P. Sutcliffe, G. Tufnell and U. Cornish (eds), *Working with the Dying and Bereaved; Systemic Approaches to Therapeutic Work.* Basingstoke, Hants: Macmillan, pp. 152–76.

Lewis, C. (2000) *A Man's Place in the Home: Fathers and Families in the UK.* York: Joseph Rowntree Foundation.

Lewis, C. (2005) 'Parenting and the family', in *Cambridge Encyclopedia of Child Development.* Cambridge: Cambridge University Press.

Lewis, C. and Lamb, M.E. (2003) 'Fathers' influences on children's development: the evidence from two-parent families', *European Journal of Psychology of Education*, 18 (2): 211–28.

Lewis, J. (1989) *Labour and Love: Women at Work and Home 1850–1939.* Oxford: Blackwell.

Lewis, J. (2002) 'Individualisation: assumptions about the existence of an adult worker model and the shift towards contractualism', in A. Carling, S. Duncan and R. Edwards (eds), *Analysing Families: Morality and Rationality in Policy and Practice.* London: Routledge.

Lewis, J. (2003) *Should We Worry About Family Change?* Toronto: University of Toronto Press.

Lewis, J. (2006) 'Men, women, work, care and policies', *Journal of European Social Policy*, 16 (4): 387–92.

Lewis, S., Brannen, J., and Nilsen A. (eds) (2009) *Work, Families and Organisations in Transition.* Bristol: Policy Press.

Liebfried, S. (ed.) (1993) 'Towards a European Welfare State?', in C. Jones (ed.), *New Perspectives on the Welfare State in Europe.* London: Routledge.

Lloyd, S.A., Few, A.L. and Allen, K.R. (2009) *Handbook of Feminist Family Studies.* Thousand Oaks: Sage.

Lopata, H.Z. (1971) *Occupation: Housewife.* New York: Oxford University Press.

references

237

Low, M. and Lawrence-Zúñiga, D. (eds) (2003) *The Anthropology of Space and Place: Locating Culture*. Oxford: Blackwell.

Lowie, R.H. (ed.) (2004) 'Unilateral descent groups', in R. Parkin and L. Stone (eds) *Kinship and Family: An Anthropological Reader*. Oxford: Blackwell.

Lucey, H. (2010) 'Families and Personal Relationships', in M. Wetherell and C. Talpade Mohanty, *The Sage Handbook of Identities*. London: Sage.

Luseke, D.R., Gelles, R.J. and Cavanaugh, M.M. (2005) *Current Controversies on Family Violence*. Thousand Oaks, CA: Sage.

Luthar, S.S., Cicchetti, D. and Becker, B. (2000) 'The construct of resilience: a critical evaluation and guidelines for future work', *Child Development*, 71 (3): 543–62.

Mackenzie, C. and Stoljar, N. (2000) 'Introduction: autonomy reconfigured', in C. Mackenzie and N. Stoljar (eds), *Relational Autonomy: Feminist Perspectives on Autonomy, Agency, and the Social Self*. New York: Oxford University Press.

Mackinnon, A. (2006) 'Fantasizing the family: women, families and the quest for an individual self', *Women's History Review*, 15 (4): 663–75.

Mahalingam, R., Balan, S. and Molina, K.M. (2009) 'Transnational intersectionality: a critical framework for theorizing motherhood', in S.A. Lloyd, A.L. Few and K.R. Allen (eds), *Handbook of Feminist Family Studies*. Los Angeles: Sage, pp. 69–80.

Mallett, S. (2004) 'Understanding home: a critical review of the literature', *Sociological Review*, 52 (1): 62–89.

Mangen, S. (1999) 'Qualitative research methods in cross-national settings', *International Journal of Research Methodology*, 2 (2): 109–124.

Marris, P. (1996) *The Politics of Uncertainty: Attachment in Private and Public Life*. London: Routledge.

Marsiglio, W. (ed.) (1995) *Fatherhood: Contemporary Theory, Research and Social Policy*. Thousand Oaks, CA: Sage.

Martin, B. (1984) '"Mother wouldn't like it!" Housework as magic', *Theory, Culture and Society*, 2: 19–36.

Martin, J. and Roberts, C. (1984) *Women and Employment: a Lifetime Perspective: The Report of the 1980 Department of Employment/Office of Population Censuses and Surveys, Great Britain Women and Employment Survey*. London: HMSO.

Mason, J. (2002) *Qualitative Researching*. London: Sage.

Mason, J. (2004) 'Personal narratives, relational selves: residential histories in the living and telling', *Sociological Review*, 52: 162–179.

Mason, J. (2008) 'Tangible affinities and the real life fascination of kinship', *Sociology*, 42 (1): 29–46.

Mason, M.A., Fine, M.A. and Carnochan, S. (2004) 'Family law for changing families in the New Millennium', in M. Coleman and L.H. Ganong (eds), *Handbook of Contemporary Families: Considering the Past, Contemplating the Future*. Thousand Oaks, CA: Sage, pp. 432–50.

Masson, J., Bailey-Harris, R. and Probert, R. (2008) *Cretney's Principles of Family Law*. London: Sweet and Maxwell.

Mauthner, M. (2002) *Sistering: Power and Change in Female Relationships*. Basingstoke, Hants: Palgrave.

McAdoo, H.P. (ed.) (2006) *Black Families*. London: Sage.

McIntosh, M. (1979) 'The welfare state and the needs of the dependent family', in S. Burman (ed.), *Fit Work for Women*. London: Croom Helm.

McLeod, J. and Thomson, R. (2009) *Researching Social Change: Qualitative Approaches*. London: Sage.

Mcquillan, J., Greil, A.L., Scheffler, K.M. and Tichenor, V. (2008) 'The importance of motherhood among women in the contemporary United States', *Gender and Society*, 22 (4): 477–96.

McRae, S. (1999) 'Introduction: family and household change in Britain' in S. McRae (ed.), *Changing Britain: Families and Households in the 1990s*. Oxford: Oxford University Press.

Mead, M. (1971) *Male and Female*. Harmondsworth: Penguin.

Melito, R. (2003) 'Values in the role of the family therapist: Self determination and justice', *Journal of Marital and Family Therapy*, 29 (1): 3–11.

Meyer, J. (1991) 'Power and love: conflicting conceptual schema', in K. Davis, M. Leijenaar and J. Oldersama (eds), *The Gender of Power*. London: Sage.

Miller, A.C. and R.J. Perelberg (1990) *Gender and Power in Families*. London: Routledge.

Miller, T. (2005) *Making Sense of Motherhood: A Narrative Approach*. Cambridge: Cambridge University Press.

Miller, T. (2007) '"Is this what motherhood is all about?" weaving experiences and discourse through transition to first-time motherhood' *Gender and Society*, 21 (3): 337–58.

Miller, T. (2010) *Making Sense of Fatherhood: Gender, Caring and Work*. Cambridge: Cambridge University Press.

Mitchell, J. (2003) *Siblings, Sex and Violence*. Cambridge: Polity Press.

Moffitt, R.A. (2000) 'Female wages, male wages, and the economic model of marriage: the evidence', in L.J. Waite (ed.), *The Ties That Bind: Perspectives on Marriage and Cohabitation*. New York: Walter de Gruyter.

Moffitt, T.E., Caspi, A. and Rutter, M. (2006) 'Measured gene–environment interactions in psychopathology: concepts, research strategies, and implications for research, intervention, and public understanding of genetics', *Perspectives on Psychological Science*, (1): 5–27.

Monaghan, J. and Just, P. (2000) *Social and Cultural Anthropology: A Very Short Introduction*. Oxford: Oxford University Press.

Montgomery, H. (2008) *An Introduction to Childhood: Anthropological Perspectives on Children's Lives*. Oxford: Wiley Blackwell.

Montgomery, H. (2009) 'Children and families in an international context' in H. Montgomery and M. Kellet (eds), *Children and Young People's Worlds: Developing Frameworks for Integrated Practice*. Bristol: Policy Press.

Mooney, J. (2000) *Gender, Violence and the Social Order*. Basingstoke: Macmillan.

Morgan, D.H.J. (1975) *Social Theory and the Family*. London: Routledge and Kegan Paul.

Morgan, D.H.J. (1985) *The Family, Politics and Social Theory*. London: Routledge and Kegan Paul.

Morgan, D.H.J. (1996) *Family Connections: An Introduction to Family Studies*. Cambridge: Polity Press.

references

239

Morgan, D.H.J. (2003) 'Introduction', in D. Cheal (ed.), *Family: Critical Concepts in Sociology*. London: Routledge, pp. 1–16.

Morgan, D.H.J. (2004) 'Men in families and households', in J. Scott, J. Treas and M. Richards (eds), *The Blackwell Companion to the Sociology of Families*. Malden, MA: Blackwell Publishing.

Morgan, D.H.J. (1999) 'Risk and family practices: accounting for change and fluidity in family life', in E.B. Silva and C. Smart (eds) *The New Family?* London: Sage.

Morgan, P. (1996) *Who Needs Parents?* London: IEA Health and Welfare Unit.

Morris, L. (1994) *Dangerous Classes: The Underclass and Social Citizenship*. London: Routledge.

Mount, F. (1982) *The Subversive Family*. London: Cape.

Munson, M. and Stelbourn, J.P. (1999) *The Lesbian Polyamory Reader: Open Relationships, Non-monogamy and Casual Sex*. Abingdon: Haworth Press.

Murdock, G.P. (2003) 'The nuclear family', in D. Cheal (ed.), *Family: Critical Concepts in Sociology*. London: Routledge, pp. 19–54.

Murray, C. (ed.) (1990) *The Emerging British Underclass*. London: IEA Health and Welfare Unit.

Neimeyer, R.A. and Anderson, A. (2002) 'Meaning reconstruction theory', in N. Thompson (ed.), *Loss and Grief: A Guide for Human Service Practitioners*. Basingstoke, Hants: Palgrave, pp. 45–64.

Nelson, M.K. (1990) 'Mothering others' children: the experiences of family day-care providers', *Signs*, 15: 586–605.

Nsamenange, A.B. (2004) *Cultures of Human Development and Education: Challenge to Growing Up African*. New York: Nova.

Nzegwu, N.U. (2006) *Family Matters: Feminist Concepts in African Philosophy of Culture*. New York: State University of New York Press.

Oakley, A. (1976) *Housewife*. Harmondsworth: Penguin.

Oates, J. (ed.) (2007) *Attachment Relationships: Quality of Care for Young Children*. Early Childhood in Focus. Milton Keynes: The Open University with the support of the Bernard van Leer Foundation.

Oates, J., Wood, C. and Grayson, A. (2005) *Psychological Development in Early Childhood*. Malden, MA: Blackwell Publishing with the Open University.

Ochieng, B.M.N. and Hylton C.L.A. (eds) (2010) *Black Families in Britain as the Site of Struggle*. Manchester: Manchester University Press.

O'Connor, P. (1991) 'Women's experience of power within marriage: an inexplicable phenomenon?', *Sociological Review*, 39 (4): 823–42.

O'Connor, T.G. and Scott, S. (2007) *Parenting and Outcomes for Children*. York: Joseph Rowntree Foundation.

O'Reilly, A. (2009) 'Introduction', in A. O'Reilly (ed.), *Maternal Thinking: Philosophy, Politics, Practice*. Toronto: Demeter Press, pp. 1–13.

Overing, J. (1985) '"Today I shall call him Mummy": multiple worlds and classificatory confusion', in J. Overing (ed.), *Reason and Morality*. London: Tavistock.

Overing, J. (2003) 'In praise of the everyday: trust and the art of social living in an Amazonian community', *Ethos*, 68: 293–316.

Paetsch, J.J., Bala, N.M., Bertrand, L.D. and Glennon, L. (2007) 'Trends in the formation and dissolution of couples', in J. Scott, J. Treas and M. Richards (eds),

The Blackwell Companion to the Sociology of Families. Malden, MA: Blackwell, pp. 289–305.

Pahl, J. (2005) 'Individualisation in couple finances: who pays for the children?', *Social Policy and Society*, 4: 381–91.

Pahl, R. (2000) *On Friendship*. Cambridge: Polity Press.

Parkes, C.M. (1996) *Bereavement: Studies of Grief in Adult Life*. London: Routledge.

Parkes, C.M. (2006) *Love and Loss: The Roots of Grief and its Complications*. London: Routledge.

Parreñas, R.S. (2005) *Children of Global Migration: Transnational Families and Gendered Woes*. Stanford: Stanford University Press.

Parsons, T. (1964) *The Social System*. London: Routledge and Kegan Paul.

Parsons, T. and Bales, R.F. (1955) *Family: Socialization and Interaction Process*. New York: Free Press.

Payne, G. (2006) *Social Divisions*. Basingstoke: Palgrave Macmillan.

Payne, G. and Payne, J. (2004) *Key Concepts in Social Research*. London: Sage.

Pearl, D. (2000) 'Ethnic diversity in family law', *Family Law: Essays for the New Millennium*. Bristol: Jordan Publishing.

Pfau-Effinger, B. (1998) 'Gender cultures and the gender arrangement – a theoretical framework for cross-national gender research', *Innovation*, 11 (2): 147–66.

Phelps, E., Furstenberg, F.F. and Colby, A. (eds) (2002) *Looking at Lives: American Longitudinal Studies of the Twentieth Century*. New York: Russell Sage Foundation.

Phoenix, A. and Husain, F. (2007) *Parenting and Ethnicity*. York: Joseph Rowntree Foundation/National Children's Bureau.

Pilcher, J. and Whelehan, I. (2004) *Fifty Key Concepts in Gender Studies*. London: Sage.

Pine, F. (1998) 'Family', in A. Barnard and J. Spencer (eds), *Encyclopedia of Social and Cultural Anthropology*. London: Routledge, pp. 223–8.

Pink, S. (2004) *Home Truths: Gender, Domestic Objects and Everyday Life*. Oxford: Berg.

Pinker, S. (1998) *How the Mind Works*. Harmondsworth: Allen Lane.

Pleck, J.H. and Masciadrelli B.P. (2004) 'Paternal involvement by US residential fathers: levels, sources and consequences', in M.E. Lamb (ed.), *The Role of the Father in Child Development*. Chichester: John Wiley and Sons, pp. 222–71.

Prout, A. (2000) 'Children's participation: control and self-realisation in British late modernity', *Children and Society*, 13: 304–15.

Pryor, J. and Trinder, L. (2007) 'Children, families and divorce', in J. Scott, J. Treas and M. Richards (eds), *The Blackwell Companion to the Sociology of Families*. Malden, MA: Blackwell.

Quest, C. (ed.) (1994) *Liberating Women … From Modern Feminism*. Choice in Welfare Series No. 19. London: Institute for Economic Affairs Health and Welfare Unit.

Qvortrup, J., Bardy, M., Sigritta, G. and Wintersberger, H. (eds) (1994) *Childhood Matters: Social Theory, Practice and Politics*. Aldershot: Avebury.

Raghuram, P., Madge, C. and Noxolo, P. (2009) 'Rethinking responsibility and care for a postcolonial world', *Geoforum*, 40: 5–13.

Rapp, R., Ross, E. and Bridenthal, R. (1979) 'Examining family history', *Feminist Studies*, 5: 174–195.

Rapport, N. and Overing, J. (2007) *Social and Cultural Anthropology: The Key Concepts*. Abingdon: Routledge.

Renzetti, C.M. (1992) *Violent Betrayal: Partner Abuse in Lesbian Relationships*. Newbury Park, CA: Sage.

Reynolds, T. (ed.) (2002) 'Re-analysing the Black family', in A. Carling, S. Duncan and R. Edwards (eds) *Analysing Families: Morality and Rationality in Policy and Practice*. London: Routledge Falmer.

Reynolds, T. (2005) *Caribbean Mothers: Identity and Experience in the UK*. London: Tufnell Press.

Reynolds, T. and Zontini, E. (eds) (2006) *Assessing Social Capital and Care Provision in Minority Ethnic Communities: A Comparative Study of Caribbean and Italian Transnational Families*. Assessing Social Capital: Concept, Policy and Practice. Newcastle: Cambridge Scholars Press.

Ribbens, J. (1994) *Mothers and Their Children: A Sociology of Childrearing*. London: Sage.

Ribbens, J. and Edwards, R. (eds) (1998) *Feminist Dilemmas in Qualitative Research: Public Knowledge and Private Lives*. London: Sage.

Ribbens McCarthy, J. (2006) *Young People's Experiences of Loss and Bereavement: Towards an Inter-disciplinary Approach*. Buckingham: Open University Press.

Ribbens McCarthy, J. (2008) 'Security, insecurity and family lives', in A. Cochrane and D. Talbot (eds), *Security: Welfare, Crime and Society*. Maidenhead: Open University Press/McGraw Hill, pp. 61–92.

Ribbens McCarthy, J. (2010) 'The powerful relational language of "family": togetherness, belonging and personhood'. Paper in progress. Open University.

Ribbens McCarthy, J. and Edwards, R. (2000) 'Moral tales of the Child and the Adult: narratives of contemporary family lives under changing circumstances', *Sociology*, 34(4): 785–804.

Ribbens McCarthy, J. and Edwards, R. (2002) 'The individual in public and private: the significance of mothers and children', in A. Carling, S. Duncan and R. Edwards (eds), *Analysing Families: Morality and Rationality in Policy and Practice*. London: Routledge.

Ribbens McCarthy, J., Edwards, R. and Gillies, V. (2003) *Making Families: Moral Tales of Parenting and Step-Parenting*. Durham: Sociology Press.

Rich, A. (1977) *Of Woman Born: Motherhood as Experience and Institution*. London: Virago.

Richards, M. (2007) 'Assisted reproduction, genetic technologies, and family life', in J. Scott, J. Treas and M. Richards (eds), *The Blackwell Companion to the Sociology of Families*. Oxford: Blackwell.

Ritzer, G. (1996) *Modern Sociological Theory*. New York: McGraw-Hill.

Riviere, P. (1985) 'Unscrambling parenthood: the Warnock report', *Anthropology Today*, 1 (4): 2–7.

Rodgers, J.J. (1996) *Family Life and Social Control: A Sociological Perspective*. Basingstoke, Hants: Macmillan.

Rogoff, B. (2003) *The Cultural Nature of Human Development*. Oxford University Press.

Rosaldo, M. (1974) 'Women, culture and Society: a theoretical overview', in M. Rosaldo and L. Lamphere (eds), *Women, Culture and Society*. Stanford: Stanford University Press.

Rose, N. (1999) *Governing the Soul: The Shaping of the Private Self*. London: Routledge.

Rose, S. (ed.) (1980) *It's Only Human Nature: The Sociobiologist's Fairyland. Sociobiology Examined*. Oxford: Oxford University Press.

Rose, S. (2006) *The 21st Century Brain: Explaining, Mending and Manipulating the Mind*. London: Vintage.

Rose, S., Lewontin, R. and Kamin L.J. (1984) *Not in Our Genes*. Harmondsworth: Penguin.

Roseneil, S. and Budgeon, S. (2004) 'Cultures of intimacy and care beyond "the family": personal life and social change in the early 21st century', *Sociology*, 52 (2): 135–59.

Ross, N., Hill, M., Sweeting, H. and Cunningham-Burley, S. (2006) Grandparents and teen grandchildren: Exploring intergenerational relationships. *Centre for Research on Families and Relationships*, http://www.crfr.ac.uk/reports/rb23grandparents.pdf (accessed 25 July 2010).

Rubin, K.H. and Chung, O.B. (2006) *Parenting Beliefs, Behaviors, and Parent-Child Relations: A Cross-Cultural Perspective*. New York: Psychology Press.

Ruddick, S. (1989/90) *Maternal Thinking: Towards a Politics of Peace*. New York: Ballantine Books.

Sahlins, M. (1977) *The Uses and Abuses of Biology*. London: Tavistock.

Scanzoni, J. (2004) 'Household diversity: the starting point for healthy families in the new century', in M. Coleman and L.H. Ganong (eds), *Handbook of Contemporary Families: Considering the Past, Contemplating the Future*. Thousand Oaks, CA: Sage, pp. 3–22.

Schalge, S. (2009) 'Maternal practice: mothering and cultural variation in anthropology', in A. O'Reilly (ed.), *Maternal Thinking: Philosophy, Politics, Practice*. Toronto: Demeter Press, pp. 239–251.

Scheper-Hughes, N. (1993) *Death Without Weeping: The Violence of Everyday Life in Brazil*. Berkeley, CA: University of California Press.

Schoon, I. (2006) *Risk and Resilience: Adaptations in Changing Times*. Cambridge: Cambridge University Press.

Schoon, I. and Parsons, S. (2002) 'Competence in the face of adversity: the impact of early family environment and long-term consequences', *Children and Society*, 16: 260–272.

Scott, J.W. and Tilly L.A. (1980) 'Women's work and the family in nineteenth century Europe', in M. Anderson (ed.), *Sociology of the Family*. Harmondsworth: Penguin.

Scott, S., Jackson, S. and Backett-Milburn, K. (1998) 'Swings and roundabouts: risk, anxiety and the everyday worlds of children', *Sociology*, 32 (4): 689–705.

Scott, S. and Jackson, S. (2000) 'Sexuality', in G. Payne (ed.), *Social Divisions*. Basingstoke, Hants: Macmillan, pp. 168–84.

Scruton, R. (1986) *Sexual Desire*. London: Widenfeld and Nicolson.

Seiffge-Krenke (2000) 'Causal links between stressful events, coping style and adolescent symptomology', *Journal of Adolescence*, 23 (6): 675–91.

Sennett, R. (2004) *Respect in an Age of Inequality*. London: W.W. Norton & Co.

Sevenhuijsen, S. (1998) *Citizenship and the Ethics of Care: Feminist Considerations on Justice*. London: Routledge.

Seymour, J. (2005) 'Entertaining guests, or entertaining the guests: children's emotional labour in hotels, pubs and boarding houses', in J. Goddard, S. McNamee, and A. James (eds), *The Politics of Childhood: International Perspectives, Contemporary Developments*. Basingstoke, Hants: Palgrave Macmillan, pp. 90–106.

Sheldon, S. (2009) *Fatherhood and Legal Change: Joint Birth Registration*. Parenting Cultures. University of Cambridge, Cambridge. http://www.parentingculturestudies.org/seminar-series/seminar2/summary.html (accessed 17 July 2009).

Shore, C. (1992) 'Virgin births and sterile debates: anthropology and the new reproductive technologies', *Current Anthropology*, 33 (3): 295–301.

Silva, E.B. (2010) *Technology, Family, Culture*. Basingstoke, Hants: Palgrave.

Smallwood, S. and Wilson, B. (2007) 'Focus on Families', http://www.statistics.gov.uk/downloads/theme_compendia/fof2007/FO_Families_2007.pdf (accessed 12 June 2009).

Smart, C. (2007) *Personal Life*. Cambridge: Polity Press.

Smart, C. and Neale, B. (1999) *Family Fragments?* Cambridge: Polity Press.

Smart, C., Neale, B. and Wade, A. (2001) *The Changing Experience of Childhood: Families and Divorce*. Cambridge: Polity Press.

Smith, D.E. (1987) *The Everyday World as Problematic: A Feminist Sociology*. Milton Keynes: Open University Press.

Sommerville, J. (2000) *Feminism and the Family: Politics and Society in the UK and USA*. Basingstoke: Macmillan.

Spencer, L. and Pahl, R. (2006) *Rethinking Friendship: Hidden Solidarities Today*. Princeton: Princeton University Press.

Stacey, J. (1990) *Brave New Families: Stories of Domestic Upheaval in Late Twentieth Century America*. New York: Basic Books.

Strach, P. (2007) *All in the Family: The Private Roots of American Public Policy*. Stanford: Stanford University Press.

Strathern, M. (1992a) *After Nature: English Kinship in the Late Twentieth Century*. Cambridge: Cambridge University Press.

Strathern, M. (1992b) *Reproducing the Future: Anthropology, Kinship and the New Reproductive Technologies*. Manchester: Manchester University Press.

Sutcliffe, P., Tufnell, G. and Cornish, U. (eds) (1998) *Working with the Dying and Bereaved: Systemic Approaches to Therapeutic Work*. London: Macmillan.

Szinovacz, M.E. (ed.) (1998) *Handbook on Grandparenthood*. Santa Barbara, CA: Greenwood Publishing.

Tadmor, N. (1996) 'The concept of the household-family in eighteenth century England', *Past and Present*, 151: 111–40.

Taylor, S. (1992) 'Measuring child abuse', *Sociology Review*, 2 (3).

Teachman, J.D., Polonko, K.A. and Scanzoni, J. (1999) 'Demography and families', in M.B. Sussman, S.K. Steinmetz and G.W. Peterson (eds), *Handbook of Marriage and the Family*. New York: Plenum Press, pp. 39–76.

Therborn, G. (2004) *Between Sex and Power: Family in the World, 1900–2000*. London: Routledge.

Thèry, I. (1989) '"The interest of the child" and the regulation of the post-divorce family', in C. Smart and S. Sevenhuijsen (eds), *Child Custody and the Politics of Gender*. London: Routledge, pp. 78–99.

Thomas, R. (1999) 'Household definition', Question Bank Commentary: http://surveynet.ac.uk/sqb/qb/topics/housedefinition/household%20definition%20thomas.pdf.

Thomson, R., Kehily, M.J., Hadfield, L. and Sharpe, S. (2008) *The Making of Modern Motherhood: Memories, Representations, Practices*. http://www.open.ac.uk/hsc/_assets/yqwnotatstun71rdbl.pdf (accessed 25 July 2010).

Thorne, B. and Yalom, M. (eds) (1992) *Rethinking the Family: Some Feminist Questions*. Boston: North Eastern University Press.

Thornton, A. and Fricke, T.E. (1987) 'Social change and the family: comparative perspectives from the West, China and South Asia', *Sociological Forum*, 2 (4): 746–79.

Tong, R.P. (2009) *Feminist Thought: A More Comprehensive Introduction* (3rd edn). Boulder, CO: Westview Press.

Tronto, J.C. (1993) *Moral Boundaries: A Political Argument for an Ethic of Care*. New York: Routledge.

Troost, K.M. and Filsinger, E. (2004) 'Emerging biosocial perspectives on the family', in P.G. Boss, W.J. Doherty, R. LaRossa, W.R. Schumm and S.K. Steinmetz (eds), *Sourcebook of Family Theories and Methods: A Contextual Approach*. New York: Springer, pp. 677–710.

Tufnell, G., Cornish, U. and Sutcliffe, P. (1998) *Death of a Parent in a Family with Young Children: Working with the Aftermath*. London: Macmillan.

Uttal, L. (2009) '(Re)visioning family ties to communities and contexts', in S.A. Lloyd, A.L. Few and K.R. Allen (eds), *Handbook of Feminist Family Studies*. Los Angeles: Sage, pp. 134–46.

Utting, D. (2007) *Parenting and the Different Ways it can Affect Children's Lives: Research Evidence*. York: Joseph Rowntree Foundation.

Van Der Geest, S. (2004) 'Grandparents and grandchildren in Kwahu, Ghana: the performance of respect', *Africa*, 74: 47–61.

Van Every, J. (1995) *Heterosexual Women Challenging The Family: Refusing to be a 'Wife'*. London: Taylor & Francis.

Van Ijzendoorn, M.H., Bakermans-Kranenburg, M.J. and Sagi-Schwartz, A. (2007) 'Attachment across diverse socio-cultural contexts: the limits of universality', in K. Rubin and O.B. Chung (eds), *Parenting Beliefs, Behaviors, and Parent-Child Relations: A Cross-Cultural Perspective*. New York: Psychology Press, pp. 108–142.

Walby, S. (1990) *Theorizing Patriarchy*. Oxford: Blackwell.

Walkerdine, V. and Lucey, H. (1989) *Democracy in the Kitchen: Regulating Mothers and Socialising Daughters*. London: Virago.

Walkover, B.C. (1992) 'The family as an overwrought object of desire', in G.C. Rosenwald and R. Ochberg (eds), *Storied Lives: The Cultural Politics of Self-Understanding*. New Haven: Yale University Press.

Walzer, S. (2004) 'Encountering oppositions: a review of scholarship about motherhood', in M. Coleman and L.H. Ganong (eds), *Handbook of Contemporary*

Families: Considering the Past, Contemplating the Future. Thousand Oaks, CA: Sage, pp. 209–23.

Warr, D.J. and P.M. Pyett (1999) 'Difficult relations: sex work, love and intimacy', *Sociology of Health and Illness*, 21 (3): 290–309.

Weeks, J., Donovan, C. and Heaphy, B. (2001) *Same Sex Intimacies: Families of Choice and Other Life Experiments.* London: Routledge.

Weintraub, J. (1997) 'The theory and politics of the public/private distinction', in J. Weintraub and K. Kumar (eds), *Public and Private in Thought and Practice: Perspectives on a Grand Dichotomy.* Chicago: Chicago University Press.

Weller, S. (2007) *Teenagers' Citizenship: Experiences and Education.* Abingdon: Routledge.

Welshman, J. (1999) 'The social history of social work: the issue of the "problem family" 1940–1970', *British Journal of Social Work*, 29: 457–76.

Welshman, J. (2007) *From Keith Joseph to Tony Blair: Transmitted Deprivation and Social Exclusion.* Bristol: Policy Press.

Weston, K. (1991) *Families We Choose: Lesbians, Gays, Kinship.* New York: Columbia Press.

Wetherell, M. (2001) 'Editor's introduction, and debates in discourse research', in M. Wetherell, S. Taylor and S.J. Yates (eds), *Discourse Theory and Practice: A Reader.* London: Sage.

White, J.M. and D.M. Klein (2008) *Family Theories.* Los Angeles: Sage.

Widmer, E.D. and Jallinoja, R. (eds) (2008) *Beyond the Nuclear Family: Families in a Configurational Perspective.* Bern: Peter Lang.

Williams, F. (2004) *Rethinking Families.* London: Calouste Gulbenkian Foundation.

Wilson, E.O. (1975) *Sociobiology: The New Synthesis.* Cambridge, MA: Harvard University Press.

Wilson, E.O. (1978) *On Human Nature.* Cambridge, MA: Harvard University Press.

Wilson, H. (2002) 'Brain science, early intervention and "at risk" families: implications for parents, professionals and social policy', *Social Policy and Society*, 1: 191–202.

Wilson, P. and Pahl, R. (1988) 'The changing sociological construct of the family', *Sociological Review*, 36: 233–72.

Woodhead, M. (2009) 'Child development and the development of childhood', in J. Qvortrup, W.A. Corsaro and M.S. Honig (eds) *The Palgrave Handbook of Childhood Studies.* Basingstoke, Hants: Palgrave Macmillan.

Yeates, N. (2009) *Globalizing Care Economies and Migrant Workers.* Basingstoke, Hants: Palgrave Macmillan.

Yeatman, A. (1986) 'Women, domestic life and sociology', in C. Pateman and E. Gross (eds), *Feminist Challenges: Social and Political Theory.* Sydney: Allen and Unwin.

Young, M. and Willmott, P. (1973) *The Symmetrical Family.* London: Routledge and Kegan Paul.

Zelitzer, V. (1985) *Pricing the Priceless Child: The Changing Social Value of Children.* New York: Basic Books.

Zelitzer, V. (2007) *The Purchase of Intimacy.* Princeton, NJ: Princeton University Press.

Zimba, R.F. (2002) 'Indigenous conceptions of childhood development and social realities in southern Africa', in H. Keller, Y.P. Poortinga and A. Scholmerish (eds),

Between Cultures and Biology: Perspectives on Ontogenetic Development. Cambridge: Cambridge University Press.

Zonabend, F. (1998) 'Marriage', in A. Barnard and J. Spencer (eds), *Encyclopedia of Social and Cultural Anthropology*. London: Routledge.

Zontini, E. (2004) 'Immigrant women in Barcelona: Coping with the consequences of transnational lives', *Journal of Ethnic and Migration Studies*, 30 (6): 1113–44.

Zvinkliene, A. (1996) 'The state of Family Studies in Lithuania', *Marriage & Family Review*, 22 (3/4): 203–32.

references